Race Bounds

The New American Canon
The Iowa Series in Contemporary Literature
and Culture

. . . .

SAMUEL COHEN, *Series Editor*

Race
sounds

· · · · · · · · · · · · · · · · ·

The Art of Listening in African American Literature

NICOLE
BRITTINGHAM
FURLONGE

University of Iowa Press
Iowa City

University of Iowa Press, Iowa City 52242
Copyright © 2018 by the University of Iowa Press
www.uipress.uiowa.edu
Printed in the United States of America

Design by Barbara Haines

The University of Iowa Press is a member of Green Press Initiative and is committed to preserving natural resources.

Printed on acid-free paper

Cataloging-in-Publication data for *Race Sounds: The Art of Listening in African American Literature*, by Nicole Brittingham Furlonge, is on file at the Library of Congress.

ISBN 978-1-60938-561-3 (pbk)
ISBN 978-1-60938-562-0 (ebk)

All living is listening for a throat to open—
The length of its silence shaping lives.

—CLAUDIA RANKINE, *Citizen: An American Lyric*

CONTENTS

ACKNOWLEDGMENTS

When I began my research on listening years ago, I heard poet Lucille Clifton speak at an event in honor of poet Sterling A. Brown. Her words resonate with me still: "One of the things I have learned to do in my life is listen. I listened to what guided me." I am grateful to her and to the myriad writers, musicians, and artists whose works have, in various ways and at various times, provoked me to listen.

Race Sounds began as a seminar paper on Sterling Brown that grew into a dissertation after Simon Gikandi asked me, "What do you mean by 'listening poet'?" I thank Professor Gikandi for listening to this phrase and encouraging me to explore its nuances more closely. I have warm memories of my time in Ann Arbor and of mind-stretching and commiserating conversations over mocha espressos, eggs Florentine, tofu dogs, and potluck meals with Jessica Lieberman, Amit Ray, Delia Coleman, Sylvia Gimenez, and Jeremy Wells. I thank Jeremy also for his generosity in reading pages of this manuscript.

I had the good fortune over the years to receive financial support from the following sources: the Horace H. Rackham Merit Fellowship at the University of Michigan, Ford Foundation Predoctoral Fellowship, Mellon Dissertation Fellowship at the University of Pennsylvania, and Johnston Faculty Enrichment Award at Princeton Day School. I am immensely grateful to the Mellon Mays Undergraduate Fellowship Program at the University of Pennsylvania and the program's administrators, Valarie Swain-Cade McCoullum and Pat Ravenell, whose mentorship and support helped shepherd me into a scholar's life. I conducted archival research and interviews at the Library of Congress, New York Public Library and its Schomburg Center for Research in Black Culture, Center for Black Music Research at Columbia College Chicago, Uri Hasson's Listening Lab at Princeton University, and the Gayl Jones Collection at the Howard Gotlieb Archival Research Center at Boston University. Many thanks to the research and technology gurus who aided me along the way: Carol-Ann Pala, Lisa Henson, Mary Kietzman, Jody Gerlock, Joanne Wernig, and Hillary Beach.

Race Sounds found a wonderful home with the University of Iowa Press. I am grateful to the entire staff for their investment in this book. Special thanks to Catherine Cocks and Elisabeth Chretien, formerly of the press, Ranjit Arab, series editor Sam Cohen, and Jim McCoy for their patience, expertise, and belief in this project. Many thanks to copyeditor Holly Carver and my anonymous readers. Their enthusiasm for this work and suggestions for revision allowed its argument to be more effectively heard.

Grateful acknowledgment to poet Claudia Rankine for permission to reprint from *Citizen*, to artist Paul Goodnight for allowing his art to grace the cover of this book, and to Bettye LaVette and Kevin Kiley for their willingness to speak with me and for the use of their photograph. Special thanks also to David Lockwood, whose listening sessions and conversations about music helped expand my understanding of the signature musical pieces examined in this book.

Herman Beavers taught me the value of learning the African American literary tradition from the ground up and pushed me to unpack my ideas. For his belief in my capacity as a scholar, I am immensely grateful. Farah Jasmine Griffin's intellectual range and creativity remain inspiring. Her comments on the early stages of this work were invaluable. Michael Gamer is the most incisive and exacting reader I know, and I thank him for his unwavering support. Mentor and friend Maghan Keita is always available to provide a precise insight, a provoking question, or a good laugh. I thank him and Nzadi Keita for being such warm listening presences—for my family and in the tradition. I am grateful to Cornel West for his feedback on and encouragement of this work. I thank, too, Lloyd Pratt and Charles Rowell for inviting me to present portions of this work to conference audiences.

I've had the great fortune to work in communities that nurtured me and supported my continued insistence on trying to write a book while teaching, advising, doing dorm duty, and sometimes even coaching: Holderness School, St. Andrew's School in Delaware, Lawrenceville School, Princeton Day School, and the Klingenstein Summer Institute. You have fed my curiosity and helped me grow as an educator. I learned from all of you the value of listening in community (sometimes while walking) and of a good laugh. I especially thank Phil and Robin Peck, Bruce and Sarah Barton, John and Marilee Lin, Jini Sparkman, John Donovan and Kara Hamill, Tad and Elizabeth Roach, Ana Ramirez and Dave Miller, Emily Pressman, Will Speers, Esther Hsiao, Eddie Chang, Brad and Lisa Bates, Jennifer and Andrew Cottone, Dave DeSalvo, John Austin and Monica Matouk, Terence Gilheany, John Burk, Caroline Lee, Kelley Nicholson-Flynn, Anthony McKinley, David LaMotte, Barbara Walker, Paul Stellato, Miriam

Folkes, Pearl Rock Kane, Eder Williams, and the KSI Collective of Liz Perry, Liz Luscombe, Suzette Duncan, Varghese Alexander, Josh Pretzer, Donald Morrison, Richard Messina, Danielle Pasno, Kelly Tracy, Steve Chan, Sara Deveaux, and Ashley Marshall.

To Kevin Mattingly and Bill Williams: immense gratitude for your discerning questions, wisdom, and care.

While Nigel worked to help build an independent school in Trenton for underserved but highly deserving students, my family and I became part of a community with vision, verve, and an entrepreneurial educational spirit. For so many good times and for their friendship, I thank Elisa and Tom Bonner, Ivy Green Jones, Marlyn Arrellano, Greg Groves, Christian Smutherman, Zaineb Hussain, Leah Hall-Hansen, and Stacey Pierre-Louis.

Over the years, my students have helped hone my listening. I especially thank Sarah Moser, Grace Awantang, Caitlin Blinkhorn, Matthew Roach, Mirte Mallory, Angel Del Villar, Matt Anderson, Andy Collado, Courtney McEleney, Emily Lockwood, Katherine Patrick, Mia Wong, Zeytun Dilan West, Sallie-Wright Milam, Brandon Ogbolu, Jessica Torres, and Spencer Jackson, whose comments on earlier stages of this work were invaluable.

To those critical, engaging listening friends who kept me grounded over the years: Todd and Leslie Engelsen, Jackie Rogers, Alex Romain, Jill O'Connor, Nika Skvir, Sharad Vivek, Charles Holder, David Akeson, Colleen Breen, Laura Cooley, and Suresh Varadarajan.

To my dear friends on the HH: Russo, Michelle, Cenk, Wendy, Kaan, Ellen, David, Sharon, Greg, Shailesh, Bhakti, Sinan, Katie, Erdal, Lisa, Tolga, Didem, Sujay, Praveen, Steve, Mona, Batur, and Lauren: thank you for your insight, wisdom, humor, and faith in the notion that ideas are important to wrestle with—definitely among friends and especially when we disagree. May we forever remain totally cognizant of the need to keep frozen patties on hand!

With the deepest love, respect, and gratitude, I thank Sapna, Samip, Kenan, and Kristin for years of soulful conversation and your unfettered care. Thank you also for introducing me to Bettye LaVette's artistry and for sharing your signature curious, nuanced, insightful minds. Most of all, thank you for always having room at the kitchen table.

I thank my family-more-than-in-laws. Yvette and McDonald Furlonge, you never cease to amaze me with your endless capacity to love and embrace family. Kris and Rhonda, Aidan, Dylan, and Brendan, I'll always have key lime pie ready for you. Crystal, keep uploading the world. Giselle and Matt, your curiosity, joy, and love help sustain me always. And Devon Dolly Kitt McAuliffe: what a joy it will be to watch you grow and get into all sorts of mischief! #keepitcritical. Thank you to the entire Tillet and Ramdoo clan, especially Annie, Suzie, Afeni and Sheldon, and, of course, Salamishah.

I am grateful for Aunt Velma, who took my call after forty years, for Uncle James, and for my birth father, John Brown.

I thank my mother, Virginia Reasonover Brittingham, and write in memory of my father, Harry Wise Brittingham. Both raised generations with love and taught me the importance of listening.

I dedicate *Race Sounds* to my partner, Nigel. Always, you listen on the lower frequencies. You are my best, most generous, and most willing listener. Your love, patience, understanding, and ability to make me laugh and laugh sustain and beautifully surprise me. Nigel, with you I am home. This book is also dedicated to our three children, Logan, Lucas, and Wyatt. You stretch my heart in unimaginable ways. Being in your lives is the most rewarding part of living I have ever known. Thank you all for finding your way to us and for pulling me away from my laptop to play, explore, and witness as you create and make magic every day. The four of you teach me continually to listen anew.

Race Sounds

"Attuned to It All"

. . . .

Embodied Listening and Listening in Print

Each time I return to Toni Morrison's *Playing in the Dark*, I linger over her reflection on Marie Cardinal's *The Words to Say It*. In her autobiographical novel of psychological illness and healing, Cardinal recalls attending a Louis Armstrong concert where she experiences what she terms "her first encounter with the Thing":

> Armstrong was going to improvise with his trumpet, to build a whole composition in which each note would be important and would contain within itself the essence of the whole. I was not disappointed. . . . The sounds of the trumpet sometimes piled up together, fusing a new musical base, a sort of matrix which gave birth to one precise, unique note tracing a sound whose path was almost painful, so absolutely necessary had its equilibrium and duration become; it tore at the nerves of those who followed it.[1]

Cardinal goes on to describe her anxious reaction to this sound, her heart beating faster and faster until it grew "more important than the music, shaking the bars of my rib cage, compressing my lungs so the air could no longer enter them."[2] Finally, she runs from the concert hall "into the street like someone possessed."[3] At this reflection, Morrison wonders: "What on earth was Louie playing that night? What was there in his music that drove this sensitive young girl hyperventilating into the street?"[4]

Cardinal's narrative works as an impetus for Morrison to listen in print. Morrison takes the time to listen to what Cardinal is listening to and models an aural imagination at work. She marvels at Cardinal's precise recall of the music and how she is able to bring the immediacy of the music from that night to the page. She wonders, too, at the power with which Armstrong's music viscerally and emotionally undoes Cardinal even as it piques her own intellectual interest as a listener attempting to imagine the specific music played. In its opening moment, not only does *Playing in the Dark* launch its project to make explicit the notion that at America's and American literature's center is blackness, it highlights the fact that such imagery is not solely visual; it is aural and sonic as well. How do these sonic constructions of literary race affect our understanding of difference? How do they help shape our reading and interpretive imagination?

Race Sounds aims to understand how listening functions to perceive and interpret bodies, ideas, and aesthetics of race, gender, and class differences. This study posits attentive, relational, and deliberate listening as a mode of aural engagement. Etymologically, the Old English word *hlysnan*, "to listen," emphasizes this notion of an intentional listening practice, distinguishing the act of listening from hearing. In Modern English, too, while the verb "to hear" usually refers to the sense of hearing, to automatic or passive physiological sound perception, the verb "to listen" connotes more purposeful use of the auditory.[5] As philosopher Jean-Luc Nancy elaborates, the French verb *entendre*, "to listen," also connects listening with intention. For Nancy, listening is a resonant structure and practice, linking sound, sense, and subjectivity in relation to each other.

Race Sounds is a literary, historical, musical, filmic, archival, and theoretical examination of how contemporary writers, artists, and intellectuals in their constructions of race, gender, and class seek to shift emphasis away from the visual toward the aural, thereby suggesting aural literacy as a significant modality of identity, representation, and engagement. By being aurally attentive to these dynamics, these contemporary writers, artists, and intellectuals explore the lower frequencies of representation, considering the ways in which aural perception can tell alternative stories and amplify sound and difference in new ways. Furthermore, the texts that I examine are sonic sites that provide opportunities for a more fully attuned, nuanced aural engagement of the ambiguities, certainties, and suggestive sonic life of difference.

More specifically, *Race Sounds* advocates for listening as an artistic, civic, and interpretive practice that emerges from a place of wonder, curiosity, and *not knowing*. In the field of scientific inquiry, Stuart Firestein explains that ignorance is a "condition of knowledge." Rather than "an individual lack of information," such ignorance is the result of "a communal gap in knowledge." This kind of "knowledgeable ignorance, perceptive ignorance, insightful ignorance," Firestein asserts, "leads us to frame better questions, [and is] the first step to getting better answers. It is the most important resource we scientists have, and using it correctly is the most important thing a scientist does."[6] At the center of listening, I suggest, is inquiry. If we listen as we read, then we will discover more fully the dynamics of an art, politics, and practice of listening in African American literary and cultural texts and uncover the different ways of knowing that emerge from aural engagement. This is the aurally inflected work that *Race Sounds* performs.

Listening in Print

Although the archive *Race Sounds* draws from is interdisciplinary and multimedia in scope, it specifically explores listening's relationship to reading and its inflection through the materiality of the book. If, as Nathaniel Mackey asserts, "The page and the ear coexist. Not only do they coexist, they can contribute to one another," then how does one read as a listener?[7]

Robert Stepto's seminal essay "Distrust of the Reader in Afro-American Narratives" takes to task mainstream reader-response critics for their failure to engage with "how acts of listening and reading may be complicated by race."[8] He examines the ways in which African American literature expresses concerns within its fictional texts about how it should be read. Stepto contends that a "discourse of distrust" runs through African American literature, leading writers of these texts to embed within their fiction heavy instruction about how to listen to each text and explicit chastisement when reading goes awry. For Stepto, black texts persuade readers to act as "storylisteners," that is, "to seek the kind of communal relationship found, for example, between preachers and congregations, musicians and audiences in certain performance venues, and between storytellers and storylisteners."[9] In this paradigm, "readers become hearers, with all that that implies in terms of how one may sustain through reading the responsibilities of listenership as they are defined in purely performative contexts."[10]

What I appreciate about Stepto's treatment of readers as storylisteners is that he points toward a treatment of reading that thinks of the printed text as sonically charged. I would like to suggest, then, that such an aurally inflected reading practice could inform our approach to reading any text, even those that are not necessarily explicitly engaged in storytelling or orality. The focus in *Race Sounds*, however, is not on texts that attempt to instruct and heavily direct a reader in a particular "correct" way of listening. The writers and their texts highlighted in this study call on us to "exercise our listening faculties" in a variety of ways and, I contend, to conceive of both author and reader as participants in a discursive community, listening through texts that yearn for readers as well as the future those readers embody.[11] These texts present opportunities to cultivate a practice of engagement that attunes readers to print as it provokes or calls forth an aurally inflected, multisensory reading practice. I build on Stepto's suggestion of listening as a potential practice for engaging with and interpreting poetry to think more broadly about how listening can do such work for African American literary and cultural texts writ large.

Rewinding to consider briefly reading culture in early modern England reminds us that literacy has not always been imagined or practiced as "a monolithic entity."[12] As Bruce Smith explains, "where twenty-first-century students are likely to see only marks imprinted on paper—or, ignoring the imprintedness entirely, the concepts that those marks encode"—readers in the early modern world "would . . . have heard traces of sound" in "woodcut illustrations, in handwriting, and in print."[13] Smith posits what he terms "unairing," a process of "learning to hear, and not just see," what is embedded in print materials.[14] While the early modern world is far removed from our visual, screen-heavy twenty-first-century one, bringing listening to reading unairs or unmutes the potential of what I refer to as listening in print.

Listening in print as a practice resonates with the desire expressed often by African American writers specifically and American writers more broadly for printed language that is as liberated, unmuted, and unmediated as spoken or musical sound is romantically perceived to be. While these writers tend to perceive a border between orality and print, this study instead insists on the intimate relationship between them. Texts such as Toni Morrison's *Jazz*, for instance, invite their readers to develop and employ a more sensory-rich reading practice. When my students encounter the first word of Morrison's novel, "Sth," they inevitably attempt to say the sound on the page or ask me how to read it and what it means. They also see this word and assume that it is a sound, something meant to be heard aloud, but one that they are not sure how to say. This utterance immediately draws them into the print to interact with it in ways that are different from those they are accustomed to. "Sth" pauses them in their reading tracks. They need to call on their powers of decoding print differently.

Beginning the novel with a sound calls on readers to listen in preparation to read. *Jazz*'s epigraph, "Thunder, Perfect Mind," from the ancient Egyptian Nag Hammadi codices, also amplifies the slippage between the presumed silence of print and the sound of language: "I am the name of the sound / and the sound of the name. / I am the sign of the letter / and the designation of the division."[15] If we consider the lines preceding those of the epigraph in the original poem, we hear printed calls to its listeners throughout: "Hear me, you hearers / and learn of my words, you who know me. / I am the hearing that is attainable to everything."[16] *Jazz*'s epigraph juxtaposes orality ("the sound of the name") and inscription ("the sign of the letter"), signifying a gap or expressive abyss into which writers like Morrison invite their readers to listen as they read. Concluding the novel in an imagined invitation for readerly-writerly collaboration with a passage that suggests a desire for the book to be able to speak and the reader to be able to listen, *Jazz*'s narrator progressively exposes her desire for listening until she makes her way to a firm imperative:

> But I can't say that aloud; I can't tell anyone that I have been waiting for this all my life and that being chosen to wait is the reason I can. If I were able I'd say it. Say make me, remake me. You are free to do it and I am free to let you because look, look. Look where your hands are. Now.[17]

In Morrison's text, we are reminded as twenty-first-century readers that if we listen, print and other visual media has, as Steven Connor suggests, "the potential to make what is visible in print audible."[18] In this model, there is a sense of the printed page as interactive and continually reconstructed through encounter. It is worth thinking about, then, how we might listen in print differently when engaging with African American cultural texts as well as how we might develop habits of listening to the various kinds of texts concerning this tradition. *Race Sounds* listens in to African American literature in order to consider how listening develops as a processual manner of engaging writing, reading, and interpretive work.

Practicing reading in this aural manner means remaining mindful of what Nathaniel Mackey refers to as discrepancies between the print surface and the sonic life of words. For instance, N., the narrator in Mackey's epistolary novel *Djbot Baghostus's Run*, practices a discrepant listening. Music plays an important role in what comprises his memory and subjectivity. What material does sound make? In one instance, N. conflates music recorded on vinyl with his "inventory of traces," a record, residue, outline of his own becoming.[19] He begins compiling this inventory by listening to Miles Davis's *Seven Steps to Heaven*, one of the older albums in his collection. As he listens, N. not only hears Davis's music, "one of the cuts which made me," but he also attends to the "places where the needle skips" on the vinyl, interpreting them not as "noisy reminders of the wear of time" but as "rickety, quixotic rungs on a discontinuous ladder—quixotic leaps or ellipses."[20] *Seven Steps to Heaven* functions not only as a vinyl archive, a recorded holding place for Davis's musical creations that can be accessed repeatedly over time and in various spaces, but it also contains, in a sense, N.'s personal evolution over time. This personal evolution in turn is informed by and perceived through how N. listens to the music. His sense of becoming, mapped through listening, involves deciphering the original recorded moments on the record, the traces of other moments spent listening to the record, and the uncertainty inherent in such cultural engagement.

As the record skips, the sound creates spaces that N. describes as a "rickety . . . discontinuous ladder."[21] As a listener, he demonstrates his ability to discern the familiar, to detect those utterances that are unfamiliar, and to develop strategies to engage with these multilevel utterances. His listening, then, is fluid, flexible, and aware of and able to engage with what Mackey refers to as discrepant. As Mackey explains, discrepant engagement operates "in the interest of opening presumably closed orders of identity and signification, accent fissure, fracture, incongruity, the rickety, imperfect fit between word and world. Such practices highlight—indeed inhabit—discrepancy, engage rather than seek to ignore it."[22] While he listens to Betty Carter perform live at the Parisian Room, N. engages in discrepant listening. He perceives the "discrepant play between facial wealth and vocal reticence" that creates "an abyss large enough at times to efface the latter's source."[23] Of this emergent abyss, "something one doesn't get on records," N. comments that Carter's "spectral, silent 'voice' . . . upstaged every now and then her actual, audible voice."[24] Listening to Carter's performance not only emphasizes the difference between engaging with live musical performance and recorded music but also reveals N.'s growing awareness as a listener of the complex interplay between various modes of expression, particularly between the aural and the visual (and aural and print in that these realizations are shared through letters in this novel) and the need to develop strategies for engaging with such nuanced cultural expressivity.

By challenging readers to listen, the texts I examine in *Race Sounds* activate listening as a dynamic aural practice of cultural, political, and intellectual engagement. In this notion of listening, critics practice cultural criticism as listening readers, attempting to think with their ears and to imagine cultural meaning through sonic attentiveness. In addition to explaining the recent preponderance of listening in literature, film, theater, visual culture, interviews, and historical archives, *Race Sounds* contends that these texts shift reading from an action solely of the eyes to one that demands an aural sensory engagement of constructions of difference. To conceive of author and reader as involved in an aural relationship is to think of them as subjects immersed in history and in particular contexts and moments.

Listening within Tradition

Black literature *sounds*. The critical power, possibility, and promise of the acoustic permeate African American and black feminist literary criticism, traditions that actively work to understand, think through, and know difference heavily through describing the sonic lives of difference.[25] In its most influential and foundational texts, sound—whether a spoken or sung voice, talking book or singing drum, the blues, trains, or hambones—functions as a key metaphoric, structural, and epistemic site of black cultural identity.[26]

In the midst of this discursive focus on sound and voice, Hortense Spillers's "Mama's Baby, Papa's Maybe" attempts to develop a new notion of subjectivity and the human. Spillers writes: "In order for me to speak a truer word concerning myself, I must strip down through layers of attenuated meanings, made in excess over time, assigned by a particular historical order, and there await whatever marvels of my own inventiveness."[27] Her brilliant exploration of an "American Grammar" offers a world of critical possibility, as is evident in its influence on a range of critical treatments of black literature and culture.[28] Her theory, though, remains within a model of the human that ultimately centers on the idea that power is best embodied by an agency-infused speaking subject—the very subject that this project's turn to listening suggests we need to question. Despite the audible culture that permeates African American literary and cultural studies, then, there is little talk of listening and little attention given to the role of listening in interpretive work.

It might seem surprising that I would advocate for a listening practice particularly in a historical and political moment that compels one to speak truth in the face of alternative facts and power. Yet alongside cultural critics such as George Lipsitz, I insist that it is precisely in such moments of "unprecedented danger and peril" that we need auditors as well as (inter)locutors.[29] Even when we act as cultural critics, Lipsitz asserts, our expertise and penchant for (and dependence on) articulating theories and overarching frameworks of tradition are not enough. Instead, critical "virtuosity entails listening as well as speaking. It requires patient explorations into spaces and silences as much as it demands bold and forthright articulation of ideas and interests."[30] Implied in Lipsitz's call for a critical listening practice is the need to shift from the prevailing notion that criticism is solely the privileged site of speech. What his challenge suggests is that we need to practice a specific and critical listening—what Gemma Corradi Fiumara calls the other side of language. In her philosophical examination of listening, Fiumara explains that the prevailing notion of logic—the Greek *logos*—

in Western thought is predominantly speech-focused, thus tending "to ignore listening processes." Her project argues for the need to understand *logos* more fully, for "there could be no saying without hearing, no speaking which is not also an integral part of listening, no speech which is not somehow received."[31] Because misunderstanding, according to Fiumara, is "deeply rooted in the exclusion of listening," the work of listening is central to the creation of the conditions necessary for true dialogue and exchange, the conditions necessary for the generation of new knowledge and understanding.[32]

I aim to restore *listening* to *logos*—to balance the relationship in our critical conversations between listening and speaking. Like Julian Henriques's "sonic logos," I examine listening in order to think about how its "multisensory nature" can explore "the relationship, connection and intertwining of body and mind together."[33] Additionally, as Mitsuye Yamada cautions, "We must remember that one of the most insidious ways of keeping women and minorities powerless is to . . . let them speak freely and not listen to them with serious intent."[34] I join Lipsitz, Fiumara, Henriques, and Yamada in their pointing to the danger of positing a voice without a listener to perceive that voice. Attempts to conceive of a personhood that does not involve an intense development of a capacity for and practice of listening are doomed to mistake an actualized voice for power and freedom.

Becoming Attuned

In this book, I intend to understand more fully the processes of critical and interpretive listening. *Race Sounds*, then, focuses on how we listen, activates listening as an interpretive and filtering practice, and argues for listening's centrality in more intentional and embodied engagement with African American expressive culture. It questions our aural assumptions concerning race, allowing us to think about how we read racial difference as it is constructed and expressed in literary texts. It contributes to African American literary and cultural studies, black feminist criticism, American literary and cultural studies, and sound studies—discourses and frames of study that are already engaged in thinking through sound. *Race Sounds* critically intervenes specifically in these discourses of literature, culture, and race as they intersect with sound studies, an interdisciplinary field of inquiry and practice concerned with how humans attribute significance to sound in various forms. I build specifically on Fred Moten's *In the Break*, Josh Kun's *Audiotopia*, and Alexander Weheliye's *Phonographies*. Moten's work in particular informs my engagement with listening, especially in his careful attention to a wide range of sonic phenomena within the black radical jazz tradition—screams, cries, groans, hollers, and whistles—and his exploration of literature's overlooked aurality. Moten also acknowledges *Invisible Man*'s call for "a new analytical way of listening and reading."[35] Like Moten, I am interested in the "ensemble of senses" from which listening emerges and in listening's capacity to disrupt the traditional separation between acts of reading (highly visual and focused on the eye) and reception of orality (highly audible and focused on the ear).[36]

This book grows out of a perceived need to shift from notions of objectively hearing race and blackness specifically to foregrounding a practice of listening that is more self-aware and allows for an examination of how aural practices have generated particularly useful but sometimes limiting notions of black racial identity over time. I am interested in how the cultural texts in this study provide the reader and critic with an apprenticeship in listening of sorts, resonant with the listening apprenticeship we witness in David Bradley's *The Chaneysville Incident* (a novel I examine at length in chapter 4) and in Fiumara's philosophical treatment of listening. As Fiumara suggests, "if we are apprentices of listening rather than masters of discourse, we might perhaps promote a different sort of coexistence among humans: not so much in the form of a utopian ideal but rather as an incipient philosophical solidarity capable of envisaging the common destiny of the species."[37] Listening, then, is not possible solely because of expertise, nor is it an unmediated means to cultural immersion and transmission. Instead, listening is process and practice, a means of considering how critics, writers, and artists frame and make meaning through situated aural cultural engagements.

Race Sounds joins a collective effort to shift from a heavy emphasis on sounding to an attention to listening practices. This shift is evident in studies such as Tsitsi Jaji's *Africa in Stereo*, Carter Mathes's *Imagine the Sound*, and Jennifer Stoever's *The Sonic Color Line*. Especially resonant with *Race Sounds*, Stoever identifies the figures of the sonic color line and the listening ear to expose sound as "visuality's doppelgänger in U.S. racial history, unacknowledged but ever present in the construction of race and the performance of racial oppression."[38] Jaji's *Africa in Stereo* posits "stereomodernism" as a way to identify and amplify a sonic politics of solidarity operating within pan-African solidarity. She explores the question "How has being modern shaped African modernism?" through an interplay of many authors and artists whose literature, poetry, music, and film form a dense but highly resonant polyphony. As in *Race Sounds*, listening for Jaji is "essential work" that "brings affiliation, affinity, and negotiated resolution into acoustic liveness, fully resonant (or equally important, muffled) across geographic, ethnic, linguistic, and technical fissures."[39] In *Imagine the Sound*, Mathes examines the sonic as "a mode of aesthetic and political resistance against external and internal oppression."[40] Focusing on the post–civil rights literary sounds of black radical thought, he asserts that "diagnosing and confronting the mythic construction of white supremacy entails shifting the focus from simply the visual dominance of race in the American public sphere to perceiving the interaction between the apparent, and more ephemeral, but no less definitive dimensions of racial formation" in the sonic.[41]

Race Sounds intervenes and provokes differently, however, from these rich works in several ways. In it, I explicitly examine listening and sustain an attention to listening for the entirety of the study. I treat writers and artists as theorists of listening and creators of complex listening texts that think aurally about black subjectivity. Throughout this treatment of black literature and culture, I posit listening as an aural form of agency, a practice of citizenship, an aural empathy, an ethics of community building, a mode of social and political action, a set of strategies for cultural revision, and a practice of historical thinking. While *Race Sounds* engages in robust ways with music, it stretches the critical ear to consider other important sounds present in the tradition. It is also invested in *unmuting* print to the reader's ear through exploring listening as a crucial element of reading, perceiving, and interpreting texts.[42] Finally, this study thinks about a listening pedagogy, engaging with issues of teaching and learning and treating the literature classroom as a valuable laboratory and archive for theorizing about and practicing listening.

While *Race Sounds* is not a history of literary listening, it does draw from cultural histories such as Jean-Luc Nancy's *Listening* and its treatment of listening as different from automatic understanding and Peter Szendy's *Listen* in its choice to attend specifically to listening, recognizing that the "critical force of listening" has often been "restrained and denied" and hidden by the focus on the oral.[43] Rather than being speculative, listening for me is historically, materially, and culturally informed and is embodied, lived, and artistically practiced. This focus on listening is not meant to suggest that aural engagement represents a higher level of logic or interpretive work. Instead, it is a mode of engagement in the continuum of sensory cultural engagement, one that enacts change. As Don Ihde asserts in his study of a phenomenology of auditory experience, *Listening and Voice*, a focus on listening is "a deliberate decentering of a dominant tradition" that "symbolizes a hope to find . . . a different understanding of experience, one which has its roots in a phenomenology of auditory experience."[44] Ihde's phenomenological approach to listening and auditory experience involves "an intense and concentrated attention to sound and listening" and raises another important issue for this study in its significant awareness of "certain 'beliefs' which intrude into . . . attempt[s] to listen 'to the things themselves.'"[45]

Keying into assumptions, misunderstandings, and biases (implicit and otherwise) matters because they can significantly impede our ability to listen, particularly since assumptions so often subconsciously frame how we listen and can determine what we are open to hearing. Implicit in Ihde's phenomenology of listening is the idea that listening is a learned activity—what Jonathan Sterne refers to as a technique—in that listening "connotes practice, virtuosity, and the possibility of failure and accident. . . . It is a learned skill, a set of repeatable activities within a limited number of framed contexts."[46] For Sterne and Ihde, listening should be considered as a process that is formed and transformed through social, cultural, and political forces, rather than treated as a fixed cultural or automatic physiological act. In this sense, listening is an active and fully engaged process that is largely dependent on the particular contexts in which it occurs.

Performing Listening: Anna Deavere Smith's
Twilight: Los Angeles, 1992

In the aftermath of the Rodney King hearings and the civil disturbances in Los Angeles in 1992, Anna Deavere Smith visited the city to listen.[47] She interviewed more than three hundred people throughout Los Angeles, including black intellectuals, Korean grocers, Beverly Hills realtors, street kids, an unnamed white juror who served in the Simi Valley trial, truck driver Reginald Denny who was pulled from his truck and beaten during the riot, a former Los Angeles gang member, then police chief Daryl Gates, and King's family members. The resulting one-woman docuplay, *Twilight: Los Angeles, 1992*, is, as Smith has described it, "first and foremost a document of what an actress heard in Los Angeles."[48] It is an innovative, highly collaborative play in that it reveals a listener being present as an active auditor for those individual voices of citizens who experienced life in Los Angeles before, during, and after the uprising, voices of citizens like Josie Morales, a woman who witnessed King's beating:

> I was scheduled to testify / . . . because I had a lot to say / and during the trial I kept in touch with the / prosecutor, / Terry White, / . . . I said, "Well are you going to call me [to the witness stand] or not?" And he says, . . . "I don't think we're going to be using you . . ." / And I faxed him a letter / and I told him that those officers were going to be acquitted / and one by

one I explained these things to him in this letter / and I told him, "If you do not put witnesses / if you don't put one resident and testify to say what they saw," / And I told him in the letter / that those officers were going to be acquitted. / But I really believe that the prosecutor was dead set / on that video / and that the video would tell all.[49]

Morales's monologue both reminds us that she ultimately was not called to testify during the trial and allows us to listen to her perspective after the fact. The perspective she shares ends up being the outcome of the trial. What we saw in the videotape could not tell all; Morales's account of what she witnessed adds a richness of witness to the captured footage. As Elizabeth Alexander argues in her response to the videotape of the Rodney King beating, "the freeze-framed Simi Valley videotape, stripped of a soundtrack in which falling blows and bystanders' screams are audible, disallows the possibility that the sounds of terror could imprint themselves on the jury's mind."[50] This stripping of sound disallowed listening; paradoxically, however, the video's muting, as Alexander notes, amplified the notion that listening is as important to witnessing as viewing: "Witnessing can be aural as well as ocular. . . . Hearing, too, is central to witnessing. Sounds here haunt the mind as much as visual images."[51] Here Alexander acknowledges listening as a mode of witness, a mode that Smith enacts as she interviews citizens of Los Angeles and that her play relies on us as the audience to perform in our seats.

Smith's decision to include Morales's interview in the play effectively restores her to the witness lineup. During the Berkeley production, following Smith's rendering of Morales's words is a ten-second video clip, run at normal speed and including the original sound of the King beating. Together, the context Morales provides and the playing of the videotape following her words restore the sound muted during the courtroom proceedings and original media coverage of the event. Smith's decision to listen—to try "to hear what they're saying"—is even more remarkable given the racially and politically charged post-uprising Los Angeles (and United States) in which she conducted her interviews.[52] *Twilight* is, in essence, what Smith has made of her listening.

Preparing to perform her own characters, Smith always uses the same method. She begins by listening to the tapes of her subjects again and again: "I often start lying down in a very relaxed position. I want to see what impact the words have on my body. Material that hits me viscerally is likely to hit the audience too."[53] She later adds physical idiosyncrasies, often working from photos of her subjects. She then provides a theatrical space that invites and challenges her audience to practice what she refers to as the difficult, heart-filled, ethical work of listening.[54] About *Twilight: Los Angeles, 1992*, Anne Cheng notes that the audience becomes "an occasion for asking the ethical question what to do at the boundaries of comprehension? How does the audience/listener operate in order to recognize an implicit context and historical past and to resist simply taking in received meanings that are already formulated?"[55]

At the center of ethics is an empathetic listening, one that recognizes the need to reach across gaps in order to understand another person. Smith continues to practice this empathetic listening in future projects, including her 2016 production, *Notes from the Field: Doing Time in Education*. For *Notes from the Field*, Smith interviewed more than a hundred people in Philadelphia, Baltimore, Oakland, and several other cities in the United States. As in *Twilight: Los Angeles, 1992*, she shifts among rendering the voices and perspectives of public officials, everyday citizens, and academics. One voice, an Oakland activist, describes how hesitant he is to include the assassination when reading a book about Dr. Martin Luther King, Jr., to first graders. He is reluctant to expose them to death. But one by one, each of the children shares that they have a relative—a brother, cousin, uncle, father—who has been shot and/or killed. While the activist worries about introducing violence and death to his students, the students are already living with close-up experiences of violence and death. The last figure Smith channels in the play is James Baldwin. With cigarette and drink in hand, she performs a moment from *A Rap on Race*, a compilation of conversations Baldwin had with the anthropologist Margaret Mead. Smith, as Baldwin, concludes act 1: "What shall we do about the children? We are responsible for them."

Instead of providing an answer to Baldwin's channeled, reverberating question and assertion of public responsibility for children, act 2 opens in the audience. As Smith explains in the show's program: "I see the theater as a convening space, where you, for the most part strangers to one another, can come together to exchange ideas, suggest solutions, and possibly when I'm gone, mobilize around what should be done."[56] Smith's decision to stage conversations, to give the theater over to civic dialogue as part of her show, reflects her desire to mobilize as active listeners the people who attend her productions. Audience members are asked to respond in writing to this question: "What would you do to help more youth succeed in school and avoid incarceration?" They are then organized into discussion groups and, with a facilitator, have a conversation about how to create change. Listening to one another begins the necessary work of what Smith calls "making the broad jump towards the other."[57]

This ethical listening is not one Smith uses to collapse the gap between herself and the people she portrays on stage.[58] Nor does she use this listening to find solutions to the problems she explores in her work. As she explains, "Sometimes there is the expectation that inasmuch as I am doing 'social drama,' I am looking for solutions to social problems. In fact, though, I am looking at the processes of the problems."[59] For Smith, then, art and social change convene in the auditory spaces she enters in interviews and represents on stage. In her theater, listening becomes a creative, necessarily social and ethical process and practice. It is ethical because it attends to the discrepancies in racial perception, meaning making, and subjectivity. Through her practice, Smith dramatizes listening as a process that demonstrates an awareness of these discrepancies while replacing those discrepant meanings with the fullness and possibilities of difference. Her listening comes to us through her theater, shifting, for instance, the discourse concerning the King beating and the trial of the offending officers from speaking to an empathetic listening that leads us back to reconstituted speech.

What sense, *Twilight: Los Angeles, 1992* asks, can we make of these un(der) heard voices when we stop to listen to them? How might texts like *Twilight* cultivate a practice of public listening in a culture of speaking? How might African American literary criticism, a tradition framed by its sounds and soundings, more explicitly engage not only in the fact that the tradition sounds but also in the manner in which we access those sounds and in how the perspectives of the critic affect what is heard there? What does listening to the literature—as opposed to hearing its soundings—reveal? *Race Sounds* attempts to, as Smith models, lean in to the difficult work of listening. By performing a play that grows from her deliberate, attuned listening, Smith implicitly calls on her audience to become aurally attuned as well.

This gesture toward a conversation among strangers that relies heavily on an intentional listening leads us to Susan Bickford's assertion that listening is "a central activity of citizenship."[60] It also leads us to Danielle Allen's *Talking to Strangers*, a study that has been crucial to my thinking about listening—particularly the ways in which listening performs as a public, civic practice. Allen asserts that it is interracial distrust rather than racism that congeals at the core of our democratic problems in the United States. For her:

> On the same page or in the same city, alongside each other without
> touching, citizens of different classes, backgrounds, and experiences
> are inevitably related to each other in networks of mutual benefaction,
> despite customary barriers between them, and despite our nearly

complete lack of awareness, or even disavowal, of these networks. This relationship is citizenship, and a democratic polity, for its own long-term health, requires practices for weighing the relative force of benefactions and for responding to them.[61]

While Allen does not speak explicitly about listening as a civic habit, her study does point to the necessary work of listening in conversation between citizens, between strangers, as a key way of developing habits that can improve the workings of democracy. Such democratic listening acts to create a curative space, one where grievances are aired and potentially cleared.

I build on Allen's and Bickford's works and their interest in listening as a practice of social, public, and civic citizenship. Uri Hasson and his team of neuroscience researchers at Princeton University's Listening Lab, too, have conducted research that demonstrates the ways in which effective communication hinges on listening.[62] Yet I am also concerned with the ways in which listening is at the core of other types of practices of citizenship or public literacies and capacities, including interpretation, reading, and writing. Among other kinds of listening practices, *Race Sounds* amplifies the vital art and practice of public listening as a way to open up the possibility for new outcomes, new opinions, and new understandings of the other—even as it recognizes the nervousness, fear, and hesitation that can also inform our listening practice.

The Structure

When reflecting on his decision to create an epic poem under the title *Song of the Andoumboulou*, Nathaniel Mackey responds provocatively with a question: "There are other pieces of music I've heard. . . . Why does that one grab me at a certain point and hold on to the point where I continue to elaborate a work under that title?" Continuing, he describes his writing as "a selection . . . an open-ended endeavor that doesn't end with one's work."[63] Mackey's framing of his poetics as "particular," "partial," and "individual" resonates with my approach in *Race Sounds*. Rather than provide a comprehensive theory of auditory engagement, I aim to amplify listening as a creative, aesthetic, and interpretive practice in ways that provoke robust motivations to develop our capacities to listen.

Throughout *Race Sounds*, listening develops iteratively. This study is organized in a way that imagines each chapter as a particular context or site in order to explicate further the complex and situational practice of listening. Chapter 1, "'Our Literary Audience': Listenership in Zora Neale Hurston's *Their Eyes Were*

Watching God and Sterling Brown's 'Ma Rainey,'" examines the ways in which these two texts model listening. This modeling reflects these authors' concerns during the Harlem Renaissance with developing a literary audience—a black reading audience or what I refer to as a listenership—specifically for African American literature. I begin this study with these authors because critics have used their works to establish sound and voice as key figures in the African American literary tradition. What understandings emerge when we approach these texts through listening as an aural way of knowing? My discussion draws on these creative texts as well as the authors' work as ethnographers in order to think through how readers of these texts are called on to do what I term "listen in print."

In chapter 2, "'To Hear the Silence of Sound': Vibrational Listening in Ralph Ellison's *Invisible Man*," I develop the idea that Ellison's novel enacts a vibrational listening as a fully embodied process, one that involves much more than the physiological ear. By extension, this chapter engages with the ways in which Ellison reflects on the role that sensory perception and sound technology—particularly the phonograph, microphone, and the tape recorder—play in constructions of racial difference. While the novel dramatizes invisibility as its key metaphor for racial dislocation, it also amplifies listening as a fully embodied experience, one that allows Invisible Man space in which to reconstitute his being. Through his vibrational listening, Invisible Man finds sonic spaces in which to potentially sense a newly materialized and more fully realized racial identity.

Chapter 3, "When Malindy Listens: Audiographic Archiving in Gayl Jones's *Corregidora*," explores the questions: What happens when Malindy *listens*? What different understandings emerge when we think of the black woman vocalist as a listener to her self? Ursa Corregidora, the novel's protagonist and a blues vocalist, performs as audience to her own singing voice, her family's orally narrated history of enslavement, and her own personal trauma. Ursa's listening results in an audiographic—auditory, autobiographical, and composed—sonic archive. This chapter concludes with a discussion of Aretha Franklin's "Respect" and Bettye LaVette's "Blackbird" as instances of interpretive musical listening.

While *Corregidora* is steeped in a history of slavery and emancipation, it is chapter 4, "'If I Allow Myself to Listen': Slavery, Historical Thinking, and Aural Encounters in David Bradley's *The Chaneysville Incident*," that focuses directly on listening and the work of the historian. This chapter contends that listening is a salient mode of historical thinking about slavery. Bradley's narrator, social historian John Washington, initially resists listening as a viable mode of historical and archival research. Eventually, he adopts listening as a way to negotiate the past and present in order to create a historical narrative that both comprehends and questions the past. Bradley's novel, I argue, presents audition as a spatial, cultural, and contested practice, one that dramatizes the dynamics of interpretation.

Chapter 5, "'New Ways to Make Us Listen': Aural Learning in the English Classroom," engages in a conversation about learning to listen and listening to learn. I share ways in which listening has informed my pedagogy and my students' learning. The chapter begins by exploring James Baldwin's "Sonny's Blues"—a text that intricately links listening and learning. I then share the multimedia and interdisciplinary curriculum I have designed in A Listening Mind, an English course that aims to develop students' habits as listeners to texts in print and other forms of cultural and social texts. The afterword to *Race Sounds*, "'All Living Is Listening': Toward an Aurally Engaged Citizenry," listens to Barack Obama's final speech as president of the United States alongside this study's epigraph from Claudia Rankine's *Citizen* in order to meditate on these persons' and texts' calls for a democratic listening.

Race Sounds is an invitation to listen—to think through sound. This project is an effort to explain why and how listening is an important critical and artistic practice. I wrote it because I wanted to situate listening as a cultural and political practice in a contemporary moment in which sound and voice serve as prevalent expressions of knowing and understanding blackness. How does thinking more intentionally about how we perceive and interpret racialized sounds refine our understanding of sonic models of black difference? How does hearing *listening* and engaging in listening studies—that is, reflecting on listening and its processes—complicate notions of racial difference? How does such attention to this aural figure push us to rethink interpretive work as an embodied practice? My hope is that this book amplifies listening as a set of intentional and persistent strategies that not only enliven how we read, write, and critique texts but also inform how we might be more effective audiences for each other and against injustice in our midst.

ONE

"Our Literary Audience"

· · · · · · · · · · · · · · · · · · · ·

Listenership in Zora Neale Hurston's *Their Eyes Were Watching God* and Sterling Brown's "Ma Rainey"

In 1973, Alice Walker, then just twenty-nine years old and still nine years from publishing *The Color Purple*, set out to Fort Pierce, Florida, to find Zora Neale Hurston's unmarked grave. Walker's essay "Looking for Zora" chronicles this challenging search for Hurston's resting place. Determined to recover this lost genius of the African American literary tradition, Walker assumes the fictional role of Hurston's niece. By doing so, not only does she build a quick trust with the townspeople she interviews, but she also develops a comfort in the role. As Walker shares, she moved "completely into being Zora's niece, and the lie [came] with perfect naturalness to my lips." She goes on to assert that "as far as I'm concerned, she is my aunt—and that of all black people as well."[1]

Walker eventually locates her cultural aunt's grave by *listening* for it. Then, when she returns to the area with a monument salesperson and attempts to locate the grave a second time, she describes to him the necessary process of discovery through listening: "You'll have to go out there with me. . . . And take a long pole and 'sound' the spot. . . . Because there's no way of telling it's a grave, except that it's sunken."[2] As they search for the gravesite, Walker calls out, "Zora! I'm here. Are you?" expressing in a sense her desire for Zora to hear and know that someone is searching for her. It is this sounding, this investigation through close, attentive listening, that leads Walker twice to Hurston's unmarked grave—a site almost completely obscured by vines and weeds and withholding any clue that anyone of importance, let alone one of the key figures in the African American literary tradition, is buried there. Walker literally listens and figuratively calls us to listen in memoriam for one of our cultural geniuses.

It is apt that Walker employs active listening as a strategy to find Hurston's gravesite, for listening was central to Hurston's practice as a writer and an anthropologist. This, too, was the case for poet Sterling Brown, whose poem "Ma Rainey" salvages a folk and a folk culture whose contours were threatened by racism and flood. In *Inventing the New Negro*, Daphne Lamothe notes similarly that "the almost seamless continuity between the folk culture [Brown]

19

observed and the poetry he wrote suggests that Brown's poetry, like an ethnographic narrative, aspired to Brown's desire to record the folk in his poetry
because of the threat of losing those very folk and the folkways they live, practice, and perform."[3] Though not a trained ethnographer, Brown conducted ethnographic fieldwork during his three years at Virginia Seminary. Like Hurston
and Jean Toomer, Brown draws on "his observations," Robert Stepto notes, "to
produce a written vernacular literature that venerated black people of the rural
South instead of championing the new order of black life being created in cities
and the North. . . . valu[ing] and practic[ing] listening as he wrote poetry about
the folk in the American South."[4] Brown was concerned with developing an audience for African American literature that could effectively appreciate the place
and sounds of the folk in this literary tradition. He was what I term a listening
poet. This generalization regarding poets is quite apt in Brown's case. He understood that his engagement as a poet with southern folk and their culture was a
multisensory, and particularly a sonic, collaboration.

For both Brown and Hurston, then, listening becomes a central means of
gathering knowledge about the folk and folkways of which they write. Writing
poetry and fiction for them becomes a means of transcribing that knowledge
gained through the sensual experience of listening. Brown and Hurston work
to narrow the perceived gap between oral and written and between the poet and
novelist and the folk in order to engage with the multivalent nature of language,
whether print or spoken.[5]

It is into the ways in which their writing cultivates a listening readership—a
listenership—that this chapter tunes. While Hurston and Brown are invested in
recording the folk in their writing, they are also interested in recording in writing *how* they listen. They are listening writers, or what Peter Szendy refers to
as *arrangers*, "listeners who have *written down their listening*."[6] Szendy writes of
arrangers,

> I love them more than all the others, the arrangers. The ones who sign
> their names *inside* the work, and don't hesitate to set their name down
> next to the author's . . . it seems to me that what arrangers are signing is
> above all a listening. *Their* hearing of a work. They may even be the only
> listeners in the history of music to *write down* their listenings, rather than
> describe them. . . . I love to listen to someone listening.[7]

While Szendy is talking about musical arrangements and their transcription to
the page specifically, I find his idea useful when examining authors like Hurston
and Brown. Both are writers who collect and then arrange in print stories and

songs in ways that preserve folk culture while also representing the folk in new ways. In particular, I read Brown's "Ma Rainey" as a literary text as transcription. In transcribing their hearing onto the page, these writers aim to provide reading instruction particularly for their black listenerships. Hurston's novel and Brown's poem position and provoke readers to do what I term listen in print. Listening and reading as both print decoding and cultural recording practices intertwine, then, providing opportunities for collaborative and performed multisensory cultural engagement to occur. At the end of this textual listening are epiphany for Pheoby, self-verification for Janie, a socially resonant performance for Ma Rainey, and a momentary soothing for Ma Rainey's audience.

Zora Neale Hurston's Ethnographic Listening

In a 1935 interview with Alan Lomax, Hurston explains her approach to ethnographic fieldwork, an approach that embodies the value she placed as anthropologist and writer not merely on orality but on aurality—that is, on listening, responding, and listening again. First, Hurston sings in this interview a song she refers to as "You May Go but This Will Bring You Back," a song she collected in Eatonville, Florida. Then she describes her process of learning and collecting songs in the field:

> I learn them. I just get in a crowd with the people if they're singing and I listen as best I can. And I start to joining in with a phrase or two and then finally I get so I can sing a verse. And then I keep on until I learn all the songs, all the verses. And then I sing them back to the people until they tell me that I can sing them just like them. And then I take part and I try it out on different people who already know the song until they are quite satisfied that I know it. And then I carry it in my memory.[8]

Hurston listens and then sings the song back to the people. The people then listen to her and provide feedback on her performance. Then she repeats the process until she is confident she holds the song in her memory. And in this recording, we witness listening as a relational process.

This recording amplifies Hurston's practice of what I refer to as a listening ethnography, a practice that itself enacts the idea of listening to someone listen. The term "listening ethnography" draws from Sarah Pink's work on sensory ethnography, what she describes as "a process of doing ethnography that accounts for how this multi-sensoriality is integral both to the lives of people who participate in our research and to how we ethnographers practice our craft."[9] While

Pink focuses mainly on visual practices, Hurston brings to the fore the sonic life of an ethnographic practice. Hurston's listening ethnography and her comments regarding it reflect such a sensorial collaboration in the field between those she is collecting material from and her self as an anthropologist. As Daphne Brooks asserts,

> For Hurston, singing not only operates as a mode of embodied cultural documentation, but it also upsets the putative boundaries between scholar and cultural informant, individual and community, folk culture and modernity, and gendered spaces of work and play. Above all else, it encourages readers to listen (again) to Hurston's vocals so as to recognize the centrality of sound as an epistemic tool in her rich, lively, and diverse career as a cultural worker.[10]

Brooks continues to describe Hurston's "ability to, like Edison's queer little late-Victorian instrument, both record and play back the sound around her."[11] Hurston's cultural negotiations demonstrate the dynamic relationship between voicing or sounding and listening. In this way, she reveals an awareness that she cannot sing—that she will never know if she has learned the song effectively—unless she listens well to the original performers of the song and to their feedback on her own performance.[12] Hurston's listening and sonic archiving in the field amplify one of her major concerns as a writer and a collector of black folk culture: how to preserve, record, and transmit this culture.

Practicing and performing a listening ethnography function as Hurston's response. Her listening ethnography emphasizes the reciprocal and aurally inflected relationship among questioning, researching, collecting, and searching. Because this recording in the field captures Hurston not only as she records a folk song but also as she demonstrates and reflects on her process of listening ethnography, it provides a template for reading literature of and about the folk. If listening is a process Hurston practices in order to preserve, record, and transmit black folk cultural meaning in writing, then it follows that at the center of the reading of that writing is listening. Hurston's aural fieldwork and aurally inflected writing in *Their Eyes Were Watching God*, I suggest, challenge us not only to listen as we read but also to consider how listening is intertwined with reading. While critics frequently identify *Their Eyes Were Watching God* as a "speakerly text," Hurston's listening ethnography calls us to think about models of listening as we read.[13] If, as Brooks asserts, Hurston's "performances underscore [her] critical acuity in the realm of listening, performing, and, by extension, arranging the sounds that she encounters, stores, and 'carr[ies] . . . in her memory' out in the field," how then does this sonic acuity resonate in her writing? How does that resonance inflect how we tune in to her writing?[14] What if we read *Their Eyes Were Watching God*, for instance, as a text of Pheoby's listening?

Listening for Pheoby

Poetic in its expressive economy, the omniscient narrator's description of the role Pheoby plays in Janie's storytelling might seem a mere statement of fact. After all, the opening moment of *Their Eyes Were Watching God* features Janie, not Pheoby, returning to the all-black community of Eatonville, Florida. After a one-and-a-half-year absence, she *must* have a story to tell (and it is, indeed, her story we learn throughout the novel). The opening scene in the town suggests as much as Janie returns at sundown, "the time to hear things and talk" when the townspeople, transformed from "tongueless, earless, eyeless conveniences" during the workday into "lords of sounds and lesser things," sit on the porches beside the main road, "their ears full of hope" to hear a good tale.[15] Yet Janie continues walking "straight on to her gate," returning the porchsitters' "good evenin'" with "speech [that] was pleasant enough" but did not meet their desire for a story.[16]

Once Janie slams the gate behind her, the porch talk recommences. We listen as four women out of the group of porchsitters converse about Janie: Pearl Stone, Mrs. Sumpkins, Lulu Moss, and Pheoby Watson. The first three women chastise Janie in her absence—both for her relationship with a younger man, Tea Cake, and for her refusal to talk to them. Pheoby, on the other hand, verbally reprimands these women, reminding them that "nobody don't know if it's anything to tell or not. Me, Ah'm her best friend, and Ah don't know."[17] Pheoby then leaves her porch to carry a hot meal to Janie and, as we know, listens hungrily as Janie tells her story. Despite, however, the straightforward brevity of this remark—"Pheoby's hungry listening helped Janie tell her story"—what Hurston describes in this line is quite striking. In order for Janie to tell her story, she must have a listener.[18] And not just any auditor. With Pheoby as model, we observe that the listener must be curiously hungry, aware of her uncertainty, and committed to listening openly, attentively, and perceptively to someone else's story.

A tall order, certainly. Yet Pheoby is well cast for this role—something her neighbors' listening in contrast makes quite clear. If we return to the big road for a moment, we witness the porchsitters waiting with "ears full of hope" for Janie's story. While they, too, are listening, their desire to hear is laced with a hungry *judging*. Their hunger is, as Saidiya Hartman decodes in a different context, an assertion of black need that positions the body "as a literal vessel of communication, attending to unmet longing and expressing dissent."[19] In this opening scene, Hurston attributes hunger to various sources: economic, psychological, racial, material. All this hunger—generated from the workday's systemic refutation of the porchsitters' humanity—is present as Janie returns to town. As they watch Janie walk into town, the porchsitters "chewed up the back parts of their minds and swallowed them with relish. They made burning statements with questions, and killing tools out of laughs. It was mass cruelty. A mood come alive. Words walking without masters; walking altogether like harmony in a song."[20] Their ears are "full" already of their need to reconstitute their own humanity, rendered null and "senseless" as they worked all day in the field. In this context, Janie's story is inconsequential. They "know" who Janie is because they know their own hunger. Figuratively and cannibalistically feasting on their own thoughts and memories, they find their own cruel song in momentary pleasure and power.[21]

Pheoby, however, positions herself as an eager yet patient, willing, and attentive listener. It is no small matter that while the porchsitters remain on the big porch, Pheoby is willing to admit "Ah don't know" and to "go there tuh know there"—to leave her porch to visit Janie and catch up. In this move, Pheoby models a notion of friendship as a practice, as what Danielle Allen describes as "a series of hard-won, complicated habits that are used to bridge trouble, difficulty, and differences of personality, experience, and aspiration."[22] Pheoby does not make assumptions even though—or perhaps because—she knows Janie well, thereby clearing the way for new, emergent information. As she sits with Janie, "eager to feel and do through [her], but hating to show her zest for fear it might be thought mere curiosity," she also "held her tongue for a long time, but she couldn't help moving her feet." At the same time, Janie, "full of that oldest human longing—self revelation"—speaks into the attentive silence Pheoby provides.[23] As Kate Lacey recognizes, communication involves a relationship in which "speaker and listener are mutually interdependent." Think of Janie's metaphor, "mah tongue is in mah friend's mouth."[24] But as Lacey asserts, "it is the openness of the listening position—on either side—which produces the space in and across which communication can take place."[25] Hurston's text demonstrates this openness when, in response to Janie's comment, "To start off wid, people like dem wastes up too much time puttin' they mouf on things they don't know nothin' about . . . ," Pheoby quickly responds, ". . . so long as they get a name to gnaw on they don't care whose it is, and what about, 'specially if they can make it sound like evil."[26] Typographically, the ellipses allow Pheoby's thoughts to pick up where Janie's leave off in a way that demonstrates her alliance with her friend.

Pheoby finishes her friend's sentence, helping to establish that she and her friend are communicating on common ground.

It also matters that this is, in fact, not the first time Janie chooses to confide in Pheoby. We know that she and Janie have been "kissin'-friends for twenty years" and that Pheoby has served as Janie's confidante in the past.[27] As Joe Starks's wife, Janie grows tired of being abused and belittled in public and decides one day to take him to verbal task on the front porch of their store. In doing so, she effectively robs "him of his illusion of irresistible maleness that all men cherish."[28] Janie feels justified in her public critique of Joe and questions why he becomes "so mad with her for making him look small when he did it to her all the time? Had been doing it for years."[29] Joe grows ill following the episode, and the town gossips that Janie has "fixed" Joe. When Joe refuses her beef-bone soup, a "stunned" and "hurt" Janie seeks out her friend, Pheoby, who insists that Janie ignore the town's gossip. Following Joe's death, Janie and Pheoby visit each other periodically and spend time fishing together. Pheoby is close enough to Janie that she knows that "a Sanford undertaker was pressing his cause" for marriage to Janie, "and Janie was listening pleasantly [to Pheoby] but [was] undisturbed," suggesting that one can listen to another without consensus existing as a result or a precondition of engagement.[30] Note, too, that this brief mention of Janie's listening to Pheoby reminds us that they are friends in conversation whose aim is not necessarily consensus. Instead, the aim is a communication at the center of which is listening.

A Critical and Cultural Politics of Listening

The critical history of *Their Eyes Were Watching God* more energetically grapples with whether or not Janie realizes her voice over the course of the novel than it does with Pheoby's hungry listening. Barbara Johnson, for instance, connects Janie's realization of a voice to her awareness of her "inside" and "outside." Karla Holloway also explains that "Janie gains her voice from the available voice of the text and subsequently learns to share it with the narrator."[31] And while she discusses Pheoby in her foreword to *Their Eyes Were Watching God*, Mary Helen Washington writes that Pheoby suggests to her "all those women readers who discovered their own tale in Janie's story and passed it on from one to another; and, certainly, as the novel represents a woman redefining and revising a male-dominated canon, these readers have, like Janie, made their voices heard in the world of letters, revising the canon while asserting their proper place in it."[32]

Critical explication of voice in *Their Eyes Were Watching God* reverberates with, as I discuss in the introduction to *Race Sounds*, efforts in the larger discourses of African American and black feminist literary criticism in the 1980s and 1990s to delimit tradition through sounding the tradition. An early generation of black feminist critics including Mae Henderson, Barbara Christian, Valerie Smith, and Cheryl Wall emphasized in their important work both the significance of recovering and sounding the too-often silenced voices of women of color in particular *and* the critical nature of dismantling the systems through which such silencing too often happens. Henderson, for instance, demonstrates the important role that oral traditions have played in African American literature through her trope "speaking in tongues"—a trope emblematic of the at once critical and spiritual work of the tradition—in order to "theorize the preeminence of voice and narration in black women's literary performance."[33]

Just as Hurston's novel signaled foundational opportunities for critics to assert and examine voice as a privileged figure of expression and knowing in the fields of black feminist, feminist, African American, and American literatures, her novel compels this study's attention, instead, to listening. Tuning in to Pheoby allows us to examine the coterminous and equally robust yet muted tropes and practices of listening and the listener in African American and black feminist letters.[34] A less audible character—both in the novel and in critical discourse about the novel—Pheoby emerges as an important practitioner and embodiment of listening as interpersonal, cultural, and communal negotiation.[35] While such a focus on listening might be heard as problematic given the ways in which the figure of voice is treated critically and politically in contrast to the figure of silence, the silence of listening actually is imbued with power, agency, and intention.

The more enduring power apparent in Pheoby's listening extends beyond its benefits in the text to suggest the potential for listening as a civic, communal, and political habit. As Hélène Cixous asserts, "Speaking is not possible without others who have such capacity to hear. With such capacity, even silence speaks. The readiness to hear difference . . . might be understood as an acceptance of the invitation to join, however temporarily, in a simultaneity of speaking and hearing, which is a game of community."[36] A key player in this interdependent model of communication, this "game of community," Pheoby is an active conduit between the porchsitters and Janie. As she leaves her porch, Pheoby promises to let the people there know what she learns from Janie, if there is anything to tell. When she visits with Janie, she assures her friend that she "hears what they say 'cause they just will collect round mah porch 'cause it's on de big road," and she makes it clear to Janie that "if you so desire Ah'll tell 'em what you tell me to tell 'em."[37] Pheoby's listening, then, is a mode of negotiation between the town and the newly returned Janie, opening a channel through which a dialogue between her and the contentious or presumptuous citizens potentially can begin.

Pheoby's fictional hungry listening also resonates for me with recent studies in cognitive neuroscience that demonstrate the significance of the behavior of listeners on personal storytelling. These studies demonstrate, for instance, that "everyday personal storytelling is a vehicle by which we and our social worlds often conspire to tell stories about a stable self in order to verify our self-perceptions," one that is fraught with social complications in that this storytelling activity necessarily "recruit[s] other people to help with the job of constructing our sense of self."[38] Researchers also have found that listening, far from being passive, is an act of co-narration. While unresponsive, disruptive, or otherwise ineffective listeners can undermine attempts at self-affirming, self-verifying storytelling, attentive listening—like Pheoby's listening—can result in experiences of verification and affirmation through storytelling.[39] We witness such an outcome, for example, as *Their Eyes Were Watching God* closes. In the novel's final moment, we listen as Janie, after benefiting from Pheoby's hungry listening, experiences catharsis:

> The day of the gun, and the bloody body, and the courthouse came and commenced to sing a sobbing sigh out of every corner in the room; out of each and every chair and thing. Commenced to sing, commenced to sob and sigh, singing and sobbing. Then Tea Cake came prancing around her where she was and the song of the sigh flew out of the window and lit in the top of the pine trees. . . . Here was peace. . . . She called in her soul to come and see.[40]

Singing, sighing, and sobbing, Janie's material surroundings are personified; her room and the objects within it become sonic sites reflective of her emotional release. The scene transforms from one of grieving into one of relief and ultimately peace in one's own fuller self.

As Pheoby decides to engage in a micropolitics of listening—the loci of which are intimate conversations with her longtime "bosom friend" and more public conversations with neighbors on the porch—she models listening as a habit of friendship *and* as a civic responsibility. We witness in Pheoby's listening performance—and Maurice Merleau-Ponty's phenomenological work on listening—the fact that listening is an active engagement with another, an "act of concentration" on someone else that is "different from trying to make of oneself an absence that does not impose on the other."[41] Rather than adopting a position of empathy or an emptying and abandoning of one's sense of self, Pheoby models for us what is ultimately a courageous listening, a practice that is "open to the opinions of others, neither refusing to listen, nor simply identifying uncritically and selflessly with the position of the speaker."[42] Such a listening, according to Kate Lacey, "takes courage because it entails the possibility of one's sense of self being challenged or changed in the process of the encounter."[43]

Pheoby finds an enduring power in her hungry listening, a listening that suggests that she embodies both a need to listen and a need to be perceived as a listener. Giving audience to Janie nourishes Pheoby, leading her to exclaim hyperbolically, "Lawd! . . . Ah done growed ten feet higher from jus' listenin' tuh you, Janie. Ah ain't satisfied wid mahself no mo'. Ah means tuh make Sam take me fishin' wid him after this. Nobody better not criticize yuh in mah hearin'."[44] Pheoby declares here a rejuvenated agency. Her articulation of a nourished self marks a movement beyond the boundaries of an already known self and suggests an appetite for meaning and sensation large enough to squeeze the last drop of sound and sense from the world and from words.[45] She demonstrates Robert Coles's notion that the way we listen reveals something of the listener: "as active listeners we give shape to what we hear, make over our stories into something of our own."[46] Further, Pheoby's hungry listening also calls into question one premise of modern epistemology: "that the knowing subject exists apart from the objects he or she perceives."[47] Pheoby's identity, in other words, is attuned to her perception of—her listening to—Janie's story. In sharing the impact of Janie's story on her, Pheoby also provides further evidence of her listening, thereby confirming Janie's perceptive choice to tell her story to this intimate audience of one.

Sterling Brown's Call for a Black Listenership

While Hurston's intimate conversation implicitly suggests a model of listenership—in relation to literary *and* social texts—grounded in friendship and trust between friends, Sterling Brown's "Ma Rainey" stages a call for a people to listen by re-creating in poetry an audience attending a live blues performance in a region struggling in the aftermath of a devastating flood. In his essay "Our Literary Audience," Brown expresses his concern about the state of black readership—a readership that, he complains, does not exist in his moment as "we are not a reading folk."[48] He elaborates: "I have . . . a deep concern with the development of a literature worthy of our past, and of our destiny; without which literature certainly, we can never come to much. I have a deep concern with the development of an audience worthy of such a literature."[49]

Brown's complaint signals the poet's firm belief in the role of a black reading audience as central to the creation, reception, and sustenance of his poetry and black literature as a larger tradition. He asserts that "without great audiences we cannot have great literature."[50] Brown was concerned with cultivating that audience and writing the great literature that his audience could both receive and assist in making. What is compelling here is his complex and fluid conception of a literary audience. His audience includes readers and listeners of literature— who will both consume and assist in creating literature—and the poet. In this move, Brown makes listening an important figure in literary and cultural perception and expression and summons an aurally inflected black readership—a *listenership*—to sustain black literary tradition building.

Brown's "Ma Rainey" presents the blues in a way that amplifies their capacity to bring into being a collective catastrophic response through the individual articulation of loss. The basis of his portrayal lies in the relationship between his poetic listening practice and the writing of this blues poem. When I first wrote about this poem, I argued that Brown was dedicated to capturing not only the intensity with which the folk (in the poem and historically) wanted to see Rainey perform but also the folk aesthetic that was a key force behind Harlem Renaissance articulations of a New Negro persona and culture.[51] Brown's poetics, I asserted, are a move away from the notion of spokespersons sounding the folk to a writing of a discourse that allows the folk to sound (like) themselves.

This is not to say that Brown was attempting to locate and reify an audible folk authenticity. In *In Search of Authenticity*, Regina Bendix examines an impulse in folklore studies to locate authenticity in order to validate the field. Validation occurs through identifying the "authentic" object of study in part because, according to Bendix, "the notion of authenticity implies the existence of its opposite, the fake, and this dichotomous construct is at the heart of what makes authenticity problematic."[52] Ironically, this search may intensify in a postmodern moment that complicates notions of fixed essences precisely because such complications create "a sense of lost authority and disciplinary fragmentation."[53] For Bendix, what should be at stake ultimately in discourses of authenticity is "not 'what is authenticity?' but . . . 'how has authenticity been used?'"[54]

This examination of "Ma Rainey" instead considers how Brown wrote his poetry to call forth and engage a black listenership, one that understands "reading" to be an active, interpretive, regenerative act of "listening." Sonya Posmentier notes similarly that Brown provides "blueprints of Negro reading" through the manner in which he composes the lyric.[55] While Posmentier turns to "When de Saints Go Ma'ching Home" and the manner in which Brown's poem and his textbook connect New Negro and New Critical concerns, my interest is in a listenership that is attuned to Brown's poetry as an arrangement of his own listening on the page.[56] As Robert Stepto suggests in an earlier reading of "When de Saints Go Ma'ching Home," Brown offers a "blueprint of a New Negro poetry" through the manner in which he evokes a "communal performance" in the poem.[57] Central to this blueprint is the practice of reading as a listener. Stepto explains, "Within the context of a specific communal performance inspired by Big Boy," the artist in the poem, "the poet has been a true listener. When the poet in turn tells his tale of Big Boy, his song, and the performance mutually created by singer, song, and audience, his act of listening in the past achieves" a poetry that emerges as "the creation of interrelated, multigeneric artistic forms."[58] Thus, the reader is called on to listen to a poem such as "Ma Rainey" as it records and performs listening in print.[59]

Jean-François Lyotard's meditation on reading and his notion that "reading listens" are useful here.[60] Lyotard explores reading as listening in *The Postmodern Explained*, asserting that "we *hear* more than we see while we are reading" and describing reading as "an exercise in listening."[61] He elaborates, noting that "forming in yourself this capacity for listening in reading is forming yourself in reverse; it is losing your proper form. It is reexamining what is presupposed or taken as read in the text and in the reading of the text."[62]

I contend that we must listen as ourselves and so, to some extent, Lyotard's notion of "losing your proper form," of emptying the self, does not resonate with this study's focus on listening as an embodied practice, informed by race, gender, class, and other social identifiers and experiences. I appreciate, however, Lyotard's connection of listening to the practice of reading. In this framing of listening, listener-readers are called upon to reevaluate prior knowledge and to reflect on their assumptions in order to make room for new possibilities and realizations. Lyotard's notion of a listening reading requires an increased attention to the text, an aural attentiveness that acts as a filter to delineate a selective and strategic reading practice.

"She Jes' Gits Hold of Us Dataway": Modeling Listenership in "Ma Rainey"

Part of what makes "Ma Rainey" a poem that depends on a listenership is that it relies itself on its poet's "literary performances of listening."[63] Brown was reportedly inspired to write "Ma Rainey" after seeing her perform "Backwater Blues," a moving blues meditation on the disastrous southern flood of 1927. As Hazel

Carby writes, "Rainey's original performance becomes in Brown's text a vocalization of the popular memory of the flood."[64] Although Brown titled his poem after the popular blues performer Ma Rainey, and although Ma Rainey did perform "Backwater Blues," Bessie Smith wrote and recorded the song following the 1926 Cumberland River flood in Nashville.[65] When she recorded the song later in 1927, "Backwater Blues" became an anthem for the Great Mississippi River Flood.[66] As Angela Davis comments: "The seasonal rains causing the Mississippi River to flood its banks are part of the unalterable course of nature, but the sufferings of untold numbers of black people who lived in towns and the countryside along the river also were attributable to racism. . . . While most white people remained safe, black people suffered the wrath of the Mississippi, nature itself having been turned into a formidable weapon of racism."[67] Smith's ability to record her music for wider distribution, the song's timeliness, and the powerful ways in which her lyrics directly spoke to her audiences' trials contributed to the immense success of her record.[68]

Paul Oliver offers a poignant account of the 1927 flood:

> No one had anticipated the full horror of the 1927 floods. Houses were washed away with their terrified occupants still clinging to the roof-tops; the carcasses of cattle and mules floated in the swirling, deep brown water; isolated figures whom none could rescue were last seen crying for help as they hung in the gaunt branches of shattered trees. Dressers and tabletops, clothes and toys were caught in the driftwood and floating timber, to twist madly in a sudden whirlpool, and then sweep out of sight in the surging, eddying, boiling waters which extended as far as the eye could see.[69]

After this flood, African Americans suffered further in part because of corrupt landlords who oversaw federal relief programs. According to Davis, black people had to pay cash for food and other aid or take out loans that they were later forced to pay back through labor, while white people received assistance for free.[70] The NAACP responded with an antiracist campaign against the relief efforts, and the black press intensely covered the unequal treatment. In the aftermath of the 1927 flood, and much like information shared following Hurricane Katrina, there were reports of widespread discrimination against black people. Officials relocated whites quickly yet placed blacks in crowded and unsafe living conditions. There was also evidence of lynchings. The flood covered more than 26,000 square miles with 30 feet of water, and 637,476 people (53.8 percent of whom were black) were aided in the relief efforts.

Like many other writers, Brown enjoyed Smith's music and heard her, too, as muse and inspiration.[71] One needs to listen no further than blues artist Bessie Smith to find an oft-mentioned musical inspiration. As a young man, for instance, August Wilson frequented thrift stores in his hometown of Pittsburgh, Pennsylvania, buying stacks at a time of old albums for a nickel each, focusing on records from the 1930s and 1940s because they were the cheapest. One day, Wilson found in his purchased pile a Bessie Smith recording of "Nobody in Town Can Bake a Sweet Jelly Roll Like Mine." He listened repeatedly to the record, so much so that he had to replace the needle on his record player often. In listening to Smith, Wilson realized that he could write in the language he heard around him—black street vernacular—rather than in the English he admired in the works of such writers as Dylan Thomas. In this defining listening moment, he noted, "The universe stuttered, and everything fell into place."[72] What Wilson heard in the blues is what, later, he would pen in the blues-inspired *Ma Rainey's Black Bottom*: "life's way of talking."[73] Wilson here enters into a listening collaborative with Smith, making literary art through listening. When James Baldwin hears "Backwater Blues" in particular, he recalls: "What struck me was the fact that [Bessie] was singing . . . about a disaster, which had almost killed her, and she accepted it and was going beyond it. The fantastic understatement in it. It is the way I want to write, you know. When she says, 'My house fell down, and I can't live there no mo'—it is a great . . . a great sentence. A great achievement."[74]

Despite Smith's authorship of the song "Backwater Blues," Brown titles his poem after her mentor, Ma Rainey, who also performed the song. Born Gertrude Pridgett in 1886, Ma Rainey began transforming blues performances as early as 1902 with her "classic blues," a combination of singing, minstrelsy, comedy, and dance. Critic Mary Bogumil describes Ma Rainey as "a flamboyant songstress." According to Bogumil, Ma Rainey would take the stage wearing costumes and accessories she designed herself. For each performance, she "paraded onto the stage with her band and situated herself in front of equally magnificent backdrops she also created, such as an enormous cut-out of a gramophone, which gave the appearance of Ma emerging right from the speaker, issuing from and manifesting the music itself."[75]

Rainey recorded at least ninety-two songs between 1923 and 1928; as Angela Davis's account of her difficulty in listening to the songs as she researched Ma Rainey attests, the technical quality of these sound recordings was poor. She was not as prolific a recording artist as other blues artists, including Smith, but Bogumil's description of Rainey's stage presence speaks to the impact of the vocalist on her audience and on the development of the blues as a commercial—

and, later, intellectual and artistic—interest.[76] In many ways, it makes sense that Rainey would figure prominently as a symbol for Brown of African American modernism.[77] During a recording session in the Library of Congress Recording Laboratory, in fact, Brown confidently states, "We can really with great accuracy say that [Ma Rainey] was the Mother of the Blues." He introduces his poem "Ma Rainey" by noting that it is "my tribute to her." Brown informs his audience: "I knew her personally and I heard her sing several times."[78] As Steven Tracy writes, "Ma's southern-drenched voice, echoing the field hollers and folk songs of sixteen-hour days among turn rows worked so unrelentingly that the laborers could see them in their dreams, had a depth of feeling matched by few other blues singers of her time."[79] In short, Rainey was heard as possessing a voice that was itself closely linked to rural folk culture.

Brown's poem "Ma Rainey" is what Gayl Jones refers to as free verse blues.[80] While the poem is a blues poem, it is not written in a traditional blues form—aa'b—where the first line introduces a theme, the second line repeats that theme with a difference, and the third line resolves the verse. Brown's "New St. Louis Blues," for instance, is a poem structured as traditional blues:

Market Street woman is known fuh to have dark days,
Market Street woman noted fuh to have dark days,
Life do her dirty in a hundred onery ways. (1–3)[81]

"Ma Rainey" opens instead with two-beat lines of irregular iambics in rhyming alternate lines. These short lines present a panoramic of the frenzy invoked upon Ma Rainey's arrival in town:

When Ma Rainey
Comes to town,
Folks from anyplace
Miles aroun',
From Cape Girardeau,
Poplar Bluff,
Flocks in to hear
Ma do her stuff. (1–8)

This folk community coheres around the common purpose of listening to Ma Rainey perform. As Stephen Henderson notes, in these lines Brown records the general geography of the Backwater region, the area devastated by the flood.[82] From these opening lines, Brown pens a poem that, as Christopher Small describes, "establishes in the place where [the musical listening] is happening a set of relationships, and it is in those relationships that the meaning of the act lies." These meanings develop, Small explains:

> not only between those organized sounds which are conventionally thought of as being the stuff of musical meaning but also between the people who are taking part, in whatever capacity, in the performance; and they model, or stand as metaphor for, ideal relationships as the participants in the performance imagine them to be: relationships between person and person, between individual and society, between humanity and the natural world and even perhaps the supernatural world.[83]

Small's discussion of musical listening amplifies the way in which Brown's poem situates the folk gathering to hear Ma "do her stuff" in order to model a listening relationship between audience and performer. Emerging from this flooded region, the audience members function en masse as intentional, willing, anticipatory listeners. The tone here is one of urgency as expressed through the high level of physical movement and the short, staccato-like lines that quicken the pace of the verse. Within these compressed lines, Brown captures the excitement of Ma Rainey's arrival and implicitly suggests the posture and habits of an effective black listenership for black literature.

Brown enacts his cultural mediation here as a listening poet; that is, through the persona in the poem, he transcribes what he hears in this scene. In the second stanza, the persona's perspective comes from within the crowd and is focused on the audience's emotional state:

> An' some jokers keeps deir laughs a-goin' in de crowded aisles,
> An' some folks sits dere waitin' wid deir aches an' miseries,
> Till Ma comes out before dem, a-smilin' gold-toofed smiles
> An' Long Boy ripples minors on de black an' yellow keys. (23–26)

While the first verse could be heard as both a general statement about Ma Rainey's popularity (anytime she comes to town) and as a comment on the current desire to hear her sing in the poem, the second verse's present tense sounds more specific to this particular event. Here, in contrast to the first verse, the lines of the second verse are longer and have a slower, seven-beat rhythm. The presence of the narrator-poet-listener in the poem does not interrupt the poem's prioritizing of the audience's perspective. There is an implied calling for the reader to listen, to be present, and to attend to this blues performance as well, one marked by the minor chords Long Boy is playing on the piano. In some ways, this is reminiscent of the uncut concert versions of recordings of contemporary singers.[84] The audience is audible, the singer performs, and the listener or consumer is "present" at the live performance.

In keeping with the natural disaster that provides the unfortunate context of this gathering, the sounds of the audience are described as comparable to the sounds of the floodwaters. The audience's audibility is the roar of the circumstances that brought them together in the first place:

> Dey stumble in de hall, jes a-laughin' an' a-cacklin',
> Cheerin' lak roarin' water, lak wind in river swamps. (21–22)

The folk, survivors of the flood, become transcriptions and recordings, replaying the hurricane's roar of wind and water within and through their bodies. Sonically intertwined with their environment, they embody the damage and force while simultaneously existing as victims of the hurricane. Here and with the description of Ma Rainey and the piano resonating with each other, it is clear that Brown is emphasizing these sounds as embodied experiences. The folk become more than a cultural sign; they are grounded, embodied, physical, situated in context. They are experiencing sounds of tragedy in the flood and in the music that reflects upon this natural catastrophe. Their listening is an embodied practice that functions as a means of engaging culture and loss. The poem becomes a recording in its own right in that it encodes Brown's listening to this event within its transcription.[85] Listeners to Brown's poem, then, are called on both to witness by listening to the aftermath and to replay the catastrophic event through his poetic treatment of these embodied folk.

Brown's representation of the folk differs from that of the ontological treatment of the folk in discourses during, and later about, the Harlem Renaissance. This audience is active and itself performing, a strategy that effectively shifts notions of the folk as a fixed and coherent whole to questions about the folk audience as embodying action and nuanced subjectivity. Further, the pronouns progress from "you" to "us" to "we," suggesting that Ma Rainey and her listeners together are a community of individuals, of subjectivities. The "we" here emerges from the shared experience of flood, displacement, and this current gathering during which they all listen. This is a significant shift, given the value placed on the folk as sign and signifier during the Harlem Renaissance. In her discussion of audience, Alice Rayner asserts,

> The questions about audience . . . need to turn away from ontology—
> what an audience or a community is—toward the listening function that

would constitute the action of audience, an action that has historical and unconscious contexts as well as intentions. . . . The contradiction between the audience that is constructed linguistically, ideologically or ideally as a sign and the audience that actively listens may be irreconcilable. But that contradiction may itself be productive insofar as it identifies the differences that comprise the social world.[86]

The audience's listening here is not one of escape; instead, it is an audition that voices and organizes the listeners' dire situations in such a way that, acoustically, they are submerged simultaneously in the loss and hope of the moment.

Brown switches the perspective and voice of the poem once again in the fourth and final verse. The voice moves from the communal, aggregate "we" of the previous stanza to that of one man who is part of the audience attending the performance. He recounts Ma Rainey's performance of "Backwater Blues," the adapted song lyrics appearing in italics that emphasize singing, and notes that "she jes' catch hold of us, somekindaway" (40):

'It rained fo' days an' de skies was dark as night,
Trouble taken place in de lowlands at night.

'Thundered an' lightened an' the storm begin to roll
Thousan's of people ain't got no place to go.

'Den I went an' stood upon some high ol' lonesome hill,
An' looked down on the place where I used to live.' (42–47)

The words are not transcribed exactly from the lyrics of "Backwater Blues." Instead, Brown captures the main point of each three-line stanza in the blues song in two condensed lines each, all the while maintaining the blues flavor of the piece. The compressed lyrics appear in italics, suggesting a transcript, a typography that both signals a recording of music in print and serves the listener as reader who is charged with decoding this song on the page. The poem also parallels the song "Backwater Blues" within its movement in the song lyrics from the individual to a collective point of view. In "Backwater Blues," for example, as the verses alternate between general and particular experience, they also alternate between a vernacular present tense ("When it rains five days") and a past tense narrative ("I woke up this mornin'"). In a particularly powerful gesture, Smith's lyrics shift their focus from the speaker to the community:

Then they rowed a little boat about five miles 'cross the pond
Then they rowed a little boat about five miles 'cross the pond
I packed all my clothes, throwed 'em in and they rowed me along

When it thunders and lightnin' and when the wind begins to blow
When it thunders and lightnin' and the wind begins to blow
There's thousands of people ain't got no place to go

The vocalist describes her own displacement in the past tense but the home-lessness of "thousands" in the continual present. To the extent that the song represents an individual story of suffering and displacement alongside the expe-rience of "thousands of people," it provokes us to listen as it powerfully juxta-poses individual loss with the continuity of collective suffering.

In the poem's third stanza, this audience of listening individuals pleads with Ma Rainey to sing her song:

O Ma Rainey,
Sing yo' song;
Now you's back
Whah you belong,
Git way inside us,
Keep us strong. . . .
O Ma Rainey,
Li'l an' low;
Sing us 'bout de hard luck
Roun' our do';
Sing us 'bout de lonesome road
We mus' go. . . . (27–38)

The folk audience requests that Ma Rainey "git way inside us," that her sung words occupy their beings, fortify them, fill them with the strength to move beyond their own losses. Their listening resonates with the hungry listening of Hurston's novel. These bodies hear their loss by embodying the external blues of the performer and her song and transforming it into an interior catalyst for mourning. In Brown's reading of this section of the poem, his tempo slows; he vocally performs the lines as he reads them. For instance, the "O," when Brown reads the poem, is stretched as an extended O sound—"ooooh Ma Rainey."[87] The "O" becomes a resonance of the pain these folks are experiencing as survivors of natural and social catastrophe. It sounds like a moan in Brown's bluesy, slowed reading, deep and low, achy like mourning. In a conversation with Paul Oliver, Brown commented that Ma Rainey "wouldn't have to sing any words; she would moan, and the audience would moan with her [because] Ma really knew these people; she was a person of the folk; she was very simple and direct."[88]

This stanza in the poem emphasizes a repeated long *O* sound throughout Brown's diction. While the lines are short and appear staccato-like in their arrangement on the page, this repetitive vowel sound slows and weighs the lines down. At the literal structural center of the poem, I would like to suggest then, are mourning and moaning.[89] If you read these lines and their repetitive *O* sounds aloud, the vibrational resonance of this moment in the poem also shakes the vocal chords in your throat, and you can listen as that deep blues sound enacts the interpenetrating quality of Ma Rainey's singing, a quality the folk recognize: "Git way inside us, / Keep us strong. . . ." This is also a quality that amplifies her performance as a collaboration between listeners; the audience members listen as she sings and they encourage her to do so, and Ma Rainey listens in order to hear the needs of the folk and then sing both those needs and some relief in the way she chooses to deliver the song to her listeners. Listening in this scene, then, becomes a circular and dynamic process.

The final verses of "Backwater Blues" include this sound of moaning and mourning in the repeated "Mmm" as the vocalist sings of the experiences of the thousands of folk affected by the flood alongside those of the "poor old girl" of the song:

Backwater blues done cause me to pack my things and go
Backwater blues done cause me to pack my things and go
'Cause my house fell down and I can't live there no more

Mmm, I can't move no more
Mmm, I can't move no more
There ain't no place for a poor old girl to go.

If you make the "Mmm" sound, it has an internal feeling of vibration as well, perhaps not as deep as the *O* but mournful nonetheless. Brown's choice to emphasize the vowel *O* deepens the sounds of loss resonating from the poem's language and potential performance out loud. The song "Backwater Blues" resonates in the fabric of the poem so that it almost literally moves into the throat of the fellow commenting on the event. In fact, this audience member shares the song as if he is remembering the performance; that is, the performance is past rather than occurring in the real time of the poem. This, in part, explains why he says, "She *sang* Backwater Blues *one day*" (my emphasis). The poem shifts from the present action of performance in the first few stanzas to one of reflection on that performance in the last section.

Brown's line here—"She sang Backwater Blues one day"—also highlights the importance of the point from which the audience listens and the point through which Ma Rainey makes an impact. As Kate Lacey insists, "The situatedness of the embodied listener is important. Since listeners cannot entirely abandon listening from their own perspective, and must recognize that the perspective of the other is doubly filtered (through the speaker's perspective and their own as listener), the act of listening opens up a space for intersubjectivity."[90] As Ma Rainey is called on to "git way inside us" and listens to and answers the call by the way "she jes' gits hold of" her listeners, this performance of poetic listening dramatizes listening as a means of confirming the effectiveness not only of her performance but also of her listening. This confirmation recalls for me Pheoby's excitement and confirmation of Janie's effective storytelling when she exclaims that she's grown taller and is going fishing with her husband. I would add, too, that this reaction signals a listening that, in Brown's view, is successful. The audience member listens to Ma Rainey sing "Backwater Blues," correctly understands the impact of her performance of this particular song, and describes effectively the effect of her song on the crowd:

An' den de folks, dey natchally bowed dey heads an' cried,
Bowed dey heavy heads, shet dey moufs up tight an' cried,
An' Ma lef' de stage, an' followed some de folks outside. (48–50)

Brown renders this portion of the fellow's commentary in the traditional blues form, suggesting the major impact Ma Rainey's blues has on the listener. The listener "sings" the blues after listening to the blues. Her performance gives the listener living the blues a way to language the blues. In turn, his report of what he heard and experienced contributes to the rendering of lived and performed moments in audible print.

In the poem's concluding line—"She jes' gits hold of us dataway"—there is a parallel change in the adverbs, from "somekindaway" to "dataway." The final adverb relates demonstratively to the preceding reaction of the audience, concluding with the sounds of loss and the possibility of renewal that the audience earlier requests from the blues vocalist. "Dataway" poignantly, albeit implicitly, suggests Rainey as an effective listener herself, responding in a moving way to the articulated request of her audience before her "performance" in the poem: "Get way inside us, / Keep us strong."

Although the poem begins with place-names, it concludes by pointing "dat-away," not toward a place but to a memory of a specific experience listening to a particular musical event. With this closing gesture, the event of Ma Rainey's performance in Brown's poem displaces the particularity of the flood and invites us to dwell instead in the local experience of listening communally. Part of what the poem "Ma Rainey" takes up is the connection between the individual virtuosic performance and the experience of the folk listening to and beginning to re-create themselves out of that listening experience. Brown's response is not so much to advocate a process of salvage, in which an endangered culture of the past is preserved and categorized, as it is to transcribe a listening process—an aural pointing toward cultural possibility grounded in a proposed aurally inflected reading practice.[91]

TWO

"To Hear the Silence of Sound"

. . . .

Vibrational Listening in Ralph Ellison's
Invisible Man

P ublished in 1952 to great critical acclaim, *Invisible Man* was touted as an immediate literary classic that placed racial issues at the center of the nation's story. Compelling in its representation of the psychological and cultural effects of segregation in the United States, *Invisible Man* highlights invisibility as a key figure of racial dislocation, a metaphor that could easily be mistaken to be solely visual in register. Certainly, our narrator is "invisible . . . simply because people refuse to see me." He further explains: "When they approach me they see only my surroundings, themselves, or figments of their imagination—indeed, everything and anything except me."[1] Invisible Man makes it clear that his invisibility is a defect of social and racial perception, one that lies not with him or his physical body but instead "occurs because of a peculiar disposition of the eyes of those with whom I come in contact. A matter of the construction of their *inner* eyes, those eyes with which they look through their physical eyes upon reality."[2]

While Invisible Man suggests there are a few advantages to being invisible, he explains that this condition "is most often rather wearing on the nerves" and leads one to "often doubt if you really exist." He also explains to his reading audience that invisibility causes you to "ache with the need to convince yourself that you do exist in the real world, that you're a part of all the sound and anguish."[3] The psychological impact of invisibility leads him to long specifically for sonic confirmation of his existence. In this turn to sonic evidence of an invisible identity, *Invisible Man* amplifies invisibility as a multimodal figure of racial disenfranchisement and social estrangement writ visually *and* aurally.[4]

This chapter examines the ways in which listening in *Invisible Man* is a fully embodied strategy of sonic engagement imbricated in efforts to potentially sense a newly materialized and more fully realized racial identity. Ellison—and the eponymous narrator of *Invisible Man*—is intensely invested in sound's ontology. In other words, he is concerned with what it means to understand one's own being—one's humanity—as a sonic phenomenon in the world. This interest in an identity confirmed through sonic perception materializes not only in the listening body that is "somehow attuned to it all," after walking "flush into the vibrations of the voices" at the Harlem Brotherhood rally and experiencing "an electric tingling along my spine."[5] This interest is also apparent in Ellison's engagement of sound technology—specifically the phonograph, microphone, and tape recorder—in his writing. Listening in his work is an aural strategy of engagement, one that negotiates a triangulated relationship among perception, sound technology, and the racial and gendered self.

"Between Hi-Fi and the Ear": Listening for Cultural Fidelity

In "Living with Music," Ellison describes himself as a writer attempting to write *Invisible Man* while under the constant attack of noise; the towering wall next to his building caught "every passing thoroughfare sound" and "rifled it straight down" to him.[6] Although Ellison finds himself undoubtedly wanting more than anything to control his sonic environment, to hear it sound a certain way, and to render it conducive to developing a quiet, introspective writing practice, he is positioned within "labyrinthine acoustics" that resist meeting his needs.[7] He battles constantly with the cacophonous sounds rifling through his Harlem basement apartment: jukebox music, howling cats, Basie's blaring brasses, barking dogs, and preaching drunks.[8] In such a constantly shifting, noisy, and sonically boundless environment, it is difficult for him to develop a sound writing practice—one that is stable *and* full of audio inspiration. The task of penning a first book while living within such "chaos of sound" was daunting for the emerging writer, although ironically Ellison's listening back in this essay on a moment that supposedly created so complete a writer's block as to render the condition itself indescribable results in an eloquent rendering of his Harlem neighborhood and of writing as an aurally imbricated creative process.[9]

In this disturbing soundscape, the sounds that most trouble him are not those of urban Harlem, though, but those of a persistently practicing vocalist. According to Ellison, no other sources of noise in the neighborhood troubled him as viscerally and intimately as his upstairs neighbor's singing. A budding vocalist, this woman was, he recalls, so "intensely devoted to her art" that she often hindered his own progress on his novel. He writes:

> From morning to night she vocalized, regardless of the condition of her
> voice, the weather or my screaming nerves. There were times when her

notes, sifting through her floor and my ceiling, bouncing down the walls and ricocheting off the building in the rear, whistled like tenpenny nails, buzzed like a saw, wheezed like the asthma of a Hercules, [and] trumpeted like an enraged African elephant.[10]

The neighbor's sung notes are at once anthropomorphic and disembodied, taking on an acoustic life energy of their own as they sift, bounce, ricochet, whistle, buzz, wheeze, and trumpet through Ellison's apartment. Implied through the singer's increasing volume in response to Ellison's stereo equipment, as evidenced through his system-building efforts to play music loud enough to drown out the sounds of his neighbor, this sonic battle is rife with desire for control and posits listening in this context as itself a figure of power negotiations.

While Ellison eventually develops a more empathetic response to his neighbor and comes to find his soundscape helping, rather than hindering, his art, living with this contentious music was by no means easy. Overwhelmed by the sound of his neighbor's voice, Ellison decides to create an "audio booby trap," amplifying music loud enough to shut out his neighbor's singing from his apartment and signal to this singer what were to his mind her own artistic shortcomings. In order to set this trap, he turns on his radio to hear Kathleen Ferrier's operatic voice singing the aria from Handel's *Rodelinda*: "Art thou troubled? Music will calm thee."[11] Ellison then goes out to purchase Ferrier's records and while shopping learns that "between the hi-fi and the ear . . . there was a new electronic world."[12]

Ellison's account of his shopping spree reveals his deep interest in what was, at the time, a listening culture emerging in the late 1940s and 1950s: high fidelity or hi-fi. Connected to high fidelity (or full frequency range recordings, as they were called in Britain) was the idea of faithfulness to the original live performance through developing equipment that would record, reproduce, and replay sound with little distortion.[13] Achieving this faithfulness would allow the recording to resemble the original performed sound as closely as possible. This growing global sound recording market featured the development and mass marketing of high-fidelity recording and listening equipment in American homes. The early 1950s, in fact, saw a surge in sales of phonograph and high-fidelity equipment, particularly in urban markets like New York City. Ellison develops such an intense interest in this new sound technology that he attends the 1949 Audio Fair in New York and eventually "built half a dozen or more preamplifiers and record compensators before finding a commercial one that satisfied my ear." Eventually he purchases a whole sound system that included a speaker system, an AM/FM tuner, a transcription turntable, and a speaker cabinet—all of high quality. He later added a preamplifier and record compensator, an arm, a magnetic cartridge, and a tape recorder.[14]

Much like his novel's narrator, Ellison is a *sound* "thinker-tinker." Recall that his narrator, just before sharing his plans to tinker with the acoustics of his hole, quips: "Yet when you have lived invisible as long as I have you develop a certain ingenuity. I'll solve the problem. . . . Though invisible, I am in the great American tradition of tinkers. That makes me kin to Ford, Edison and Franklin. Call me, since I have a theory and a concept, a 'thinker-tinker.'"[15] Akin to his narrator in this moment, Ellison tinkers: he plays with stereo components and configurations in an attempt to manipulate the sonics of his environment.[16] His tinkering—his listening—is situational, inventive, exploratory, and adaptive.

High-fidelity culture was intricately connected with high cultural forms of music like classical, operatic, and orchestral music, yet Ellison's use of the equipment expands this relationship between high culture and high recording to include jazz, blues, gospel, and Latin music. He selects music by musicians representing a plethora of traditions including opera, blues, and jazz: Bidu Sayão, Marian Anderson, Kathleen Ferrier, Lotte Lehmann, Maggie Teyte, Jennie Tourel, Bessie Smith, Richard Strauss, Béla Bartók, Duke Ellington, and Louis Armstrong—a list that gives us a clue to his own inner ear's aesthetic range and particular musical preferences.[17] Ellison's motivation to "plunge into electronics" largely stems from his desire to enjoy and "to reproduce sound with such fidelity that even when using music as a defense behind which I could write, it would reach the unconscious levels of the mind [read: inner ear] with the least distortion."[18] He builds a defense for his writing—its practice, production, and aesthetic—through a listening that is fully mediated by sound technology.

While high-fidelity culture and Ellison's sonic hobby promise listening experiences that collapse the difference between the *here* and the *there* of the concert hall and the living room, I hear in his description of his technical pursuit of high fidelity a coterminous desire to experience music in the privacy of his home as he would a live performance coupled with a recognition that the access he is purchasing and tinkering his way toward is actually not to the concert hall or jazz club performance, not to live performance itself, but to, as he writes, the enjoyment of "*recorded* music as it was intended to be heard."[19] Ellison's conflict here is, as Jonathan Sterne notes, the "conflicted aesthetic of recorded sound" expressed in the high-fidelity movement by musical professionals and by the music industry more broadly through an insistence on "technology as a vanishing mediator continually . . . set in conflict with the reality that sound reproduction technologies had their own sonic character."[20] Ellison's sound system does not vanish; its material presence remains quite visible and persistent; and his seeming obsession with amassing the best, most effective equipment possible admittedly "didn't come easily . . . there were wires and pieces of equipment all over the tiny apartment."[21]

Ellison's listening relationship with his invisible yet audible neighbor is one that ranges from a listening fraught with sonic warfare to one infused with artistic appreciation and even influence. Alexander Weheliye describes their dynamic as a democratic sharing in music between the neighbors, while Mark Goble, noting that the race of the singing neighbor is never mentioned, suggests that the "scene of musical assault and pedagogy, protection and programming" in "Living with Music" gives context to a listening relationship that "is at once color-blind and racially involved," and that Ellison seems to hear his neighbor as white.[22]

I would like to suggest another possibility, one that Weheliye and Goble do not consider: What we are audience to in "Living with Music" is a triangulated relationship—in this instance among gender, sonic technology, and the embodied listening self—negotiated largely by phonograph and the strength of "her diaphragm."[23] As the neighbors exchange music selected from an impressive array of musical traditions, Ellison admits, "Once in a while I'd forget completely that I was supposed to be a gentleman and blast her with Strauss' *Zarathustra*, Bartók's *Concerto for Orchestra*, Ellington's 'Flaming Sword,' the fame crescendo from *The Pines of Rome*, or Satchmo scatting 'I'll Be Glad When You're Dead (you rascal you!).' Oh, I was living with music with a sweet vengeance."[24] His mention that he "was supposed to be a gentleman" coupled with his keen awareness of her gender identity marks this pair's sonic exchanges. Although both neighbors end up in a place where each appreciates the sonic contributions of the other over the building's soundscape, what Ellison's essay highlights are the ways in which listening can function as a mode of cultural and social power negotiations writ aurally.

"I Want to *Feel* Its Vibration": Invisible Man's Listening Body

Given Ellison's struggles to control and then engage with the acoustics of his basement apartment, it is perhaps no wonder that the resulting novel features a protagonist who struggles to control the light, sound, and feel of his hibernating hole beneath the streets of Harlem. Following his descent into hibernation, Invisible Man paradoxically begins to use his invisibility to become increasingly a more perceptive listener. His home underneath and on the edge of Harlem suffers from, he says, "a certain acoustical deadness." This deadness makes him long to own five stereos so that he can fill his home with Louis Armstrong's music and "*feel* its vibration, not only with my ear but with my whole body."[25] Here Invisible Man explicitly names the multimodal, "whole body" listening with which this chapter is concerned. Infusing his acoustically dead "hole" with vibration would be a technical feat, allowing him to enliven the acoustics of his space and, more importantly, enliven his very being. As Weheliye argues in his study of sound and Afro-modernity, Ellison's attempts at phonographing or, literally, writing sound result in the expression of a modern African American subject.[26] According to Weheliye, sound is significant in Ellison's novel specifically and in black cultural production generally for its ability to "augment an inferior black subjectivity—a subjectivity created by racist ideologies and practices in the field of vision—establishing venues for the constitution of new modes of existence."[27] While I agree with Weheliye's astute examination of sonic Afro-modernity in Ellison's novel, I am also drawn to the ways in which these sonic moments dramatize sensation of and in sound. Ellison amplifies blues, jazz, vernacular, and other instances of sonic cultural production in ways that provide his protagonist and his reader with opportunities to listen.

One such instance occurs when the eponymous narrator of Ellison's novel prepares to deliver his first Brotherhood speech at a protest rally in Harlem. As he waits, he listens and catalogues the sounds of the scene: the audience's droning and churning; alternatively murmuring, hushed, and edgy voices; "an impatient splatter of hand claps"; chairs scraping and clattering; the "newness" of the song "John Brown's Body"; and synchronized breathing and speaking. Into the midst of these perceived sounds, Invisible Man eventually takes the platform: "I walked flush into the vibrations of the voices and felt an electric tingling along my spine."[28] He sits onstage, anxiously waiting for his turn at the microphone, listening as "songs flared between speeches [and] chants exploded as spontaneously as shouts at a southern revival."[29] Of this "high keyed event," Invisible Man recalls, "I was somehow attuned to it all, could feel it physically. Sitting with my feet on the soiled canvas I felt as though I had wandered into the percussion section of a symphony orchestra."[30]

Invisible Man's declaration mixed with wonder, "I was *somehow* attuned to it all," amplifies the focus of this study (my emphasis).[31] His body in a sense becomes his ear as he experiences a full-bodied listening *within* sound. Because Invisible Man links his listening at the Harlem rally to his perception of sound through not only his ears but also his entire body, he becomes attuned to and squarely posits listening as a fully embodied practice. Further, his embodied, aware, intentional, and query-inflected performance of listening at a protest rally points to listening as a public practice and a cultural, political, and civic responsibility.

What is striking about Invisible Man's reaction to this embodied listening experience is his decision essentially to listen to what guides him. Although Brother Jack initially instructs him to "listen carefully to the rest of us . . . so that you can get the pointers for your remarks,"[32] Invisible Man notes that this sensing and perceiving of sound "worked on me so thoroughly that I soon gave up trying to memorize phrases and simply allowed the excitement to carry me along."[33] He flips the script, so to speak, in his decision to listen his way along, thereby emphasizing a listening that is informed by anticipation and stretches the listener toward a process of discovery and new ways of knowing. In this moment, Invisible Man demonstrates a deep attentiveness to sound, an experience of listening as a fully embodied experience, and a sense of wonder and slight uncertainty at how this experience is happening and where it might lead.

Different from the vibrational experience at the Harlem rally, where merely walking into the collective sounds of the crowd provided for him a vibrational, full-bodied listening experience, Invisible Man's project from underground instead calls for a specifically modern listening enabled through listening in isolation to recorded music via phonograph.[34] For Ellison, it is such technologically mediated listening that enables—sometimes wholeheartedly and sometimes ambivalently—the reconstitution of a fractured racial self.[35] The phonograph is positioned here as a technology capable of transforming acoustical deadness into resonance and isolation into an approximate experience of listening as if hearing the original performance. Such collapsing of *there* and *here* as in a high-fidelity listening culture provides Invisible Man with a listening experience that makes him feel *present*.

Invisible Man imbues this vibratory listening experience with such importance, recalling for me Julian Henriques's notion of sonic dominance. In his discussion of the physical characteristics of the sound system used in Jamaican dance hall culture, Henriques explains that within sonic dominance "the sound pervades, or even invades the body. . . . It's not just heard in the ears, but felt over the entire surface of the skin."[36] If we apply the reggae sound system aesthetics Henriques describes here to Invisible Man's desire to feel music's vibration, then we understand him to desire a listening that enfolds him in sound and potentially allows his very body to become part of the phonograph system he would like to possess. In other words, Invisible Man imagines a merging of listening technology with an embodied listening self, resulting in his becoming "a part of all the sound and anguish" he perceives in Armstrong's performance, one that "made poetry out of being invisible."[37]

Equipped, however, with just one phonograph, Invisible Man uses his simple system to play Louis Armstrong's "(What Did I Do to Be So) Black and Blue?" in his underground home, a listening experience he describes as an aural plunge into sound.[38] While Ethel Waters also recorded the tune for Columbia Records in 1930, Armstrong recorded "Black and Blue" twice—once in 1929 and again in 1955.[39] Armstrong's performance of lower-frequency scatting enfolds Invisible Man in sound, creating a surround sound effect.[40] He descends Dante-like into the depths of the music, level by level, listening to sound at previously unperceived lower frequencies—all the while learning how to listen anew: "I discovered a new analytical way of listening to music."[41] As he listens deeper to this recorded song, Invisible Man sharpens his aural perception; his body becomes increasingly attuned to the music. Sound technology for Ellison provides opportunities for a listener—for his narrator—to learn to listen differently, more acutely, and more intentionally to the sounds that, in this case, the phonograph emits.

It is important to note, too, that Invisible Man is listening to recorded music that has been engineered and captured in a way that allows the listener the opportunity to appreciate musical details made more perceptible through its recording. As Invisible Man notes, "The unheard sounds came through, and each melodic line existed of itself, stood out clearly from all the rest, said its piece, and waited patiently for the other voices to speak."[42] Invisible Man's imagined immersion in sound coupled with access to recorded and amplified music allows him to participate in a transformative listening to Armstrong's signature tune.

The first few melodic lines Invisible Man listens to are the sounds of an older woman singing a spiritual, a pleading voice of a woman who is being bid on at a slave auction, the haunting sounds of slavery, and then the sermon "Blackness of Blackness," an allusion, with a difference, to Herman Melville's "Whiteness of Whiteness" sermon in *Moby-Dick*.[43] The italicized text of the sermon is also heavily punctuated with ellipses:

"In the beginning . . ."
"At the very start," they cried.
". . . there was blackness . . ."
"Preach it . . ."
". . . and the sun . . ."
"The sun, Lawd . . ."

"... was bloody red ..."
"Red ..."

And the sermon's concluding lines:

"Black will make you ..."
"Black ..."
"... or black will unmake you."
"Ain't it the truth, Lawd?"[44]

Pause over, unmute, and listen to the ellipses here, the speculative space between an exploratory call-and-response practice. Such punctuation acts as provocation, an awakening for the reader that parallels a deep listening experience for the narrator. Ellison's use of ellipses enacts a cognitive shift. Our sensory perception of print on the page, traditionally thought of in terms of the visual, sits flattened without our listening, our reading as a multisensory practice. We are reminded that we are audience to a church gathering, performed by preacher and congregation. Listening, in the face of the ellipses, then, becomes a collaboratively speculative endeavor; reading shifts from an activity that aims to yield full comprehension to a process that renders the lucid an outlier of reading's goals. Rather than marking gaps solely, the ellipses mark punctuated spaces of potential speculation, communal exploration, and meaning making.[45]

What Invisible Man describes as a disembodied *"voice of trombone timbre"* screams, disrupting the sermon, telling him to leave.[46] He then continues his travels, listening more deeply into a return to the old slave woman. During this aural encounter, he asks the woman, *"Why do you moan?"*[47] The question, one that keys in on her moan, a sound whose vibrations are felt within a body and heard beyond it, begins a dialogue between Invisible Man and the once-enslaved woman about freedom and ambivalence.[48] She shares the fact that she loved her master because he was the father of her sons, but she hated him, too, for refusing to free them. She poisoned her master, and in response she produces an ambivalent moan mixed with happiness, sadness, and resistance. The woman's wordless moan signals her struggle to exercise her freedom and to speak eloquently, a struggle that resonates in many ways with the difficulty involved in listening. For in order to translate her inner thoughts to spoken language—to "remember how to say ..."—she needs to open a frequency that will allow her to access what she needs psychically to articulate. This suggests that through his encounter with the depths of music and his conversation with the enslaved woman, Invisible Man is led to consider how, even as an invisible man, what he listens to and how he listens pose a challenge to act. His dialogue with the enslaved woman in particular pushes him to another place to examine social—and aural—responsibility. Invisible Man's experience of listening to "Black and Blue" and all those voices beneath the surface of the notes played, sung, and scatted underscores his auditory experience as paradoxically an intensely inward yet socially connecting one.

Emerging from his plunge into an "underworld of sound," Invisible Man reflects on his listening experience: "At first I was afraid; this familiar music had demanded action, the kind of which I was incapable, and yet had I lingered there beneath the surface I might have attempted to act. Nevertheless, I know now that few really listen to this music."[49] This individual plunge into listening carries with it the potential for public action, an action our narrator is not yet ready to take but one he nonetheless recognizes in this moment to be possible. If more people really listened, Invisible Man implies, that listening would lead to more action.

Invisible Man's sense of the potential for public action changes by the epilogue into an imperative to act: "I must come out, I must emerge."[50] He asserts, "Perhaps . . . my greatest social crime" is that "I've overstayed my hibernation, since there's a possibility that even an invisible man has a socially responsible role to play."[51] As he conceives it, part of his social responsibility involves posing his final question to his reader, an opportunity the novel presents for aural participation. But if we also reflect on the notion of social and aural action in relation to Invisible Man's desire to feel the vibration produced by Armstrong's music, we hear a longing for the music to touch him, for audition that is felt as well as heard.

Why is Invisible Man interested, though, in feeling specifically music's *vibration*? Vibrations are foundational to sound; they make sound material in that they are the form in which it passes through matter at particular frequencies. In his discussion of vibrations, John Shepherd suggests that "it is the vibratory essence that puts the world of sound in motion and reminds us, as individuals, that we are alive, sentient and experiencing."[52] It is no wonder, then, that Ellison focuses on sonic vibrations in his search for a way to make his invisible narrator present. Invisible Man imagines that he may restore himself by becoming a vibrational presence as he listens from within sound—and as we listen to him from his hibernating space. If Invisible Man's multisensory listening entails feeling the vibration of the music, then it follows that listening itself becomes not only a multisensory process but also a vibrational practice of sonic engagement. Bodies as listeners and while listening, then, are placed in a relational networking system of sound, reminding us that attentiveness to the vibrations of sound and their perception leads to an attentiveness toward the body—especially, in this case, social bodies rendered invisible, unseen, non-sensed—toward the material that sound makes vibrate and vibrant.

From Inner Eye to Inner Ear:
Invisible Man and the Electric Microphone

If we rewind to the moment when Invisible Man explains that his invisibility "occurs because of a peculiar disposition of the eyes of those with whom I come in contact. A matter of the construction of their *inner* eyes, those eyes with which they look through their physical eyes upon reality," we are reminded that the inner eye is an offending member. To counter the impact of the inner eye of others on his subjectivity, Invisible Man implies what I refer to as an inner ear. This figure of the inner ear is not literally the anatomical inner ear, though physiologically the inner ear allows humans to maintain balance, a function that translates figuratively to address the imbalanced ways in which Invisible Man is perceived. The inner ear is more figurative and is not necessarily without the implicit bias or aesthetic preference carried in the inner eye that animates the narrator's invisibility.[53] Nor is it a metaphorical or enacted panacea for the racial disenfranchisement the novel chronicles. I tune in to the implied figure of the inner ear in order to think through the microphone as a notable yet rarely examined sound technology—either in sound studies treatments of audio technology or in examinations of Ellison's novel, where the phonograph garners more attention. In this turn to the inner ear and the microphone, I posit a listening figure that is perhaps hampered by implicit and cultural biases but that has the potential to function as a counter to the inner eye that renders Invisible Man invisible.

As with the phonograph, Invisible Man's discourse concerning his relationship and technique with the electric microphone resonates with 1950s' discourse around this sonic technology. The microphone is particularly intertwined historically and culturally with the physiological ear. According to historian Susan Schmidt Horning, electric microphones originated in the 1860s and 1870s alongside other new inventions like the telephone and the phonograph. New and more sensitive microphones were introduced following World War II. By the 1950s, "the choice and placement of microphones became an art form, assuming greater importance in the 1950s than before."[54] Of the telephone, phonograph, and microphone, Horning notes, "the microphone most exactly imitates the anatomical ear, and earlier primordial, pre-electrical microphones were often cast as prostheses for the ear."[55] The microphone, then, becomes a modern site of extended human hearing.

While we may think of the microphone as a sound technology focused on voice and sound amplification, it is actually a transducer; it imitates the anatomical inner ear as it receives and translates sound vibrations. In *The Audible Past*, Jonathan Sterne does not examine the microphone but does connect transduction—particularly as it occurs with the vibration of the eardrum—to technological transducers. Sterne refers to transducers as cultural artifacts, generating a shift in sound studies from thinking about sound largely through its production to thinking about sound in terms of its reception.[56] Ellison's brief engagement with the microphone in his novel provides an opportunity to think about the microphone as a technology of listening.

When it is time for him to speak at the Harlem rally, Invisible Man approaches the microphone. The narrator never used a microphone when he spoke at the College in the South, where speakers and singers spoke and performed without microphones, using their full diaphragmatic force to amplify their voices. Not knowing how to speak into the microphone correctly, Invisible Man approaches it with his "voice sounding raspy and full of air," as if he is about to speak in a hall in which he has to self-project his voice. But what he has not yet learned is that the microphone changes not only how we hear but also how we speak when using it. For instance, crooning, a singing style made popular from the 1920s to the 1950s and mastered by such singers as Frank Sinatra and Sammy Davis, Jr., is possible only with the microphone. As Mark Katz explains, "Crooning is akin to whispering, which under normal circumstances can be heard only when one is physically very close to the speaker; crooning thus provides a sense of intimacy between artist and audience, collapsing the technologically imposed distance that would seem to preclude such a relationship. . . . Without amplification [crooning] would be expressively flat and nearly inaudible."[57] The microphone, then, creates a paradox: in order to be listened to effectively, the user of the microphone must quiet her or his voice relative, of course, to speaking without a microphone.

After someone comes to adjust the microphone and advises Invisible Man, "Don't stand too close," he attempts to speak again, and he stands, "hearing my voice boom deep and vibrant over the arena."[58] Through the microphone as a mediator, Invisible Man hears his vibrant voice—emotional, energetic, stirring, vibrating, and resonant—spread throughout the arena, existing separate from his self, despite his projecting with less volume and with less force. With the microphone, the audience hears the speaker, and the speaker—in this case, Invisible Man—hears himself. This experience of public listening and speaking is quite different from Invisible Man's experiences in similar arenas before his migration north. He recalls attending a Founders' Day service at the college and listening to a young woman sing *a cappella*. As she gradually increases her volume, there are times when he hears her voice as "a disembodied force that sought to enter her, to violate her, shaking her, rocking her rhythmically, as though it had become the source of her being, rather than the fluid web of her own creation."[59] Invisible Man perceives this voice as uncontrollable, with nowhere to travel but in violation of and within the body of its creator. The sound (the singing voice) is imagined as both intimately and violently linked to and remaining with the source of the sound (the vocalist). What he experiences at the Brotherhood rally while using the microphone is a listening mediated by modern sound technology: his voice carries from his body, becoming disembodied while traveling to the ears in the crowd.

At this first contact with the microphone, Invisible Man thinks it "strange and unnerving." He describes his perception of the microphone to the audience, saying, "it looks like the steel skull of a man!"[60] While the microphone allows Invisible Man to be heard during this rally, it also interestingly serves as an excuse for the disruption of his unscripted message. While "pretending to adjust the microphone," Brother Jack cautions Invisible Man not to "end your usefulness before you've begun."[61] This access to sound technology, then, does not come without a potential cost. Invisible Man has to perfect his technique on the spot. When he walks toward the microphone, he finds himself

> entering the spot of light that surrounded me like a seamless cage of
> stainless steel. I halted. The light was so strong that I could no longer
> see the audience, the bowl of human faces. It was as though a semi-
> transparent curtain had dropped between us, but through which they
> could see me—for they were applauding—without themselves being seen.
> . . . I stood, barely hearing Brother Jack's introduction.[62]

The narrator is engulfed in an electrified field that recalls his hibernating hole, but with a difference: instead of granting him vision, the light renders him incapable of seeing the audience he is to address. There is an inversion of sensing: the audience is invisible *to him*; the "vague audience closest to the platform" is the most he can perceive.[63] To be seen without seeing makes Invisible Man feel trapped, similar to the feeling of being in the hospital lobotomy machine a few days earlier. It is his voice that is able to travel, even as he is caught in the blinding light of the stage. He is invisible, yet his sound is heard. Ellison is interested in sound technology, but here his narrator feels anxious in the face of all this electrification in the form of light and microphone. Where is he—the self—in this new soundscape? What power and agency can he practice within it? What happens when the self, amplified through the figure of the electrified voice, reverberates boundlessly beyond the source of its sound? How does one listen to sound transduced in this way?

At the end of his speech, Invisible Man listens as "the applause struck like a clap of thunder." He reports that, in the moment, he "stood transfixed, unable to see, my body quivering with the roar. . . . The sound seemed to roar up in waves. . . . It grew in volume. . . . It was a deafening demonstration"—the choice of the word "deafening" being particularly resonant in this discussion of listening and attempting to listen.[64] As Invisible Man chronicles the crowd's response, he emphasizes a sense of reciprocity between him as speaker and the audience he just addressed. Throughout his speech, in fact, he makes note through a call-and-response of how his listeners are receiving his words and how he, in turn, adjusts moment to moment to try to garner their approval. The microphone, then, not only allows Invisible Man to be heard—to project his voice through the soundscape the audience constructs—and the protesters to hear, but also becomes a site through which the speaker and the group work toward some accord, since Invisible Man is only successful and only has a reason to speak if the crowd remains willing both to talk back—or provide feedback—and to listen.

If we consider again Invisible Man's experience of immersive listening when playing Armstrong's "Black and Blue" in the context of a vibrational listening, it is clear that Ellison imagines his narrator's body as a transducer, its own inner ear of sorts, being washed over with and receiving music that he interprets through listening. And if we consider that he is immersed in recorded music, then we might think of our narrator as being his own iteration of listening technology. Invisible Man is so enveloped in sound that he is able to experience, like quite sensitive tape recorders and microphones, the satisfaction of accessing even silent sound, a kind of sound that in the previous "acoustical deadness" of his hole did not resonate and certainly would not be perceptible to the human ear alone: "it was a strangely satisfying experience for an invisible man to hear the silence of sound," a silence otherwise unheard, unspoken, unrecorded, and deemed as empty of meaning or void of significance.[65] If we can listen to the sound of invisibility as a musician plays and sings unseen through recorded music, how might the listener listen to the silence, then, of perceived sound? Invisible Man's body is fully immersed in a practice of listening to recorded sound, thus acting as a transducer, an inner ear, recording the significance of silence as such. In this, he asserts silence to be meaningful, remarkable, and part of the lower frequencies.

A Cultural Politics of Frequency

The novel ends with Invisible Man's query from underground: "Who knows but that, on the lower frequencies, I speak for you?"[66] This question raises the possibility that, while he has been recording his own unique experience, that experience is resonant with those within hearing. I call attention to this interactive and reciprocal line because, implicitly, it gestures toward the listening function of the reader. In what other way are we to determine the resonance of the narrator's story on the lower frequencies but to tune in and listen? Invisible Man's focus specifically on the lower frequencies also brings to mind R. Murray Schafer's connection between hearing and touch. Schafer explains: "Hearing and touch meet where the lower frequencies of audible sound pass over to tactile vibrations (at about 20 hertz). Hearing is a way of touching at a distance and . . . is fused with sociability whenever people gather together to hear something special."[67] The question reverberates with the focus on vibration within the novel, understanding that multisensory, vibrational listening moves us from a self-in-isolation toward becoming a self-in-relation to others.

The lower frequencies, then, recall Invisible Man's concerns with feeling musical vibration and with noting the vibrations he becomes attuned to at the Brotherhood rally as they are specifically linked to a tactile listening. Additionally, as Shelley Trower notes, "vibration appears to cross distances between things, between people, between self and environment, between the senses and society, promising (or threatening) to shrink or break down such distances."[68] Here Trower suggests that vibration produces a social and experiential space, one that listens to the possibility of resonance from one person to another. We might say, also, that Invisible Man's lower frequencies constitute a cultural politics of frequency, one that relies heavily on an embodied, vibrational listening in order to examine the possibilities and limitations of such listening toward public action.[69] Further, in order to perceive lower-frequency sound, the listener must intentionally and closely listen. The novel's reading audience is activated here as a listening community—one that connects, gives audience, listens in—drawn together by the social and communal possibilities of listening.

Invisible Man's question also suggests the material book as a space of aural encounter. Reminiscent of Morrison's narrator in *Jazz*, Invisible Man directly addresses his listenership even before his concluding question. He informs us through a rhetorical question that he has been writing throughout his hibernation: "So why do I write, torturing myself to put it down?" His response: "Because in spite of myself I've learned some things."[70] He shares with his listeners that he can hear them complaining: "Ah . . . so it was all a build-up to bore us with his buggy jiving. He only wanted us to listen to him rave!"[71] While he admits that this is "only partially true," Invisible Man also asks, "Being invisible and without substance, a disembodied voice, as it were, what else could I do? What else but try to tell you what was really happening when your eyes were looking through?"[72] He seems to have a sense of responsibility to tell those who will listen "what was really happening." And though he is afraid of the answer to his final question, he longs to know that what he has taken great pains to record is worth a listen. In his fearful query, Invisible Man suggests, too, the possibility of his listening's public purpose.

"Most Sensitive Recorders of Sound": Invisible Man's Ethical Listening

Following the death of his Brotherhood colleague, Tod Clifton, and prior to his hibernation, Invisible Man wanders down Harlem's 125th Street, listening to sounds blasting mainly from storefront speakers. When he reaches the train station, he stands on the platform, watching the "transitory ones" who, like him, are waiting for the next train. In this moment of waiting, Invisible Man questions the ability of those traditionally in charge of writing history and fiction to hear, listen to, and record those "too silent for the most sensitive recorders of sound."[73] Struck by their "noisy silence" in the midst of blaring city sounds, he wonders why even he did not hear them before, why, despite his job in the Brotherhood to do otherwise, he had left these people stuck, unrecorded "outside the groove of history."[74] Ellison implies a parallel between the tape recorder and his narrator's ear, both discussed as instruments capable of capturing sound yet not quite sensitive enough to detect the young zoot-suiters he observes on the subway platform.

Like the phonograph and the microphone, the tape recorder developed in the 1950s and was an element of Ellison's phonograph system that he was quite pleased to be able to purchase. In terms of personal recording devices, critics of sound recording equipment in the 1950s "saw the tape recorder as the more advanced, and hence more desirable, technology" over the alternative—the wire recorder.[75] Emily Thompson explains that "the tape recorder (and allied technologies such as the phonograph and the radio) made possible a new mode of lis-

Ralph Ellison in his study with print and tape-recorded manuscript. Still from the 2002 PBS documentary "Ralph Ellison: An American Journey," directed by Avon Kirkland and Elise Robertson as part of the *American Masters* series.

tening" referred to as acousmatic listening: "Listening to sounds in the absence of their original sources and visual contexts, a listening that thus gives access to sound-as-such."[76]

The tape recorder is the technology that allows Ellison to focus on the sound of his writing during revision. The PBS documentary "Ralph Ellison: An American Journey" features Ellison in his home office, where he is captured on film revising a manuscript.[77] Surrounded by piles of paper and shelves brimming with books, he sits at his desk, recording himself reading his manuscript. He speaks into a handheld microphone connected to a large tape recorder atop his desk. In another shot, we hear the playback, Ellison's voice faint. Ellison focuses intently on his voice reading portions of his thick manuscript, which also sits in front of him on the desk. With pen in hand, he listens, pauses the tape reel, then makes a note on the page. He resumes listening. Ellison began to revise his manuscripts in this manner after working with his editor, Albert Erskine, on the revision of *Invisible Man*. The two men read the manuscript aloud, editing and revising as they went. Ellison found this revising and editing process valuable and began recording and then replaying these recordings to help him "hear the rhythm of the sound" of his writing. He also used the tape recorder to refine his narrative listening strategies as a Works Progress Administration interviewer. He explains, "I tried to use my ear for dialogue to give an impression of just how people sounded."[78]

Considering the scene on the train platform alongside Ellison's work with his tape-recorded writing highlights a parallel relationship between Invisible Man as he wanders through Harlem considering the difficulty of recording "the silence of sound" in the people he watches and Ellison's attempts to capture fully the sounds of the people he encounters in his writing. Another way to put this is that Invisible Man in particular is struck perhaps by the unease he feels at how simple it is to miss these quieter frequencies even with the most delicate of recording technology and the most sensitive of ears. How could he miss them even though he was one of them? As a writer, how might Ellison create literature that fully captures the sound and humanity of those about whom he writes?

Invisible Man contemplates the human ear, technologies of sound recording, and writers like himself as a triangulated liberating and restorative racial and cultural practice. Despite exciting developments in sound technology, however, such developments do not serve to remedy racial disenfranchisement through misperception. Nor do these innovations erase the still-figurative and literally limited ability to record (read: value, be aware of and attentive to) those who reside in more silent sound registers—those who are disenfranchised. While Veit Erlmann argues that modernity is marked by the notion that because of technology "we listen all too well," Invisible Man suggests here that the modern subject, despite this sonic technology, does not listen well enough.[79] For Ellison and his protagonist, then, there is much at stake in this modern listening. Here listening emerges as an ethical practice, one whose purpose largely is to hear and record those who are inaudible and, therefore, ignored. In light of this sonic exclusion, Invisible Man's deliberate attuning to "the silence of sound" becomes even more significant.

THREE

When Malindy Listens

· ·

Audiographic Archiving in Gayl Jones's
Corregidora

In her essay "When Malindy Sings," Farah Jasmine Griffin meditates on black women vocalists—their voice and performing presence—as prominent persons on the national stage. Citing such monumental performances as Marian Anderson's appearance at the Lincoln Memorial in 1939 or Whitney Houston's rendition of "The Star-Spangled Banner" at the Super Bowl in 1991 during the Gulf War, Griffin suggests that "this singing spectacle offers an alternative vision of a more inclusive America."[1] Despite her own limited privileges in this space, the black woman vocalist, according to Griffin, performs an important service to the nation in such moments "as she pulls together and helps to heal national rifts."[2] This same iconic figure performs also a different kind of national and cultural work, serving as muse for black male writers and musicians; as Griffin writes, the black woman vocalist's "voice, linked to nature, inspires cultural memory in the hearer and sets him on his own path of creative discovery."[3] Whether singing for the state of our nation or inspiring black writers and musicians to infuse the nation with story and song, this singing voice, she asserts, provides "an aural space where listeners can momentarily experience themselves as outside of themselves, as 'home' or as 'free.' The space can be simultaneously political, spiritual, and sensual. It is the context of the listening or the hearing that embodies the voice with meaning."[4]

Griffin illuminates the black woman's singing voice as a point of mythical creative origin. In doing so, she emphasizes the interconnected and interdependent relationship between audition and vocalization, or what we might refer to as audible reciprocity. Additionally, she suggests that listening functions as a catalytic, generative, and constructive process, an accessing by the listener of possibility in the voice of the singer. While this practice actively constructs meaning, Griffin's listener, however, is largely positioned exterior to the performing self—as an audience member, a cultural critic, the writer or (female or male) musician.

In this chapter, I wish to build on Griffin's meditation on the cultural politics of black female vocality by exploring this question: What happens when Malindy *listens*? More precisely, what happens when, in fictional texts such as Gayl Jones's *Corregidora*, "the storyteller becomes her own hearer"?[5] By tuning in to *Corregidora* with these questions, I aim to understand listening not only as a practice of agency that imbues each individual's voice with meaning but also as a method of cultural critique and remaking—a strategy that is itself political. Further, this chapter considers how listening is necessarily strategic in the ways in which it allows the listener to filter and discern what is listened to. Within Jones's novel, history and the blues become story stored in and lived through the body, resulting in an assembling of an audiographic—auditory, autobiographical, and composed—archive, one that Ursa assembles through storytelling and music as she engages both with her family history and her own vocalizations of personal and familial story through a filtered listening.[6] If Sterling Brown's Ma Rainey is a blues woman who is perceived as knowing the folk and their sufferings so well that she can sing in collaboration with them to enable their momentary relief, Jones's Ursa struggles with how to bear witness to historical abuses even as she labors to understand and make musical her own present, intimate pains. At chapter's end, I listen closely to black women vocalists Aretha Franklin and Bettye LaVette as listeners. *Corregidora*, I want to suggest, helps amplify these famous vocalists' acts of listening—to themselves and to others—as culturally political work.

Storytellers and Storyhearers in the Flesh

In her first novel, *Corregidora*, Jones presents Ursa Corregidora, a blues vocalist who negotiates a continuum of historical, familial, and personal creative trauma that is shared among characters continually through storytelling. While the novel is set in Kentucky in the mid-1940s to the late 1960s, the historical traces of slavery, particularly the experiences of enslaved women in nineteenth-century Brazil, are resonant still in the lives of the Corregidora women. Ursa, the fourth generation of Corregidora women, grows up with the matriarchal edict to bear witness to slavery's atrocities by giving birth to a (female) child and passing on orally the evidentiary narrative to her offspring. The traumatically repeated concern of the Corregidora women is insistent in part because despite the abolition of slavery in Brazil, the control over future generations was contestable, particularly because the state burned all the records of slavery. There is no account for lived life, then, only for that which is spoken and listened to.[7] The novel speaks simultaneously to historical horror and personal loss primarily through her fore-mothers, with Ursa serving as their audience.

With the publication of *Corregidora* in 1975, Jones was heralded as an innovative, major new author. Toni Morrison, then an editor at Random House, signed Jones after learning about her work from Jones's mentor, Michael Harper.[8] Morrison heard Jones's novel as one in which "there was no separation between the storyteller and the hearer."[9] In an interview with Harper, Jones shares that she "learned to write by listening to people talk." She elaborates, "I still feel that the best of my writing comes from having heard rather than having read."[10] She extends this distinction between hearing stories and reading stories in her reflections on the difference between being a story*writer* versus a story*teller*, explaining:

> I say I'm a fiction writer if I'm asked, but I really think of myself as
> a storyteller. When I say 'fiction,' it evokes a lot of different kinds
> of abstractions, but when I say 'storyteller,' it always has its human
> connections. . . . There is always that kind of relationship between a
> storyteller and a hearer—the seeing of each other. The hearer has to see/
> hear the storyteller, but the storyteller has to see/hear the hearer.[11]

Moving away from the acousmatic sound of *Invisible Man*, Jones's novel relies heavily on a reciprocally grounded sense of story*tellers* and story*hearers*—those who have discernible shape, face, and context—in creating her novel. By enacting a storyteller-storyhearer relationship in her experiment with "the 'form' of oral storytelling," she invites us to listen as we read.[12] As the reading audience, storyhearers to the novel's pages, we are called on to tune in to an explicitly aural, gender-inflected, materially and historically situated embodied experience.

Ursa's body is quite palpable throughout this novel, particularly with regard to loss experienced through it. The first loss the reader encounters—the loss that initiates the narrative and one that emphasizes this novel's focus on an embodied experience negotiated through listening—is Ursa's miscarriage; she loses her child and has an emergency hysterectomy after her husband, Mutt, pushes her down the stairs. Even as I write "pushes" here, the verbs Jones chooses to mark this act are important to pause over, for at various times in the narrative the event is reported not only as a "push" but also a "throw" and named in the noun as a "fall." These words, though, all lead directly to the same consequence: following the incident, Ursa is admitted to the hospital and doctors perform an emergency hysterectomy that renders her unable to bear children.

What is also haunting and resonant particularly concerning Ursa's hysterectomy is the political context around women's reproductive rights in the 1970s.

Corregidora was published two years after the Roe v. Wade decision concerning a woman's right to regulate her own reproductive life. In her discussion of the social context in which Ursa undergoes this medical procedure, Stephanie Li suggests that "given the growing attention to the number of women of colour subjected to involuntary sterilization through hysterectomy and tubal ligation, Ursa's chilly 'the doctors said . . . my womb would have to come out' is not so simply an indictment of Mutt's battery; the hysterectomy is written over with many possible medical, social and racial lines of interpretation."[13] The issue of reproductive rights is also present in Ursa's equation of sex with creativity, articulated in her angry question: "And what if I'd thrown Mutt Thomas down those stairs instead, and done away with the source of his sex, or inspiration?"[14] Previously taboo in public discourse, issues such as female fertility, reproductive rights, sexual desire, incest, and domestic violence are central to Jones's novel; these concerns were the focus of what is known now as the first wave of contemporary black feminism. Through such scribal texts as Toni Cade Bambara's anthology *The Black Woman* and Roseann Bell, Bettye Parker, and Beverly Guy-Sheftall's *Sturdy Black Bridges* and such organizations as the Combahee River Collective with its "Black Feminist Statement," African American women attempted to establish a racial political and social agenda that recognized women's reproductive rights.

The implications of Ursa's hysterectomy reach far beyond her reproductive health, as she comments that it was "as if something more than the womb had been taken out."[15] After her surgery, Ursa describes her womb as comparable to her self; she describes it metaphorically as broken musical instruments and other objects: "The center of a woman's being. Is it? No seeds. Is that what snaps away my music, a harp string broken, guitar string, string of my banjo belly. Strain in my voice. . . . That old man still howls inside me. . . . My veins are centuries meeting."[16] Ursa does, indeed, seem to embody Michael Harper's poetic notion that "history is your own heartbeat."[17] Hers are horrific and complex bloodlines, their aural imagery striking. Ursa listens to sounds her body makes and imagines a physiological soundscape. Her perception of the impact of loss on her body and the desire (or lack thereof) and grief she carries all inform what she perceives in her voice. She compares her removed womb to broken strings, no longer resonant, and imagines her loss as fractured sound, symbolic of a lost ability to reproduce a new generation of listeners. Her blood also courses with noises. Yet what is broken also seems to possess the ability to sound, for it is what is heard in Ursa's voice: the strain. The abruptness of this loss is reflected as well, particularly in the quick snapping away sound of her music. The strain results from these snapped string fragments, the snapping suggesting a limited resonance. This limited resonance has implications for Ursa's notion of self.

In these lines, too, we hear the burden of an aural historical witnessing and the coursing of historical continuity as well. As readers, we are witness to an intense somatic experience that we access throughout this audiomusical text as we listen. Carolyn Cooper discusses this notion of "noises in the blood and reverberating echoes in the bone" as genealogical discourses of race, a discussion that resonates with the ways in which Jones explores issues of race and history in her novel.[18] The body in *Corregidora* becomes a necessary, living archive: Ursa's "veins are centuries meeting." This is, indeed, a blues novel. Ursa describes her blood here not only as a recording of her biological and racial self but also as a historical archive. As a Corregidora—from the Spanish *corregidor*, "magistrate and corrector," and the Portuguese *carregador*, "laden, to load or carry, to overdo"—Ursa literally and ethically embodies and bears law and justice, burden and strain. The howling of old man Corregidora—the man who, animal-like and imaginatively animated across time, "still howls inside me," and who owned Ursa's great-grandmother and sexually abused both her and Ursa's grandmother—sounds in counterpoint to the broken strings. His howling is vocalized through Ursa's body, creating a sense of the past abuse living on in her present pain.

Considering the historical context from which *Corregidora* draws, the womb additionally becomes a site of personhood. The 1871 Free Womb Law in Brazil was a law that emancipated the wombs of enslaved mothers, thereby freeing the children born of those mothers. This law also made it illegal to sell enslaved children under the age of eight away from their mothers and ensured that slave owners provided for those children ages eight to twenty-one to whom they did not grant freedom. What was "at stake was a legal claim that a slave master, like Corregidora, might have on the bodily and psychic life of future generations."[19] Ursa's personal loss is amplified as it is tied intimately to historical and familial concerns. Through her fiction, Jones thinks through the impact of historical trauma on future generations and understands this trauma's ability to travel in erratic ways, marking bodies and persons despite their geographical and temporal separation. Further, locating historical knowledge about racial and sexual trauma in the body rather than in national archives or legal and governmental documents like those lost in the process of emancipation in Brazil offers bodily memory as an alternative site through which and to which we tune in for historical evidence and understanding.

Listening to Loss

Rather than treat the haunting sonic breaks in Ursa's voice as completely debilitating, Jones begins to recast them as Ursa listens to her voice after surgery. There is emphasis in the novel on ensuring that Ursa has the opportunity to learn how she sounds—to others and to herself. Ursa is part of her own first audience following her hysterectomy. She is returning to work soon after her surgery and is worried about how she is going to sound. She begins with her throat: "They didn't say anything about my throat. They didn't say it did anything to my throat."[20] While we listen for Ursa to sing her song, she tunes us in to her interior sound—her unique resonance.[21] For the first time in the novel, we hear her sing: *"Trouble in mind, I'm blue, but I won't be blue always."*[22] The lyrics appear italicized in the text, emphasizing these words as song. Many black women vocalists have sung this song. Here the fictional Ursa joins these women, giving voice to a balanced blues line—declaring her current situation and pointing to a promise that the trouble, one day, will be over. Interestingly, Ursa's reading audience attends to her singing voice while situating it within an archive of black women's singing voices. As a listening reader, for instance, Toni Morrison describes Ursa's voice as a cross between Billie Holiday and Fannie Lou Hamer, both voices of resistance.[23] In this moment, Ursa's voice is treated similarly to the description Sherley Anne Williams offers in her meditation on Esther Phillips, "like an open wound, proclaiming that its owner had survived unspeakable things."[24] The singing voice I hear when I revisit Ursa's singing of "Trouble in Mind" is Nina Simone's.[25]

As Ursa tests her voice in her own listening, her friend Cat is listening, too. When Ursa stops singing in response to the difference she hears in her own voice—"It didn't sound like it used to"—Cat urges her to continue and Ursa finishes the song. Cat responds with a smile and applauds, noting, "Your voice sounds a little strained, that's all. But if I hadn't heard you before, I wouldn't notice anything. I'd still be moved. Maybe even moved more, because it sounds like you been through something. Before it was beautiful too, but you sound like you been through more now. You know what I mean?"[26] Here Cat checks in to make sure Ursa understands what she is saying, a gesture of a listener. Again, Ursa's voice is heard as strained, which Cat infuses with positive meaning, significance, and the presence and recording of Ursa's experience. The strain marks Ursa as having endured trauma, having "been through something." It is the sung voice that we are acculturated to hear when listening to blues and jazz vocalists, a voice that makes audible the wounds that otherwise would live hidden in the body. We are called on to sustain our listening here—not just during performance but also during musings of varied expressiveness.[27]

While Cat's comments focus on the past nature of this strain—"you been through something"—I suggest along with Elizabeth Goldberg that this strain also reveals the physical and psychological pain Ursa continues to feel. Goldberg notes that Jones's novel contains "a pained present, symptomatic of the representation of a body still in pain rather than of a traumatized subject attempting to grasp a pain which sustains itself upon living memory."[28] My reading extends Goldberg's here: Ursa's voice sounds in the sonic hinge between historical memory and personal experience. The story she sings is audiographical, an aurality of the flesh. If Ursa's singing vocalizes both the horrific past that her foremothers experienced and traces of her mother's life as they elide with that historic past, it also articulates the pain she has experienced and continues to experience.

Cat is not the only listener in the novel to interpret Ursa's post-traumatic vocality as carrying traumatic traces. Max Monroe, the owner of the Spider, Ursa's second place of employment, hears hardness in her voice and describes what he hears in ways that emphasize listening as an embodied act. In fact, his description seems to project his own body into her vocal timbre. Max describes her voice as "callused hands. Strong and hard but gentle underneath. Strong but gentle too. The kind of voice that can hurt you. I can't explain it. Hurt you and make you still want to listen."[29] For Max, Ursa's voice generates pain and vocal engagement. The voice she amplifies from her body can act physically on another. Mutt, in contrast, hears this hardness negatively and tells Ursa, "You try to sing hard, but you not hard."[30] Tadpole, Ursa's second husband, says that her voice "sounded like it had sweat in it. Like you were pulling everything out of yourself."[31]

Cat, however, also hears beauty interlaced with painful experience in this strain. At the nexus of beauty and pain is meaning in Cat's description. While Ursa worries that her voice has changed, Cat assures her, "Not for the worse. Like Ma [Rainey], for instance, after all the alcohol and men, the strain made it better, because you could tell what she'd been through. You could hear what she'd been through."[32] The strain becomes an audiographical archive of the singer's experience writ musically and a collection of gender-inflected listening. Further, drawing this similarity to Ma Rainey provides Ursa with a familiar model with and against which to hear the strain in her own voice. By comparing Ursa's voice to that of this powerful blues icon, Cat makes it clear that she does not hear this change in voice as negative. Cat's listening gives confirmation to Ursa's experience.

Before Ursa realizes it herself, her audience of one locates the potential of her strained, broken, wounded voice. The voice, that is, becomes meaning-filled in its own right, making what Ursa has "been through" impossible to ignore because what she has been through is audible with every note she produces. Here the voice is clearly material, with the history of the body's experiences affecting how it sounds. Rather than a problem, the record of her loss and pain in her voice functions as an empowering difference throughout the text. Loss, then, functions ironically as a potentially productive process, becoming a palpable agent for engagement of the past and how it now figures in Ursa's present. This loss changes how Ursa sounds. Also, importantly, it changes how she listens.

"Trouble in Mind": Ursa's Inner Listening

In her room, Ursa continues vocalizing for the first time since her accident, humming another portion of the song "Trouble in Mind"—"the part about taking my rocking chair down by the river and rocking my blues away." She then reflects, "What [Cat] said about the voice being better because it tells what you've been through. Consequences. It seems as if you're not singing the past, you're humming it. Consequences of what? Shit, we're all consequences of something. Stained with another's past as well as our own. Their past in my blood."[33] Ursa's voice is both strained and stained. Rather than a final erasure of Ursa from a historical or familial record, then, her miscarriage and subsequent hysterectomy serve as the impetus for a change in her blues art, her relationship to her maternal forebears and their narrative, and her position as a witness—a listener to the past and an aural agent in the present. In this moment of humming "Trouble in Mind," she calls attention to a distinction between singing—the voice of the vocalist traveling beyond the body to her audience—and humming—the voice heard by an audience but reverberating in the body of the vocalist. Here we witness Ursa's listening, and that listening attunes our reading ears to her interior acoustics made public.

This tuning to an interior acoustics made public is an important one, for it allows Ursa to filter her foremothers' process of archiving the trauma of slavery. Ursa's grandmother insists: *They burned all the documents, Ursa, but they didn't burn what they put in their minds. We got to burn out what they put in our minds, like you burn out a wound. Except we got to keep what we need to bear witness. That scar that's left to bear witness. We got to keep it as visible as our blood.*[34] According to Gram, for the Corregidora women the trauma of slavery must be internalized, archived, branded on their "conscious" through perpetual, imperative storytelling.[35] Emancipation is insufficient to remove the suffering, sexual exploitation, and incest endured during and after slavery and leads the Corregidora women to create another scar, seared into memory and the "conscious" in order to produce intergenerational memory as evidence. The documents burned upon emancipation in Brazil destroy only external objects.

While Ursa's foremothers also point to the significance of the internal record of the mind—the socioemotional, psychosocial archive—their conceptualization of the interior is quite different from Ursa's emerging interior acoustics made public. For Gram and Great Gram, as long as the record of that original historical and traumatic memory passed on is intact, evidence remains. What they also assert is that what was put in the slaves' minds, their "trouble in mind," what was internalized of the harm done, should be burned out like a wound. The language of healing here is both provocative and invasive. We burn a wound to sterilize it, close it, and help it heal. So the call is to burn out the harm, the pain, and the hurt but to keep the scar as a record—what is left over, what remains. Evidence of historical atrocity, then, becomes physical and material—blood, visible body, scar on the mind. But it is also psychological and psychical—scar *on the mind*, a personal experience internalized as historical record. The destroyed legal record resurfaces here as both spoken and indelible evidence on the mind.

For the Corregidora women, the perpetuation of this internal evidence also takes the form of offspring, creating conscious beings to retell and maintain the evidence until it comes time to produce it: *"The important thing is making generations. They can burn the papers but they can't burn conscious, Ursa. And that what makes the evidence. And that's what makes the verdict."*[36] The offspring become "conscious" multiplied, making the scar visible and, as interlocutors, amplifying its audibility.[37] With Ursa's inability to bear children, then, comes a break in the family's trail of storytelling evidence: "My great-grandmama told my grandmama the part she lived through that my grandmama didn't live through and my grandmama told my mama what they both lived through and my mama told me what they all lived through and we were suppose to pass it down like that from generation to generation so we'd never forget. . . . Yeah, and where's the next generation?"[38] For Ursa, this is a poignant and high-stakes question. Without the next generation, she does not have children to pass the story on to or to bear witness for her. Less obvious is the way the question also emphasizes her own absence from the narrative. In order for Ursa to engage in her family's codifying narrative, she must bear children. Because she cannot, her story cannot move in the ways this familial contract demands. The text suggests a crisis of witnessing, for without the next generation of listeners Ursa is erased except as a possessor of evidence through habitual listening.

The crisis of witnessing does not stop there. When discussing her mother, Correy (her name a diminutive of Corregidora and a name her husband, Martin, used to call her), Ursa wonders at the *interior* story Correy never told her: "*Mother still . . . carried their evidence, screaming, fury in her eyes, but she wouldn't give me that, not that one. Not her private memory.*"[39] As Ursa tries to figure out other possibilities for herself in terms of her responsibility for bearing witness, she visits Correy, longing to talk with her: "I could feel the strain and wondered if she could. I'd always loved her and knew she loved me, but still somehow we'd never 'talked' things before, and I wanted to talk things now."[40] This moment of talk between mother and daughter carries with it the strain that Ursa mentions in relation to her postaccident singing voice. Quiet also frames this exchange: Correy "asked quietly" what Ursa wanted; Ursa regards her mother with "a quiet look."[41]

During this visit home, Correy shares parts of her own story with Ursa, particularly her experiences with Ursa's father, Martin. Correy becomes pregnant after her first sexual encounter with Martin; Great Gram then forces Martin to marry Correy, and they live together in the same house with Gram and Great Gram. As Correy describes her life with Martin, her story emerges "in pieces, instead of telling one long thing."[42] While much of her story focuses on her time with Martin, Correy slips between her story and that of Great Gram and Gram, interweaving the two narratives as if they are one. More striking, according to Ursa, Correy shifts from herself telling her own story and morphs into what seems to Ursa like Great Gram telling her own story: "Mama kept talking until it wasn't her that was talking, but Great Gram. I stared at her because she wasn't Mama now, she was Great Gram talking."[43] Although Correy is able to share portions of her "own private memory" with her daughter, she is unable to disentangle her memory completely from that of her foremothers.[44] Her storytelling leaves Ursa noting that "it was as if their memory, the memory of all the Corregidora women, was her memory too, as strong with her as her own private memory, or almost as strong."[45] Correy also stops short of sharing the circumstances of her current life with her daughter, leaving Ursa wanting "to ask what about her now, how lonely was *she*. She'd told me about *then*, but what about *now*."[46] The punctuation here—periods instead of question marks—underlines the fact that these are questions left unasked.

While Ursa is still left wondering after her conversation with Correy, we can still listen and perceive Correy's decision not to share certain experiences with Ursa as an empowering choice. As Kevin Quashie reminds us, while African American culture is often considered expressive, dramatic, and even defiant, quiet can be heard here as a different kind of expressiveness, particularly one that speaks to Correy's vulnerabilities and fears. Strategic silence, as Quashie explains, "is often aware of an audience, a watcher or a listener whose presence is the reason for the withholding."[47] While Correy strategically withholds information about her current life, she plants the seed for questioning, for the possibility of an inheritance that differs markedly from the evidence-building narrative of Great-Gram and Gram, a narrative that makes no room for questions. We listen as Ursa shares that once, when Ursa was still a child, Correy questioned her mother's and grandmother's narrative: "*How can it be?*" Ursa reflects, Correy was "*the only one who asked that question, though. For the others it was just something that was, something they had, and something they told. But when she talked, it was like she was asking that question for them, and for herself too.*"[48] Posing questions is quite a different listening habit from the one that Ursa was raised to practice. Growing up, hers was a rote listening in which posing questions was not only discouraged but also punished.[49] Correy's question "How can it be?" signals her openness to listen toward another possibility, specifically toward an altered storytelling and storylistening practice.[50]

After visiting with her mother, Ursa reflects: "*Still it was as if my mother's whole body shook with that first birth and memories and she wouldn't give those to me, though she passed the other ones down, the monstrous ones, but she wouldn't give me her own terrible ones. . . . How could she bear witness to what she'd never lived, and refuse me what she had lived? . . . What was their life then? Only a life spoken to the sounds of my breathing or a low-playing Victrola. . . . What's a life always spoken, and only spoken?*"[51] Ursa, in her quiet questioning, is defiant in her own way. Her questions trouble the narrative repetition of the Corregidora women. Understood partly is the implication that a life only spoken and not lived is not a full life. I would add, however, that Ursa's questioning also gestures toward a lack of conscious listening to the life repeatedly spoken. That is, the Corregidora women live as if a spoken, witnessing voice is proof enough—all at the expense of a cultivated personal and interior life.

Ursa's questioning and listening here are necessarily discerning and reflective and resonate with Lauri Siisiäinen's notion of listening: "The art of listening . . . has a certain sense of paradox to it. . . . One must know how to listen attentively and silently, how to actively direct, fix, and concentrate one's listening to the logos transported by speech, as well as how to discriminate and exclude the ambient, surrounding sounds."[52] On the bus ride home, for instance, Ursa notes,

"I was thinking that now that Mama had gotten it all out, her own memory—at least to me anyway—maybe she and *some man.* . . . But then, I was thinking, what had I done about my *own* life?"[53] Ursa's question signals that the listening practice she now brings to bear is one that does not accept narratives without reflecting on them. She instead embraces in her listening the need to filter and discern what she hears as she determines the new story she then wishes to sing.

Inner Listening for a New World Song

Ursa's questioning also enacts a commitment to disrupting the world as it is in order to imagine, through listening, a new (future) world. Her particular query early on in the novel—"where's the next generation?"—underscores, in fact, her position as a willing, urgent listener. Rather than perpetually reenact a process of identification so intense as to erase the individual's "own private memory," because the stakes are too high to forget the past, Ursa questions and re-creates the evidence based on how she listens to what she hears and what feedback she receives from her multiple audiences. In Ursa's listening, evidence is no longer fixed, questioning no longer stifled.

Through Ursa, Jones posits listening as aural action. Ursa is an attuned listener, one who actively, intentionally, and artistically constructs meaning through her music. While "listening" is a verb, often listening practices are not imagined as ways of taking social or other kinds of action; as discussed earlier in this study, speaking tends to function as the default for sonic social action. Yet throughout *Corregidora* Ursa practices listening not as object but as action, understanding a query-driven and discerning listening to be a crucial practice of subjecthood. For instance, she poses the ultimate question: "But I *am* different now, I was thinking. I have everything they had, except the generations. I can't make generations. And even if I still had my womb, even if the first baby *had* come—what would I have done then? Would I have kept it up? Would I have been like *her*, or *them*?"[54] While losing the physical ability to bear children immediately prompts Ursa's quest to locate her self differently in the context of her familial narrative, this moment suggests that the question of whether or not to pass on the evidence and pass it on in the same manner is just that: a question, not a given.

Functioning as her own listener, Ursa wades through her inwardly explored and outwardly expressed thoughts, concluding that bearing witness to her familial past will morph into musical composition. She decides to write a song that reflects her present *and* their past: "I wanted a song that would touch me, touch my life and theirs. A Portuguese song, but not a Portuguese song. A new world song. A song branded with the new world."[55] Her description of her new world song takes branding or being branded—a widespread practice of punishment and ownership inscription that slaveholders used on the bodies of enslaved women and men—as a figurative postemancipation (and, given the publication date of the novel, post–civil rights) marker of memory and potential healing. Ursa's description of her emerging musical composition also recalls Ellison's explication of the cultural work of the blues. This new song—and Jones's novel—dramatizes the "impulse" Ellison identifies in the blues "to keep the painful details and episodes of a brutal experience alive in one's aching consciousness, to finger its jagged grain, and to transcend it, not by the consolation of philosophy but by squeezing from it a near-tragic, near-comic lyricism."[56] Ursa's proposed new world song enlivens the space where the personal (read: individual, familial, communal) and the historical chronicle or archive merge. Jones's novel and specifically this new world song, however, expand Ellison's notion of the blues in that the ultimate goal is conscious attuning to, rather than transcending of, painful experience.

An inner listening, one that tunes in to the "jagged grain" of an "aching consciousness," is quite prevalent throughout *Corregidora*. Ursa listens to her thoughts, dreams, and memories, struggling along the way with her personal loss as well as the familial and historical loss branded on her "conscious." This inner listening takes the form of an internal dialogue—a dynamic conversation *in mind*. As listeners in print, we are made privy to conversations she has with herself throughout the novel. For instance, listen as she wonders about her mother's decision to keep her own private memory from her: "*I would have rather sung her memory if I'd had to sing any. What about my own? Don't ask me that now.*"[57] The last sentence here emphasizes a self listening to and in conversation with herself. Ursa poses a poignant question, "*What about my own?*" It is a question, though, with which she is unable to come to terms and so defers its consideration: "*Don't ask me that now.*" While Ursa is certain of her preferential desire to bear witness to her mother's narrative instead of the story that Gram and Great Gram "squeeze" into her during her childhood, she is uncertain of what to make of her own memory and experience. Throughout the novel, Jones distinguishes these internal spoken thoughts and dreams from the rest of the text by italicizing them, thus marking them as a sort of "imaginative modal counterpart to spoken voice" in print, a mode that requires its own type of representation and engagement and, I would add, listening to on the page.[58] Ursa's inner voice arms her for resistance.[59]

After marrying her second husband, Tadpole, Ursa composes blues lines in a dream sequence. The verbal changes—as if she is trying out different words and is not ready to transcribe them as finished with complete punctuation—suggest revision and improvisational play during the songwriting process:

> O Mister who come to my house You do not come to visit You do not come to
> see me to visit You come to hear me sing with my thighs You come to see me
> open my door and sing with my thighs You come to see me open my door and
> sing with my thighs Perhaps you watch me when I am sleeping. Who are you?[60]

How should she think of the mister's trip to the slave woman's house? Should the mister in the song "come to see me" or "come to visit"? More importantly, there is an interweaving between Ursa's story and the story she wishes to vocalize in her new world song. First, the slave woman metaphorically sings with her thighs as Ursa sings a song of sexual abuse in slavery. Further, she speaks and listens to herself in her dream, defining herself as *"the daughter of the daughter of the daughter of Ursa of currents, steel wool and electric wire for hair."*[61] Here Ursa notes four generations of women, paralleling the four generations of Corregidora women in the novel. She begets these generations through her art as opposed to being the descendant of these generations. In short, she recalls her foremothers' narrative of making new generations in her remaking, remembering, and in a sense rebirthing of past generations in her art. The self that she earlier suggests is lost through the loss of her womb is reconstructed through her artistic listening.

In this description, Jones also recalls in my listening Medusa, most widely recognized as the Greek character Perseus beheads in order to squelch her power. If any archetypal figure embodies the blues, it is the ancient, resistant Medusa. Medusa originated in North Africa and is a tripartite figure, appearing in different manifestations in African, Indian, and Greek myths. Her name is connected with wisdom and expression, and she is also connected with fertility and menstruation. Earlier in the novel, Ursa alludes to Medusa in talking about her womb: *"Vinegar and water. Barbed wire where a womb should be. Curdled milk."*[62] In alluding to Medusa, Jones recuperates this violently silenced female mythic figure, reclaiming her power of creation through Ursa's musical authoring. This moment requires the reader to listen—and in a way that recognizes that this speaking and singing are not words of resolution. Instead, this moment dreams the sense of traditional and continual revision that Jones purports throughout the novel: *"Everything said in the beginning must be said better than in the beginning,"* an aesthetic of necessary repetition but with an improved difference.[63]

Ursa's dream composing culminates in a portion of her new world song. *Italics*—the typographical marker of the dreamscape in Jones's novel—remain as the lyrics tell the story of an enslaved married woman who would not take her master for a lover. In response to her master's sexual advances, she castrates him and he bleeds to death. Her punishment is death, but before dying she is forced to witness her husband's castration and death:

While mama be sleeping, the ole man he crawl into bed
While mama be sleeping, the ole man he crawl into bed
When mama have wake up, he shaking his nasty ole head

Don't come here to my house, don't come here to my house I said
Don't come here to my house, don't come here to my house I said
Fore you get any this booty, you gon have to lay down dead
Fore you get any this booty, you gon have to lay down dead[64]

The presence of these lines, heard as sung within a dream, suggests that Ursa is listening to herself even as she composes while dreaming. We can hear the continuum between the lyrics of resistance and her resisting anger. There are layers of listening suggested here as well: Ursa hears the song as she "performs" it and the readers listen to the song as they read it on the page. Ursa's desire for a new world song is realized in what Homi Bhabha refers to as "revisionary time," a sort of time that allows for "an encounter with 'newness' that is not part of the continuum of past and present."[65] For Bhabha, art that enacts revisionary time "does not merely recall the past as social cause or aesthetic precedent; it renews the past, refiguring it as a contingent 'in-between' space, that innovates and interrupts the performance of the present. The 'past-present' becomes part of the necessity, not the nostalgia, of living."[66] In Jones's "past-present," Ursa's new world song commences a new process of listening, one that positions the listener as the hinge between the pasts and presents that circulate in the novel—a listening that is processual, not procedural.

At novel's end, Ursa comments: "It was like I didn't know how much was me and Mutt and how much was Great Gram and Corregidora—like Mama when she started talking like Great Gram. But was what Corregidora had done to her, to them, any worse than what Mutt had done to me, than what we had done to each other, than what Mama had done to Daddy, or what he had done to her in return, making her walk down the street looking like a whore?"[67] Then we listen as both Ursa's and Mutt's capacities to vocalize their pains and fears to each other expand. Mutt and Ursa are reunited and have a blues exchange:

"I don't want a kind of woman that hurt you," he said.

"Then you don't want me."

"I don't want a kind of woman that hurt you."

"Then you don't want me."

"I don't want a kind of woman that hurt you."

"Then you don't want me."

He shook me till I fell against him crying. "I don't want a kind of man that'll hurt me neither," I said.[68]

Note the unitalicized typography here. Ursa and Mutt are able to express directly to each other their negative desire—what they do not want—thereby gesturing toward an alternative future, one that perhaps yields what they do want. This desire to end the repetitive cycle of wounding contains the impossibility of its own imperative—"I don't want a kind of woman that hurt you. . . . Then you don't want me." Ursa's return to Mutt is not redemptive. She notes, "I knew what I still felt. I knew that I hated him. Not as bad as then, not with that first feeling, but an after feeling, an aftertaste, or like an odor still in a room when you come back to it, and it's your own."[69] This return is a result of her perception of Mutt as her witness, her auditor—regardless of whether or not readers consider him an ethical one. As Mutt's cousin Jim notes, "Once you told me that when you sang you always had to pick out a man to sing to. And when Mutt started coming in, you kept picking out him to sing to. And then when y'all was married, you had your man to sing to. You said that you felt that the others only listened, but that he heard you."[70]

And perhaps Ursa is Mutt's listener as well. When they reunite after twenty-two years, he reminds Ursa of his "great-grandfather I told you about . . . the one with the wife."[71] The wife of Mutt's great-grandfather is taken from him, and Mutt shares, "After they took her, when he went crazy he wouldn't eat nothing but onions and peppermint. Eat the onions so people wouldn't come around him, and then eat the peppermint so they would."[72] Mutt then reveals that he tries his great-grandfather's strategy: "I tried it but it didn't do nothing but make me sick."[73] This exchange might seem out of place in this moment when Mutt and Ursa are reunited. Yet Mutt's memory of the story of his great-grandfather's trauma reminds us that as Ursa notes earlier in the novel, "we're all consequences of something. Stained with another's past as well as our own."[74] Ursa and Mutt are stained with their families' traumatic pasts and with their own shared past. Mutt's—and his great-grandfather's—attempt alternatively to repel and attract others, too, reads as a blues, a pulling in and a pushing away. We hear that bluesy negotiation again in Ursa's and Mutt's exchange. At the heart of the novel is this grappling with a desire and a need, laced with ambivalence, to be with someone in order to listen and be listened to. In this blues conversation, Ursa and Mutt revise, communicate, and listen for a potentially new future resonant not with what is but with the possibility of audaciously hoping for what may be.[75]

To Hear My Self Sing: Listening to "Respect" and "Blackbird"

While the end of *Corregidora* is not a resolution, one thread that resonates throughout the novel and in this conclusion is the desire, in addition to listen to others, to actively listen to one's *self*, in music and on the written page. Listening, then, is an action-filled process involved in remaking and reinterpreting one's own new world song. Listening in this way is resonant with Christopher Small's musicking as "an activity by means of which we bring into existence a set of relationships that model the relationships of our world, not as they are but as we would wish them to be."[76] Small emphasizes musicking as "a way of knowing" that allows us to "learn about and explore those relationships" in ways that help us "learn how to live well" in our world.[77] *Corregidora*, then, is concerned with creating conditions not only to be heard by others and not only to listen to others but ultimately to listen to one's self in ways that generate the possibility of new ways of knowing. This cultural work of active, discerning, and reinterpretive listening in *Corregidora* recalls for me the artistry of Aretha Franklin and Bettye LaVette, two vocalists who are highly accomplished listeners and reinterpreters.

African American writers often cite Aretha Franklin, the Queen of Soul, as a musical muse. Baldwin identifies Franklin's song "That's Life" as an example of "the way I wanted to write." He continues, "You know, there is something fantastically pure and sad, heart-breaking, and yet peaceful in all this horror. What a triumph—to be able to sing about it—to give it back to the world—to save the world, or simply another person (which is the world) by making the person look at the person."[78] On April 10, 1967—in the midst of a failed truce and a newly fueled Vietnam War, fully mobilized civil rights and women's rights movements, and President Lyndon Johnson's call to end racism, what he termed "man's ancient curse and man's present shame"—Franklin released her hit recording turned anthem, a cover of Otis Redding's "Respect."[79]

While both artists enjoyed chart-topping success with their versions of the song (Redding just two years prior on his 1965 album, *Otis Blue: Otis Redding Sings Soul*), it was Franklin's soulful vocals and additional unique elements that introduced to the ears of her audience soul's social and political potential. In her autobiography, *Aretha: From These Roots*, she recalls, "so many people identified with and related to 'Respect.'" She continues:

> It was the need of a nation, the need of the average man and woman in the street, the businessman, the mother, the fireman, the teacher— everyone wanted respect. It was also one of the battle cries of the civil rights movement. The song took on monumental significance. It became the "Respect" women expected from men and men expected from women, the inherent right of all human beings.[80]

Franklin impressively played the piano and sang at the same time during the song's recording. It is, in fact, the piano and syncopated bass that drive this song, whereas in Redding's version the horn section and emphatic drumbeat are more prominent. Redding sings lead vocals in the key of D with no backup, his "respect" punctuated by the repetitive phrases "gotta, gotta, gotta; give it, give it, give it." His vocals are robust and slightly deeper than Franklin's. His version of the song contains no bridge.

On Franklin's recording, other musicians joining her include guitarist Jimmy Johnson, bassist Tommy Cogbill, drummer Roger Hawkins, cornet player Melvin Lastie, and Franklin's sisters, Carolyn and Erma, as backup singers delivering a fast-paced chant of "sock it to me." Aretha and Carolyn are key in reinterpreting this song. In contrast to Redding, Franklin sings in the key of C, incorporates more blues notes, plays more with tempo, sings behind the tempo, and builds in prominent backup vocals. In addition, the unexpected saxophone break and the spelling of "R-E-S-P-E-C-T" with full band stops coupled with the overall persistent energy of the song led listeners to interpret the song as a cry for racial and gender equality.

The effect Franklin had on her listeners was so powerful that *Ebony* declared the civil rights summer of 1967 as "the summer of 'Retha, Rap [Brown], and Revolt."[81] Often cultural historians cite Franklin's version of the song as a tipping point in the history of soul music.[82] Brian Ward, for instance, suggests that Franklin's version of "Respect" and its reception on the R&B *and* pop charts are good examples of "the ways in which the meanings of a particular song could be amplified, manipulated, or simply imposed thanks to acts of creative consumption by its listeners."[83] While Ward thoroughly accounts for the song's audience in his comments, I would add that Franklin's own creative listening—to Redding's original lyrics and music, that is—leads her to arrange and perform "Respect" in ways that contribute importantly to generating new meaning. For Franklin and her audience, then, creative listening performs an act of politicized reading that allows us to locate this song in what was by most accounts a moment of swelling desire to hear the civil rights and feminist struggles in popular music. Listening, in this context, became a potential means of thinking about group identity and enacting collective action, answering implicitly the audience's desire for "Aretha to set this to music."[84]

While Bettye LaVette has enjoyed a different musical career, her interpretations also amplify this energy and commitment to hearing one's self sing. An American soul singer–songwriter and consummate song interpreter, LaVette began her career at age sixteen when she recorded the single "My Man—He's a Lovin' Man," which became a Top Ten R&B hit.[85] She has had a prolific and storied career, recording at major studios including the iconic Muscle Shoals in Alabama, where she cut her first full-length album, *Child of the Seventies*. She performed in the Broadway musical revue *Bubbling Brown Sugar*, nominated for a Tony Award for Best Musical and an Olivier Award for Best New Musical. LaVette's "surgence," as she terms it, was solidified with her 2005 album *I've Got My Own Hell to Raise*, showcasing her eclectic combination of soul, blues, country, funk, rock and roll, and gospel music.[86] Her entire body of work, dating from the 1960s, has finally made it into print.

I first heard LaVette perform at the famed Café Carlyle in New York City in February 2012. I sat with my spouse and friends at our after-dinner table, listening as LaVette steadily shared a program of interpreted songs framed by her humor-filled storytelling about her decades of hard luck in the music business. Throughout her set, her unmatched skill as an interpreter was clear. Whether performing Lucinda Williams's "Joy," George Harrison's "Isn't It a Pity," or Bruce Springsteen's "Streets of Philadelphia," she worries a lyric like no other; her raspy delivery pushes, bends, and recasts a phrase until it is etched on the listener's ear. Despite these songs' long recording and performance histories, LaVette made them sound in that intimate café setting as if they were written with her listening in mind.

On stage and in her memoir, *A Woman Like Me*, LaVette reiterates as much. Her show that night at the Café Carlyle was like an arrangement, as in Peter Szendy's notion, a transcript of her listening—part of her artistry involves her listening in order to recompose and sing; we, in turn, listen as she shares and performs that creation.[87] She transforms what she has listened to into a new articulation of her artistic, singing, personal self as her band masterfully accompanies her in the

Bettye LaVette at Water Studios, Hoboken, New Jersey, recording *Interpretations: The British Rock Songbook* in 2009. Photo by Kevin Kiley.

transformation: drummer Darryl Pierce, bassist Chuck Bartels, guitarist Brett Lucas, and keyboardist Alan Hill. Although LaVette's voice is often described as raw—what we have been trained to hear when we listen to hard-luck singers—and she employs minimal vocal embellishment, she infuses it with the narrative acuity of a storyteller who has survived to share the tale and a listener who understands how to set that story to music.

A particular song that captured my ear was LaVette's interpretation of the Beatles' song "Blackbird." Originally, Paul McCartney recorded "Blackbird" alone in June 1968, with just a guitar for accompaniment. After recording thirty-two takes, only eleven of which were complete, McCartney decided he wanted the song to sound as if he were singing outdoors. So he and his sound engineer ultimately recorded "Blackbird" outside Abbey Road Studios.[88] At Café Carlyle, LaVette reminded the audience that so many recording artists have remade the song except "the person the song was written for." Before singing "Blackbird," she began with a story delivered in time with the music—transformed from McCartney's mostly 4/4 with shifting meters into a slow anthem in 12/8 time, or what might be more popularly understood as a slow Ray Charles ballad tempo.[89]

When LaVette performed "Blackbird," her arms outstretched, subtly flapping with grace as she urges the singing blackbird to learn how to fly with broken wings, she embodied the song. Her "Blackbird" builds on a less busy chord progression and adds instrumentation—electric guitar, synth strings, and bass—which creates a sound quite different from the acoustic guitar and bird sounds of the Beatles' version. When LaVette performed "Blackbird" at the Hollywood Bowl on July 9, 2010, for a Beatles tribute, the instrumentation was even more striking. As she recalls: "Stepping in front of a symphony orchestra and singing 'Blackbird' to the lush accompaniment of a thousand and one strings brought tears to my eyes."[90]

Characteristic of blues and rhythm-and-blues vocality, LaVette sang the song at the Café Carlyle that night a bit out of time throughout, but in the same key of G as McCartney. She methodically moved her way through the song, employing melisma—an element absent from the original "Blackbird," where McCartney sings one syllable per note and employs no reverb on vocal—and freeing the melody up to make room for vocal improvisation. The song culminates in a transcendent vocal crescendo: "All of *my* life, *I've* been waiting for this moment to arrive" (my emphasis). With her shift in lyrics from the third to the first person and her striking vocal delivery, LaVette makes this song her own. She virtually creates a new melody with melisma, lyric repetitions, and live reverb. During her performance that evening, she recalled that her inspiration to interpret "Blackbird" came from listening to the song itself and to a story about McCartney noticing a black woman sitting alone on a bench, singing at the top of her lungs, which gave him the impetus for the song.[91] While she admitted that she could not confirm the veracity of this specific tale, it made a good story. Nonetheless, LaVette felt a strong connection to this song—one that compelled her to work with her band to rewrite and perform it as a theme for her own life.[92] Ultimately, as she explained onstage and reiterated later in a conversation with me, she interpreted "Blackbird" because she wanted "that black girl to finally sing herself—and hear her self sing."

This phrasing is striking. In it, LaVette calls attention to herself as a vocalist listening back to a song and choosing to revise it. What she calls our attention to here is her awareness of her self as a listener not only to other musicians but also notably to her own voice and its performance. This self-reflective, desire-filled listening that LaVette describes here and that Franklin also enacts in her artistry adds a new possibility to the discourse concerning the figure of the black woman vocalist in African American literature and expressive culture. LaVette's assertion that she chose to sing "Blackbird" to "hear her self sing" challenges us to listen further to the role of vocal musician as co-creative listener. Listening to Franklin's and LaVette's artistry in the context of this conversation about Ursa's listening and her desire for a new world song aims also to amplify these vocalists' cultural work as political.[93] These cultural politics involve not only musical artistry but also historical and personal remembering, all aiming to recast the self as an interpretive listener in public.

FOUR

"If I Allow Myself to Listen"

· ·

Slavery, Historical Thinking, and Aural Encounters
in David Bradley's *The Chaneysville Incident*

At a particularly arresting moment in David Bradley's 1981 novel, *The Chaneysville Incident*, narrator and historian John Washington ruminates on the potential eternal consequences of a brutal slave trade for both the enslaver and the enslaved. According to John, "even so knowledgeable a historian probably does not understand the African Slave Trade" fully because she or he understands the moment as completed, "that whatever its effects were, they are existing now in and of themselves."[1] Yet he asserts that in order to understand death itself as the central issue plaguing the African slave trade, historians need to shift the terms of inquiry when considering this historical trauma. In his estimation, the slave trade was a moment when European notions of death as the end of life collided with African notions of death as the beginning of an afterlife. John makes it clear that he is not calling for historians to resolve "some dialectical battle between African thesis and European antithesis."[2] Instead, he is concerned with how, ultimately, we come to engage with and think about slavery, a violent institution and practice not past but quite present.[3] Slavery is in fact so present that as John confides, "When the wind is right, I think that I can smell the awful odor of eternal misery. And I know for certain that if I allow myself to listen, I can hear the sound of it. Oh yes. Surely, I can hear."[4] John's olfactory and auditory faculties awaken at the stench and pain of slavery's violence. It is his role as historian, he suggests, to make sense of—and to *sense*—these smells and sounds of eternal misery, pungent and audible in the present.

Throughout *The Chaneysville Incident*, a novel ten years in the making, Bradley stages sensory-rich encounters with the past. As he reveals in his brief acknowledgment before the novel, Bradley—like his industrious narrator—consulted a diverse array of historical archives, documents, published sources, and persons while writing this novel. While Bradley describes the novel as a collective effort, not "the product of one person's imagination, or determination, or skill," his narrator does not accept with ease the role of a collaborative and sensing historian.[5] In fact, he struggles particularly against imaginative audition as a viable mode of historical thinking. Sensing the past, however, particularly in all its auditory complexity, becomes crucial to John's attempts to research and understand what happened to his father, Moses Washington, when he apparently committed suicide in 1958 and, by extension, the fate of his great-grandfather, C. K. Washington, and a group of twelve fugitive slaves who in 1858 chose suicide over returning to enslavement.

This chapter listens closely to Bradley's *The Chaneysville Incident* as a novel invested in practicing what I refer to as historical listening. I use "historical listening" to describe a sensory-inflected mode of historical thinking, a practice particularly attuned to sound and sonic perception. It is through John's grappling with what constitutes historical thinking concerning the slave trade and slavery in particular—historical moments that historians and cultural critics alike have noted were "made to be heard"—that we witness the crucial role listening plays in this fictional historian's thinking.[6] Listening, positioned as the most contentious and explicitly dramatized mode of sensory engagement in the novel, emerges eventually as central to John's reasoning and, by extension, his production of a historical account of the Chaneysville Incident. I write "eventually" because, for much of the novel, John regularly resists or completely dismisses historical listening as a viable habit of mind for a historian.

Part of John's struggle, in fact, may be the nature of historical thinking itself. Sam Wineburg describes historical thinking as "unnatural," for it "goes against the grain of how we ordinarily think."[7] Despite our expectations for clear, complete, and informing historical narratives, Wineburg explains that historical texts "come not to convey information, to tell stories, or even to set the record straight. Instead, they are slippery, cagey, and protean, reflecting the uncertainty and disingenuity of the real world."[8] Such texts behave less like fixed, containable, and completely knowable objects of study and more like material that fuels investigation and iterative inquiry. For Wineburg, of utmost importance is the shift from memorizing dates or thinking in dichotomous ways to a dynamic interpretive process, for "achieving mature historical thought depends precisely on our ability to navigate the uneven landscape of history, to traverse the rugged terrain that lies between the poles of familiarity and distance from the past."[9] Like historical thinking, historical listening is an unnatural, intentional, amplified practice. John suggests as much when he returns to his boyhood home—an area in rural Pennsylvania referred to as the Hill—after living for some time in Philadelphia. Upon his return to the Hill, he reflects on "where the lie had been: I had stopped hearing, but I had not stopped listening."[10] John's realization reminds us that, of course, listening is not the same as hearing. While hearing is a physiological form of reception, listening is interpretive, situated, and reflective.

Bradley's treatment of historical listening in *The Chaneysville Incident* dramatizes historical listening as a set of interpretive acts that are not without challenge and are never, according to John and postmodern notions of knowledge, complete. About historians specifically, John shares that "most of us have learned to accept the idea that we will never know everything, so long as we labor here below. . . . It's just that we want to, really, truly, utterly, absolutely, completely, finally, *know*."[11] The desire to know motivates John—and, by extension, the novel's readers—even as the archive we listen through with him complicates the realization of that very desire. Compelling in its imagining of historical work as giving audience to the past, *The Chaneysville Incident* dramatizes John Washington's ever-evolving, complex development as an aural historian. Further, listening in *The Chaneysville Incident* performs as an epistemological and methodological approach to the construction of an inevitably incomplete and at times inaudible history and historical fiction. Together, the impossibility of reaching the past and the ensuing desire to return to it at turns confirm and complicate the inescapably interpretive dimension of history.

Listening for a Sound (Hi)Story

African American writers and artists have been highly engaged with, in Hortense Spillers's term, "reinventing slavery" in their work.[12] This attention to slavery is far from irrelevant for, as Salamishah Tillet asserts, although African Americans possess the full rights of citizenship in the post–civil rights United States, they nonetheless and paradoxically live as estranged citizens. It is this "crisis of citizenship," Tillet argues, that drives African American artists and intellectuals to revisit and recast "sites of slavery"—"the objects, texts, figures, places, and narratives from the American past that provide tangible links between present day Americans and American chattel slavery"—in order both to imbue enslaved persons with a fuller subjectivity than the historical record suggests and to claim a more realized American democracy.[13] I am interested in the ways in which this turn to slavery often entails listening as a mode of fictional expression, representation, and historical recasting of black subjectivity.

Two iconic slave narratives, Frederick Douglass' 1845 *Narrative of the Life of Frederick Douglass* and Harriet Jacobs's 1861 *Incidents in the Life of a Slave Girl*, demonstrate the investment in and power of the ear when narrating the horror of bondage and the complexities of freedom. For instance, Douglass recounts that when chosen to do work at what they called Great House Farm, thereby earning an opportunity to be away from the overseer, the slaves would sing songs while traveling there: "They would make the dense old woods, for miles around, reverberate with their wild songs, revealing at once the highest joy and the deepest sadness."[14] While Douglass shares that he did not understand fully the meanings of these songs when he was enslaved, upon reflection he believes that hearing them would "do more to impress some minds with the horrible character of slavery, than the reading of whole volumes of philosophy on the subject could do. . . . Every tone was a testimony against slavery, and a prayer to God for deliverance from chains."[15] As he recalls, listening to "those wild notes . . . always depressed my spirit, and filled me with ineffable sadness."[16] The sonic power of these songs is so intense that merely writing about them caused "an expression of feeling" to roll "down my cheek."[17] Douglass attributes to these songs his "first glimmering conception of the dehumanizing character of slavery."[18] For him, the songs, sung and heard, are the ultimate vehicles for communicating the horrors of slavery. He imbues sound with the affective strength of moving one to fight to abolish slavery.[19]

Similarly, Linda Brent, Jacobs's heroine and the pseudonym under which she writes, presents her ear as conduit and sonic site for the recounting of her sexual abuse when enslaved. She shares with her audience the regular advances of her aggressive master, Dr. Flint, whose "stinging, scorching words . . . scathe ear and brain like fire," transforming her from an innocent girl into a "prematurely knowing" enslaved woman.[20] Such assaults through the ear came from Jacobs's mistress as well. After her mistress moved Jacobs's bedroom to a "room adjoining her own," Jacobs became "an object of her especial care, though not of her especial comfort." "Sometimes," Jacobs reports, "I woke up, and found her bending over me. At other times she whispered in my ear, as though it was her husband who was speaking to me, and listened to hear what I would answer. . . . At last, I began to be fearful for my life."[21] By calling on primarily white women to "hear my voice, ye careless daughters!" Jacobs challenges her audience to serve as "earwitness" to her enslavement even as they listen through ears that are, by contrast, deemed pure and in need of protection from defiling language and incidents.[22] More recently, Daphne Brooks's archival listening to musician and bondsman Blind Tom as an acoustic "musical analogue" to the discursive slave narrative reveals a narrative of enslavement that encourages us "to forge new critical methodologies to consider the multisensory dimensions of enslavement as well as the dissident, sonic modes of enslaved narration."[23]

Part of the aural affective power of these sonic sites of slavery is that they place the listener in the present moment. Language spoken and sung is presented as media that grants intensified and immediate access to slavery's injustice. In such texts, what is audible often is imagined and experienced as existing in the present.[24] Robin Kelley's reflections on the audio series *Remembering Slavery* echo this sense of the past as present *and* presence in the audible; in his case, he expresses a desire for historical immediacy and an imagination of sound as the medium through which such immediacy can make the past live in the present. *Remembering Slavery* features restored recorded interviews with former slaves conducted by the Works Progress Administration in the 1920s and 1930s.[25] In addition to hearing the voices of formerly enslaved African Americans, the audience for these recordings hears African American actors, including Debbie Allen, Louis Gossett, Jr., and James Earl Jones, dramatically render some of the interviews available only in transcript form from the Library of Congress archives. About these recordings, Kelley asserts: "The immediacy of the voices of men and women who had experienced enslavement provided listeners a link to a world of slaves and slave owners—a world often relegated to the distant past. Through the medium of the spoken word, the slaves' memory exploded out of the archives into the here and now."[26] For Kelley, *Remembering Slavery*—its immediacy of recording technology and its ability to render the voice of the slave with such veracity—figuratively removes historical and other distance as contemporary audience members listen. Consequently, these taped voices take on presence and significance in the current moment. Not only do these interviews amplify the past, they also enliven the past event of enslavement in the moment in which they are re/wound and replayed.[27]

The ways in which these slave narratives embrace the sonic as an expressive site of slavery recalls for me Haile Gerima's 1993 independent film, *Sankofa*. *Sankofa* dramatically demonstrates the sonically animated slave past and compels audience members to listen as intently as they watch. An Akan word meaning "to remember the past, to go forward," *Sankofa* opens with a montage of African sculpture coupled with a repeated incantation: "Spirit of the Dead, rise up, lingering Spirit of the Dead, to claim your story." The incantation permeates the dark space around the images, filling the screen with sound. The film then moves to the site of the Cape Coast slave fort in modern Ghana. There a divine drummer (Kofi Ghanaba)—later we learn his name is Sankofa—chants and drums to summon the spirits of ancestors. Concurrently, a tour guide lectures about the pivotal role this fort played in the slave trade as Mona (Oyafunmike Ogunlano), a contemporary African American model, poses for a photo shoot. A whispered offscreen voice urgently insists, "Wute!": "Listen!" This call maintains our attention to the sonic texture of the film. Abruptly, the drummer interrupts the tour, chastising the tourists, their guide, the photographer, and Mona for desecrating the fort's sacred ground: "Get away from here. Leave this ground." To Mona, he demands, "Back to your past! Return to your source!" Mona stands transfixed by the drummer's words.

In the film's next scene, Mona follows white tourists into the slave dungeons of Cape Coast Castle. As the tour guide's voice fades into the background, she hears the sound of a heavy door slam shut, enveloping her in pitch-darkness. When the lights return, we see African men, women, and children in chains encircling Mona. Mona bangs on the door, demanding to be released. Horrified, she insists, "I'm not an African!"—implicitly insisting that she should be released from capture. She is then stripped to the waist and her back is seared with a hot poker. Nondiegetic music changes from West African drumming and chanting to a live recording of Aretha Franklin prayerfully singing the gospel song "Take My Hand, Precious Lord."

Composer Thomas A. Dorsey wrote this hymnal plea in 1932 as he struggled with depression following the death of his wife during childbirth and of their newborn son the following day. The song would become iconic. It was a favorite song of Dr. Martin Luther King, Jr.; Mahalia Jackson sang this hymn at his funeral and, in turn, Franklin sang it at Jackson's memorial service.[28] "Take My Hand, Precious Lord" has been recorded by hundreds of musicians from Jackson and Franklin to Nina Simone, Al Green, and Whitney Houston.[29]

Dorsey came to church music through his practice as a blues pianist. As gospel music historian Michael Harris explains, "urban African American churches were moving a lot toward trying to emulate white worship standards, and particularly in their singing. They were also bringing in a number of rather well trained choirs and choir directors to sing European classical music as part of the service."[30] Wanting instead to bring a southern black aesthetic into church music, Reverend J. H. L. Smith, a pastor from Alabama who was newly appointed to Chicago's Ebenezer Missionary Baptist Church, invited Dorsey in 1931 to play during church. Soon after the soul-stirring service enlivened by Dorsey's energetic playing, Smith named him director of what would become the first so-named church gospel choir.

While Dorsey is often called the father of gospel music, Harris suggests that rather than infusing church music with the blues, this composer and musician took secular blues music back to its spiritual roots. Harris shares:

I like to tell people that if we could go back to a slave gathering on a plantation, the singing you would hear there would not be like the spirituals we know sung by a Marian Anderson or Leontyne Price. The singing would be a bit more bluesy. So actually Dorsey wasn't so much bringing blues in as he was restoring what we associate with as the blues sound back to African American religious music.[31]

If we build on Harris's comments here, Gerima's decision to use Franklin's recording of "Take My Hand, Precious Lord" allows the audience to listen back to a sonic site of a return to slavery. This song resonates with the songs of slavery and speaks to the pain Shola will experience in slavery, the trauma of Mona's return to her roots, and the need for a divine hand to hold hers as she travels these routes there and back again.

Despite its temporal dissonance, the use of "Precious Lord" in this moment in *Sankofa* when Mona transforms into the enslaved Shola sonically transports the film's audience from contemporary Ghana to a nineteenth-century plantation in the American South, where Shola shows no awareness of her former self in this new naming. In Dorsey's use of the adjective "precious" and the lyrics that call out from the first-person "I," "Precious Lord" makes the traditional move of spirituals at the time to call on divine help in order to transcend pain. Yet the song couples that plea for divine intervention with the presence of the weak and worn—and, in the context of the film, enslaved—body in agony. Although the song calls out for heavenly grace, it remains grounded in the pain of lived experience. It is a song immersed in the yearning of the speaker for an earthly listener to heed this soulful cry.

Sankofa's opening racialized and gendered soundscape features robust sounds that span cultural and technological spaces and time: incantation, drumming, electronic rhythms, jazz and blues rhythms, gospel music, and the snap of a bullwhip. These sounds emanate from various moments in the African diasporic soundscape and together create an audio montage that fills space—between stolen lives and lost memories, between the past and the present, between geographically distant spaces, between those once enslaved and those never enslaved—in such a way that present and past sounds merge. This sonic mash between present and past—and between Mona and the enslaved Shola into whom Mona transforms—creates a filmic space through which we as audience members are called upon to see the film's imperative as provocation: "Return to your source!" We are challenged to listen to the sounds that carry traces of intentionally framed Afro-sonic moments, and we encounter time as enfolded by sound and witness the insistence of a sonic continuity of time. According to Mark Smith, unlike the visual, sound "dissipates, modulates, infiltrates other sounds, becomes absorbed by actual objects, and fills a space surrounding them."[32] To extend this idea, the characters Mona/Shola absorb the nondiegetic sounds in the film, connecting both personas even as the same actress plays quite distinct roles. The present cannot ignore the force of the past, nor can the past speak without the present. At film's end, Mona will return to a soundscape filled again with drumming, incantation, and a welcoming African crowd. A shared act of audience listening binds the past and the present in the film's conclusion. By listening, *Sankofa* suggests to its audience, you may return.

While *Sankofa* risks ignoring temporal specificity in its musical choices, the film's opening audioscape provides an opportunity for the audience, inviting listeners to return to a story of slavery that insists on being told and heard. Further, listening to slavery creates an experiencing—and, by extension, a remembering—of slavery by those who have never been enslaved. Cultural texts like *Sankofa* provide opportunities for us to think about what Steven Feld refers to as "acoustemology" or "theorizing sound as a way of knowing."[33] They suggest listening as an intimate way of knowing and understanding a slave past that transforms the temporal and psychic distance between now and then in such a way that the act of remembering slavery becomes imbricated in contemporary racial identity. One consequence of a slave past that is organized and imagined through aural structures of knowing is that listeners gain memory and perhaps increased consciousness of a horrific event that they have not actually lived nor are actually required to live firsthand. In other words, these texts imagine and dramatize proximate listening to slavery as at least empathizing with, if not sonically experiencing, slavery.

"A Time Not for Talking but for Listening": John Washington's Aural Apprenticeship

After his father's passing, John becomes an apprentice of Old Jack Crawley, a storyteller and masterful resident tracker of the rural landscape of the Hill.[34] Old Jack first appears in the novel when, following the burial of his old friend Moses Washington, he arrives at the home of John's grandmother, the site of the repast:

> Old Jack came. It was as if a boulder dropped into a pool; the silence had
> that same hollow sound to it that water makes as it swallows a stone.

He stepped into the middle of the room and looked around, swaying drunkenly, blinking like some weird sleepy reptile. There was a collective gasp throughout the room. Old Mrs. Turner, who was noted for seeing signs and omens in nearly everything—she claimed to have foreseen Moses Washington's death in the actions of a flock of birds—stood up and raised her hands above her head and began to wail, her voice rising from a low, barely audible whisper to a keening that was painful to the ear. I heard a rush of feet as my mother came in from the kitchen.[35]

The acoustics of this brief moment are arresting. Like Ellison in *Invisible Man*, Bradley writes silence here in a manner that reminds us that it is, indeed, audible, perceptible sound—a hollow, thudding, low resonant sound mindful of Old Jack's deep connection to the natural landscape, but a sound nonetheless.[36] Shocked by his noticeably drunken appearance, the bereaved emit a choral gasp, clearing the air for a solo—Old Mrs. Turner's wail, growing from a "barely audible whisper" to a "keening . . . painful to the ear." This emitted keening is described here as a sonic weapon, a sharp, slicing sound that brings pain to those whose ears perceive it. This wail, made room for by the collective gasp of the other mourners, also carries sonic traces of Mrs. Turner's horror at Old Jack's class difference made hypervisible as he, a black lower-class man from the "other side of the Hill," drunkenly sways in the center of her pristine living room.[37] When Old Jack finally states his reason for appearing—"Mose tole me. . . . Tole me to come here for this here boy. An' I come"—his resolute statement of Moses's wishes finds no welcome audience, and he is sent away.[38] In the guests' gasp and especially in Mrs. Turner's wail, I perceive sonic rupture.[39] This wail records intraracial class prejudice, amplifying the social distance—and disdain—between Old Jack and the invited guests. In this moment in his grandmother's living room, John initially stands in frozen fear of Old Jack and then suddenly thaws enough to punch him and run away.

Rather than have Mrs. Turner's wail stand only as a calling out and distancing from difference, though, it also unintentionally draws attention to race and class difference in a way that piques John's curiosity enough to cause him to put aside his frozen fear and visit Old Jack. That evening, John sneaks out of his mother's house to visit Old Jack. When he reaches the other side of the Hill, it is dark; he cannot see where he is going. On his journey, he loses his footing and falls, rolling until he hits a pine tree. He then recalls "listening to the night. I had never done that before. I had heard the sounds . . . but I had never lain in the darkness listening to them."[40] He feels secure in this listening and becomes unsettled only when the night suddenly grows silent, right before he encounters Old Jack at his then unfamiliar cabin. Notice again that an audible silence accompanies Old Jack's appearance, a sonic clearing of sorts, an audio signal emphasizing both the silence of listening and Old Jack as listener and instructor of listening.

This moment in the evening woods commences the training John gains under Old Jack's tutelage. John comes to understand signals for listening: "I had learned that when he spoke in that voice, it was a time not for talking but for listening."[41] On his eleventh birthday, also, John remembers Old Jack retelling the story of the Chaneysville fugitive slaves, and how he listened "with only half my mind, filling in the details on my own," because he already knew the story.[42] Yet Old Jack surprises John by adding something new and, like the musicians in James Baldwin's "Sonny's Blues," he finds a way to make a familiar story new all over again, a way to renew active interest in his listener: "But that night had been different; he had added something new. His voice had come clearly to me, coming, it had seemed, out of the flames."[43] That "something new" is the dispute over the status of a group of fugitive slaves—that is, whether they were killed or killed themselves—and, more intriguing, Old Jack's resolution of the legendary dispute: "I doubt the killin' part of it myself. On accounta they ain't dead. They're still here. Still runnin' from them dogs an' whatnot. I know, on accounta I heard 'em. I ain't never heard 'em that often—maybe five, six times in ma whole life. Funny times. . . . An' the sound you hear is the sound of 'em pantin'."[44]

As I read this passage, I am reminded of the opening moments of Bradley's novel. There John offers a chilling description of the sounds he perceives as he listens to the telephone wire during an early morning conversation: "Sometimes you can hear the wire, hear it reaching out across the miles; whining with its own weight, crying from the cold, panting at the distance, humming with the phantom sounds of someone else's conversation."[45] He notes that these wire sounds are not always perceived by the human ear; instead, the listener hears them only when the conditions are right, "when the night is deep and the room is dark and the sound of the phone's ringing has come slicing through uneasy sleep; when you are lying there, shivering, with the cold plastic of the receiver pressed tight against your ear." Only then, and only after "the rasping of your breathing fades and the hammering of your heartbeat slows," are the sounds of the wire's "whining, crying, panting, humming, moaning like a live thing" audible.[46]

The precision with which Bradley constructs this moment rich with subtle sonic detail positions the reader and the narrator-historian as engaged in a listening practice, one that in Jean-Luc Nancy's words "calls up consciousness, anticipation, curiosity, awareness, and . . . a stretching [*tendre*] towards possible understanding, one that is not immediately accessible."[47] John couples sound and hearing here, demonstrating that sound relies on being heard to exist. His voice, articulated in a second-person address ("Sometimes *you* can hear the wire"), acts less as an inanimate description than as the activation of speaking and listening in print. This audible figure of the wire, coupled with the novel's use of the second-person "you," is meant to draw its readers in to work in league with the text, establishing this moment in the novel—and, more precisely, the past(s) the novel constructs—as continuously and audibly present.[48] Here as readers we are enveloped in the soundscape of the novel from the start as John makes us welcome and imaginative auditors to what he hears on the wire. That is, as we listen to John's aural perceptions, we are simultaneously able to enact our own listening, a method of reading the text that, implied in Bradley's decision to begin his novel *in medias res*, we should sustain for the duration of our reading.

While voicing the text's joint concerns with audition and historical knowing, John's description of the sounds reverberating on the wire also activates his voice as narrator. At this scene of his early morning listening, the reader witnesses John as he engages with voice as a dynamic and occasional figure. His narration depends on his listening to these sounds preserved on the telephone wire. It is helpful to recall that in its inception the telephone was thought of as a technological re-creation of the human ear. "Perhaps the most important feature of the wire," Steven Connor writes,

> was that it embodied the possibility of two allotropic states: the coiled, or compacted, and the extended. The extended wire gave an image of the voice thinned almost to nothing; the coiled wire is an image of the voice stored, concentrated, and magnified by compression. The coil of wire recalls the whorls of the inner ear. From the earliest times, the idea that such coiled structures might detain sound, preserving it from decay, has been in evidence.[49]

If we apply this technological information about the telephone to this novel, the telephone wire becomes another listener in the text. This description of the telephone materially supports the reading of the wire in Bradley's novel as preserving voices—potentially of the Chaneysville fugitive slaves. The telephone connects and disconnects, allowing a sonic inventory of history's traces (qua Nathaniel Mackey) to ebb and flow throughout the novel. The wire, then, functions as a metonym for the entire novel, embodying the mix of certainty, flux, and (im)possibility that this novel presents with regard to fully knowing the past. In this opening moment of the novel, John enacts his challenging work as a historian as he negotiates the wire—and, to some extent, the novel—as a fluctu-ating audiohistorical archive.

Listening Again on the Wind

We return to listen to the wind as it sounds through the description of Old Jack: "The sound you hear is the sound of 'em pantin'." Notice that as he tells this story to John, Old Jack also adopts the direct address "you," gesturing with his voice toward what we are to perceive on the wind. This use of "you" also rhetor-ically links the cultural work Old Jack does orally and aurally by the fire with the work John does in constructing a historical narrative in the novel and with the work Bradley does as the writer of the novel. You/we listen to the panting of the still-running fugitives resisting a return to enslavement.

Despite the direction the listener receives from the text with regard to lis-tening and what to hear, listening still asserts itself as a complex, individual, and sometimes conflicting practice—even among listeners who are close to each other, even between individuals who are listening to and within the same sound-scape. During their visits, for instance, Old Jack and John often work on honing their perceptions of the contours of their environment, revealing the landscape as a space to hear, listen to, and attempt to understand. Of special significance to them are the west wind and the sounds it makes on Old Jack's side of the Hill. As a child, John listens to the west wind and hears singing. For Old Jack, however, the wind sounds with the panting of "the souls of the Indians who lived and died in the mountains, long before the white man came, panting as they ran in pursuit of deer and bear and catamount in their hunting grounds beyond the grave."[50] Here, with a difference from the panting of the Chaneysville slaves, panting is the sound of lives lived and self-framed, expressing active self-determination.

When he returns home years later to the Hill to attend to Old Jack in his final days, John reflects on his apprenticeship in listening with his father's friend and recalls that, while they both perceived different meanings in the wind's sound, the two of them never argued about their differing interpretations because "it was not the kind of thing you could argue about. He heard panting, I heard sing-ing; we both heard something, and believed what we wanted to believe."[51] Fur-ther, Old Jack does not impose an interpretation on John, even when John is a child. Instead, in Old Jack, we witness a willingness to accept the existence of dif-ferent versions of a story and the potential validity of a different reading—even from a novice listener. He models, albeit implicitly, interpretation as a dynamic of historical and cultural listening in context and grounded in the various experiences of a listener.[52]

The idea that interpretation is dynamic rather than fixed proves crucial to the work John does as a historian. Yet he does not understand this lesson until much later in his life and much deeper into the novel. As a senior in high school, John studies physics—specifically, the physics of sound—and this educational experience shifts his perception of sound from something one believes to something one could know. Despite the nonargumentative manner in which he and Old Jack interact, John relishes his sense of possessing what he believes to be final, confirmable, and indisputable knowledge. This knowledge empowers him. Following the next winter storm, John heads over to Old Jack's cabin, armed with his new technical knowledge of sound production. The pair sit in the cabin engaging in their usual ritual: drinking toddies before a fire and listening to the sound the wind makes. This time, however, John intends "to glory in the power of knowing what [the sound of the wind] was."[53] When he shares his information with Old Jack, Old Jack responds incredulously and maintains his belief that the wind is the sound of "the Indians." Now hearing Old Jack's interpretation as a sign of ignorance, John recalls: "And I had realized for the first time that even though I loved him, he was an ignorant old man, no better than the savages who thought that thunder was the sound of some god's anger, and for the first time, I had argued with him about it."[54] Even while recognizing that epistemologies are more complex than that, John desires an easy method of interpretation, one that produces meanings that are certain—that confirm rather than complicate his understanding.

In this moment in *The Chaneysville Incident*, the sense of a psychoacoustic perception of sound as a metaphysical manifestation of those who are gone yet still present begins to exist in tension with the physics of sound—concrete, material, and representing a different set of knowledge than Old Jack offers. This moment signals a shift in John's negotiations of the soundscape with Old Jack. As an active element of the novel, the landscape, George Henderson explains, acts "contingently on the characters that cross it in the act of their own spatial practice—for which landscape is a set of structuring possibilities in the first place. Landscape has to be understood not just as a visual arrangement, then, but as the set of conditions for practice and agency."[55] If we extend Henderson's discussion of landscape to consider the dynamics of a soundscape, then we come to focus on the aural dynamics at play in these men's engagement with sound. Ultimately, listening in Bradley's novel is a spatial, cultural, contested process, one that dramatizes the dynamics of interpretation, a significant practice of historical narration that resonates beyond its ability to engage us with a discrete, fixed present. Listening also allows for or challenges us toward an aural engagement with the past. Rather than a distanced and removed reflection, our posture toward The Past is one of a proximate and sympathetic resonance. Old Jack's cabin changes from a soundscape in which multiple audible possibilities are allowed to circulate as options among infinite possibilities into an active site of contested audition.

When the wind sounds itself, though, John stops arguing with Old Jack and listens. In spite of John's conviction about his newly learned knowledge, his ears do not confirm what he thinks he knows. As the wind blows, John, as before, hears singing:

> And what I had heard had filled me with cold fear. For I had not heard
> a sound like a car honking; I had not heard vibrations of a frequency that
> varied directly or inversely with anything at all; I had heard singing.
> I had sat there, clutching my toddy, trying to perceive that sound as I had
> known I should, trying not to hear voices in it, trying not to hear words.
> But I had heard them anyway.[56]

John considers this moment a failed listening and responds as an intensely conscientious student might: he returns to his textbooks and studies furiously. Despite his motivation to transfer book knowledge to perception, his efforts do not change what he hears. John sees his listening as a failure of his (historian's) ear to make sense or interpret well his world. But this "failure" actually invites him to open up to the very world he is trying to decipher. For John, what is at stake is far more crucial than passing a test. His very sense of himself as a knowing self and as an individual who can move about with certainty in his ability to interpret his world is in jeopardy.

Although John responds to this moment of listening to the wind as a failed listening because he falls short of hearing what he scientifically should hear in the wind, I do not take this moment to suggest that what he and Old Jack heard is the correct way to hear and listen. Nor do I think this moment reveals John as an incapable listener in the context of scientific proof. Instead, I see his intense study of sound as dramatizing his emerging understanding of listening as a mode of engaging with the world—both his own and that of the past, both personally and as a practicing historian. Listening emerges here as a learned, developing practice. In order to avoid uncertainty and the ebb and flow of understanding that Old Jack introduces him to in their ritualized interactions, John leaves the mountains and goes "down to the flat land, where there were no irregularities of surface," armed with a promise to himself that he "would never go up into the mountains again."[57]

John breaks that promise when he learns of Old Jack's illness; he also releases the illusions he possessed that allowed him to believe that, even though he could not hear the wind, he was beyond earshot of listening. *The Chaneysville Incident* grapples with the interplay between traditional notions of hearing and listening and, more precisely, with processes of audition. Throughout the novel, the role of historian is dramatized as a listening mediator between past and present. The historian, then, employs a reflective practice. The implication is that John is not as distant from the practices of the Hill as either he or Old Jack thinks. While John removed himself from the Hill and, therefore, from the singing wind, the lessons he learned during his childhood through listening, in a step-by-step engagement with changing contexts, remain with him, most significantly in his work as a historian. Listening also allows for the auditor—in this case, John—to attend to what is possible. In fact, the "cold fear" John experiences as he hears singing against his will recalls for me (again) the scene of listening to the telephone wire at the start of the novel. If listening is framed by the context in which it is practiced, then the listening John never stopped doing continues when he moves away from the Hill to Philadelphia. Instead of the contours of the Hill's geography, however, sound travels on the telephone wire, altering yet maintaining John's auditory imagination.

Listening across the Wire

The singing John hears in the wind, then, is linked to the moans, whines, cries, panting, and humming he listens to on the telephone wire. The wire sings, reverberating with the sounds of the wind throughout the novel. For instance, when Judith, John's longtime girlfriend, calls him after he has reached the Hill, he sits, listening to "sighing wire" as they each say nothing.[58] At the end of their conversation, Judith sighs, her voice joining the sighing wire. Despite the apparent disconnections and missed uttered connections that occur during the telephone conversations in this novel—for instance, John repeatedly notes while "talking" with Judith on the telephone that "I didn't say anything," "She didn't say anything," "She was silent"—his description of the wire and Judith's voice as "sighing" suggests that first, he hears Judith as well as he hears the wire; second, the audible response that she offers is one that he presumably needs to focus on intentionally in order to hear; and third, in this description he listens toward scenes later in the novel that find him listening to her in increasingly attentive ways as she provides an open audience for his reconstruction of a historical narrative.[59]

John increasingly moves from a distrust of Judith's auditory ability to a willingness to imagine her as an effective auditor. He actually puzzles over the evidentiary fragments he possesses with regard to the Chaneysville Incident despite his sometimes resistant, sometimes discounting posture toward what to him are less valid, traditional forms of evidence.[60] As he does so, Judith is there, encouraging him to imagine the information that occupies the gaps or that would help bring the fragments together in a mash-up or audio collage of history.[61] Additionally, John's return to the Hill finds him reentering a rural black community already heavily associated with death, dying, and fragmentation. He reenters a community, then, that resists any desire the reader might have to locate an idyllic southern folk space.

During Old Jack's last days, the stories he tells John were "breaking up inside him; he coughed out fragments." John listens to these fragments "sitting by the roaring stove, sipping whiskey and feeding the fire."[62] His conversations with Old Jack provide a context for reception in and through which they negotiate how John is to figure out the truth of his father's death and his ancestor's fate. Old Jack's fragments are the form in which the Hill seems to provide raw evidence. The man to whom critics often attach a locus of organic, coherent blackness speaks his folk stories in disconnected pieces, requiring a listening that performs with a reflective desire to approach understanding.[63] Likewise, John's mother represents her community as dying and blames the telephone for arresting the existence of the black community and destroying a "uniquely black epistemology."[64] In an account as chilling as the freeze John feels while listening to the wire at the start of the novel, Mrs. Washington describes the effect of modern technology, of progress, in terms of death:

> We're all dying. . . . I remember we used to have a chain. Just like an old bucket brigade, only it was for news. Every woman would have two others to get word to, and each one of them would have two more. That was the old way. When I moved here [to the Hill] it had been going on as long as Negroes had been living here. The thing that changed it was the telephone; folks started listening in on the party lines. You'd hear your ring, and soon as you picked up you'd hear the other phones, click, click, click, all down the line. When all the Negroes had telephones, or most did, well, the system just died. And then they brought in the dial phones, and you didn't know when your neighbor's phone was ringing anymore,

and we needed that old way again. But it was too late then, we'd forgotten how to do it, and we had to get our news like everybody else, over the radio, or in the paper. Just like everybody else.[65]

Mrs. Washington's discussion of technological change reveals that the telephone alters how people listen, which in turn links to how people identify as part of a larger community. Listening here has a social—and socializing—function. While she is initially pleased with this progress "while it was happening" because the change gave the black community access to a telephone system "just like the white folks" had, Mrs. Washington eventually hears the something lost of modernization; she begins to understand that the telephone "poles marching up the Hill weren't progress, they were death. Just like Moses said."[66] She feels and lives a kind of civic estrangement for which the telephone becomes an object of blame. She additionally identifies a special way of knowing: Black people communicated differently; hence, they listened differently. The telephone wire—first its existence and then its silencing—harbors loss figured as death, not only of lives passed away but also, according to her, of a community's lost cohesion. Mrs. Washington listens to this absence in communication as a complete loss of community.[67]

Listening to the Archive

As I mentioned earlier, John asserts not only that he does not have an imagination but also that history is exclusive of listening for imaginative possibility. Earlier in the novel, he recalls how he "learned history" by visiting and studying the materials in Moses's attic and the failure he felt when he could not make sense of the facts he collected from that rich archive. He comments, "There were, it seemed, too many gaps. But what I had feared was that there were not too many gaps; only too many for me. . . . I could not imagine. And if you cannot imagine, you can discover only cold facts, and more cold facts; you will never know the truth."[68] Because he is unable to access the frequencies of history that require imaginative access—or, to draw on his language, to warm the historical record—the plethora of information remains at the "limits of the unthinkable," imperceptible to him. Despite his already hard work, John's assumptions and prior understanding of the work of the historian leave him—to use Michel-Rolph Trouillot's phrase differently—out of tune with the "frequenc[ies] of retrieval" necessary to construct a history from the evidence and sources before him.[69] Furthermore, his dismissal of the role of imagination in historiography and his failure to make audible the silences of history demonstrate history not as truth writ large but as discourse running on multiple, though frequently intertwining and overlapping, historical frequencies.[70] This moment constitutes an interpretive emergency that, albeit uncomfortable, creates the dissonance necessary for cognitive discovery.[71]

As John's practice as a historian develops, he later recasts the pieces missing from his store of historical materials as an opportunity. He explains to Judith, "You can't create facts. But you can discover the connections."[72] We are still mindful of his fear as he works to discover connections—hence the bone-deep, death-like cold he feels often in the novel and the "cold facts" that block "the truth."[73] But we witness an aural historiography enacted in the concluding moments of the novel as John demonstrates the role of imagination in his interpretive work. He listens intensely, openly, and speculatively to the "evidence" the wind sings, drawing on what Don Ihde hears as "the possibility of a synthesis of imagined and perceived sound" in auditory imagination.[74] Armed with his note cards full of historical facts, John enters a culminating listening sequence and invites Judith to join him in the listening: "Listen . . . because the time is right: the leaves are off the trees and the ground is covered with snow and the west wind is blowing. Listen."[75] It is in this moment when he is willing to listen imaginatively to and for it that John is able to hear his version of history and begin sharing it with Judith.

Moments like this have led critics to read Bradley's novel as confirming the singular significance of oral traditions in the telling and knowing of black history, particularly a slave past. In his essay "The African American Historian: David Bradley's *The Chaneysville Incident*," for instance, Matthew Wilson argues that Bradley privileges oral history and African American vernacular culture in his novel, presenting these traditions as "alternative ways to encode and represent" history. Bradley's valuing of oral and vernacular traditions, according to Wilson, is demonstrated by John's decision at the end of the novel to listen for the history he is constructing. For Wilson, "Washington can only understand his own position in the world by delineating the enduring conditions of oppression, and by grounding that understanding in African American vernacular culture."[76] In this reading, Wilson reaffirms the dichotomous notion of Eurocentric knowledge as inscribed and Afrocentric knowledge as spoken.

While John does at times present ways of knowing as an exclusive proposition and ultimately uses an imaginative listening to assist in historical reconstruction, Wilson's assertion that his final victory in constructing a new history comes with his complete and singular embrace of oral and vernacular (and, therefore, African-inflected) knowing ignores his dynamic relationship with historical discourse and the confluence of written, oral, and aural modes in the novel. Rather than drawing sharp distinctions between writing and orality, between supposed European and African epistemologies, I find Bradley attempting to enact and account for the dynamics between these modes of knowledge transfer and the slippery and sometimes unwieldy nature of evidence. This novel is not a "rift . . . between the written and spoken word" but rather one "between the archive of supposedly enduring materials (i.e., texts, documents, buildings, bones) and the so-called ephemeral repertoire of embodied practice/knowledge (i.e., spoken language, dance, sports, ritual)."[77]

In Bradley's novel, "enduring" documents or the materials of a chronicled history—newspapers, libraries, diaries, ledgers, maps, John's meticulously catalogued index cards and history lectures—abound alongside the sounds of storytelling, nature, bodies, and communications technology. John actively creates other enduring documents as he records facts. He describes his method of cataloguing index cards by year, month, date, time, and then day. An example is the last chapter title, "197903121800 (Monday)," a method he devises after seeing the materials in his father's attic: "I had developed a system of color-coded index cards on which I recorded events, and which I ordered by carefully noting the time of their occurrence, the time dating expressed as a string of numbers, year, month (in two digits), date (in two digits), and time of day (in a twenty-four-hour military-style expression), followed by the day of the week. That was how I learned history. That was where the magic came from."[78]

From an early age, John acts as the consummate reader, interpreter, and tracker in the novel. As a young child, he is portrayed as almost obsessive in his search for materials to read. It bothers him that his grandfather has a library full of beautiful volumes that he will not allow anyone to touch. His grandfather, John recalls, does not even read these volumes himself. That John steals from the library and reads books that are thought to be beyond his reading level and inappropriate for his age is something that Moses admires about his younger son. When John climbs into the attic after his father's death and sees the voluminous stack of books there—"a seemingly endless array of notebooks of every size, shape, and color"—he recalls that he

> had never realized that Moses Washington had loved books as much as I did: it was a side of him that it had never occurred to me existed, that I had never heard about. Knowing about it made me feel easier about my own passion. And, like mine, his had been a passion for using books, not just owning them; every one of those books had been read, and reread.

The colors of their bindings were faded, and any stamping on the spines had long since been worn away.[79]

Unlike John's maternal grandfather, Moses collects books to use, not merely to display. This relationship with books, too, suggests the intimate connection between history as record and history as interpretation.

Listening Alternatively/Alternative Listeners

As John reconstructs his version of the Chaneysville Incident from the evidence he has at hand and ear, Judith, who is a psychiatrist, functions as his intratextual listener.[80] John develops a willingness to share his version of the incident with her, suggesting the possibility of an expanded idea of who can listen—and listen well—particularly with regard to discourses of racial difference. During a gap in John's narrative, for instance, Judith helps him figure out how Bijou, one of the escaped Chaneysville slaves, may have obtained his great-grandfather's book of poetry and journal. Judith reasons that Bijou loved him, an interpretation that John is unable to devise himself. In coming to the Hill (Judith follows John there after he leaves Philadelphia to care for Old Jack), Judith becomes a cooperative audience to his storytelling. This partnership emerges because John's ability to imagine Judith as a listener also shifts.

For much of the novel, however, John assumes that Judith's race and gender preclude her from ever understanding, marking, at least momentarily, historical listening in this novel as a uniquely black male activity and, perhaps, the only unique surviving black epistemology in the novel.[81] For instance, as John sits in Old Jack's cabin, holding the coffee Judith just made for him, he comments: "I did not want coffee. I wanted a toddy. I needed one. But I could not expect Judith to understand that. There was a lot that I needed that she would never understand. For she was a woman and she was white, and though I loved her there were points of reference that we did not share. And never would."[82] John later tempers his judgment, considering the possibility that Judith might be able to listen and understand—at least he desires this posture of listening from her and opens himself to the possibility that she has the capacity to listen. After Judith prepares a toddy for John, mixing the drink as he would, he "knew then that I had underestimated her, and had done it in a way that cheated us both."[83] John begins to recognize Judith as a good listener—as the best listener he has available. While she cannot listen exactly as he does and willingly admits where her understanding begins and ends—"I don't know how to listen that way"—her listening provides a self-reflective, honest, vulnerable model for auditory engagement that performs while generating feedback about the limitations and possibilities of that audio performance.[84]

It is significant also that John's capacity to listen and to hear Judith increases as the novel concludes. The last time the reader sees the couple together, they are in Old Jack's cabin drinking hot toddies, talking about the information they have discovered. Judith asks for a toddy—the first time we see her consume one.[85] She engages in the ritual of talk that John often practiced with Old Jack. Judith has earned her place as John's audience, even as John earned that role with Old Jack. Her presence on the Hill—and on the other side of the Hill at that—provides John with a witness to his witnessing, allowing historical cognition to emerge through his narrative and paralleling his work as an audience for and of other audiences.

John's and Judith's cooperative listening involves his imaginative listening and storytelling and her attentive listening—both to the emerging historical narrative and to his need for toddies (that is, the ritual contexts in which to story*tell* and story*listen*, as Stepto and Jones would say) to spur on his listening.[86] John and Judith travel to the South County so that he can attempt to reconstruct the Chaneysville Incident. He is trying to make sense of the facts he has about C. K. Washington, his great-grandfather, the man whom Moses had been tracking. C. K. is a black moonshiner who was also involved in organizing the Chaneysville group of slaves on their journey on the Underground Railroad to freedom in the North. At the moment the narrative opens, C. K. has been devising a plan to protect the group of slaves, twelve in all, from recapture and potential death at the hands of expert slave catchers who are actually trying to capture him and are using the group as a trap.

When John perceives the song of this group in the west wind, he listens eagerly, no longer resisting the song he hears. He composes a slave narrative in Judith's hearing that picks up with C. K., who in turn is listening to a group of runaway slaves he has been tracking. John shares with Judith:

> I can hear them as they pass. I can't see them—it's misty. But I can hear them. They're running quietly, like Indians, never breaking the silence, never snapping a twig or turning a stone. You couldn't hear them at all if it wasn't for one thing: the breathing. They're running hard and they're breathing hard, and that's what you can hear, that's the sound that goes floating through the mist. That's what [C. K.] hears.[87]

John's language resonates with his second-person address at the novel's opening. "You"—Judith and the novel's reading audience—are again made privy to what he hears, thereby becoming listeners to his listening. Further, John shifts at the end of this description of the sound in the wind from noting what he hears to claiming that he shares the same hearing with C. K. He continues, saying that C. K.'s been "listening for them. . . . He's been listening for a long time."[88] These words imagine a C. K. performing listening in order to track the endangered fugitives he is trying to save. They also reflect John's personal and historical work in this novel. John has been listening to historical fragments for a long time in his attempt to explain how events occurred. His listening becomes C. K.'s listening in this fictive historical audioscape, rendering John's explanation of the past, at least momentarily, animated, enlivened, and validated as C. K.'s narrative. In this moment, *The Chaneysville Incident* suggests an affirmative response to Peter Szendy's question, "Can one *make a listening listened to?* Can I transmit *my* listening, unique as it is?"[89]

Not only does John listen to C. K.'s listening, he also becomes a witness to the voices of the enslaved persons traveling with him. John's aural senses are heightened and aware. Now that he is far from the naive historian who, while attempting to examine Moses Washington's materials in his attic study, "fell prey to one of the greatest fallacies that surrounds the study of the past: the notion that there is such a thing as a detached researcher, that it is possible to discover and analyze and interpret without getting caught up and swept away . . . unaffected, unchanged, unharmed," John's historical listening and knowledge of the event at hand function to bear witness through his embodied self.[90] John, in fact, notes at one point that his voice has grown hoarse, his throat dry. Perhaps, like the scars and breaks perceived in Ursa Corregidora's voice, John's voice as mode of historical transfer bears the immediate physiological impact of this narrative. This moment also reminds us that John listens to himself—he hears his own hoarseness—as he speaks this history; that is, Bradley does not represent this telling as C. K.'s overtaking John's voice or speaking through John. Instead, we are aware always that this is John's interpretation of events, mediated through his listening, his understanding of the facts, and intertwined with the novel's concerns with the dynamics of historiography—with the history of history. No longer the objective historian, John makes his presence known as he generates this new historical narrative.

Historical cognition emerges within and from the soundscape that John imagines. We—and Judith—listen as John reports what C. K. figuratively hears: hounds, tracking men, running slaves, the wind. When C. K. finally locates the group of slaves at Iiames Mill, he visits with each individual runaway, asking each to recount his or her reasons for escaping. As John retells these stories, Judith and the reader become privy to an imagined firsthand testimony of persons in search of freedom. In this moment, these Chaneysville slaves become men, women, and children with names and stories: Lydia; Juda (who gave birth during this escape); Azacca (his master called him Jacob); Linda and her three sons, Daniel, Robert, and Francis; and Harriette Brewer, the woman whom C. K. loved and the mother of three children, Cara, Mara, and William. They are humanized and we are their belated auditors.

We listen until their voices fade into the wind in the silence of death. The voices of the Chaneysville slaves, John reports, were at first strong. Then they "grew weaker . . . until at last there was only one voice, a strong soprano voice, carrying the song. And then that voice, too, fell silent. But the song went on . . . because now the wind sang."[91] Through listening to the wind, John reasons that Iiames, the white mill owner, carefully buried the slaves according to family groupings. This explanation surprises Judith, who presumably would have no reason to believe that John could ever imagine that a white man would show such compassion and humanity to a group of slaves. John's listening, then, leads him to figure possibility where before he heard none. He encounters an incomplete historical narrative that he eventually must recognize as such in order to construct a narrative in the moment.

What are the consequences of John's aural witnessing of the past? For his father, Moses Washington, the search for historical "truth" ended in suicide: he kills himself on the very spot where he believes his enslaved and deceased ancestor, C. K., died. Moses fails to remember the past as separate from his own existence; he assumes that John will pick up the task of telling the remainder of the story, similar to the way in which he discovered and constructed the narrative about C. K. In his dying, the need to maintain and understand distinctions between the past and the present is clear, not only for the sake of the living present but also, and equally importantly, for the sake of honoring and valuing the past.[92]

John's end, however, is a bit ambiguous. The morning following his interpretation of the Chaneysville Incident finds John and Judith preparing for their return to Philadelphia. John restores the cabin to its original condition and then asks Judith to leave him alone to complete some other tasks. When she leaves, John sets about preparing to burn the material evidence he accumulated during his investigation. His narration of his actions here is meticulous:

> I took the folio down and put the books and pamphlets and diaries and
> maps back where they belonged, ready for the next man who would need

them. I sealed the folio with candle wax, as my father had done for me. Then I gathered up the tools of my trade, the pens and inks and pencils, the pads and the cards, and carried them out into the clearing. I kicked a clear space in the snow and set them down, and over them I built a small edifice of kindling, and then a frame of wood. I went back inside the cabin and got the kerosene and brought it back and poured it freely over the pyre, making sure to soak the cards thoroughly.[93]

John proceeds to burn the papers in the kerosene-fed fire, an act that highlights the fact that there is not solely one way to understand the events he wrestles with in the book.[94] This act of burning renders the historical evidence absent, and that absence becomes the impetus for "the next man" to discover the moment anew. John's notes are burned and yet the possibility of historical narrative is renewed through the flames. As he lights the pyre, he says, "it came to me how strange it would all look to someone else, someone from far away," and he wonders if Judith will understand as she watches the smoke rise from the other side of the Hill.[95] John's question about Judith's understanding is ambiguous: What, indeed, does he want her to understand? If he wants to dramatize history as a narrative that requires an imaginative listening to negotiate its ever-evolving meanings, then apparently all he would have to do is reunite with her on the other side of the Hill and return to Philadelphia with her, where he could reiterate that point.

Yet there are details in John's description that complicate my desire to read him as a historian who has experienced an aural return to the past and has survived the experience of doing so—unlike his father and great-grandfather before him. For instance, as John pours the kerosene over the pyre, he notes that "I was a bit careless, and got some of it on my boots, but that would make no difference."[96] There is an emphasis on doing things "one last time": "I left the cabin for the last time and went and stood before the pyre and stood looking at the cards and the papers, and thinking about all of it, one last time."[97] Finally, he stands close enough to the pyre that he merely "dropped the match to the wood and watched the flames go twisting."[98]

In this reading, we are left with a possible act of self- and historical immolation, recalling the earlier act of the group of slaves who would rather die than lose their freedom. We are left with John's performance of the past resonating with that of his father, his great-grandfather, and his grandfather. For his grandfather, the "fairly prominent black mortician" Lamen Washington, burns Moses's copy of C. K.'s book, *Sketches*, in order to prevent him from learning about his ancestor. This act of burning piques Moses's curiosity, and he obtains another copy of the book, rereads it, and takes notes, paralleling what John does with Moses's papers. If John burns the papers and himself, we are left, then, with death, resonating with the figure of the lost souls reverberating on the telephone wire at the start of the novel and with the dead souls in *Sankofa* calling for a recuperative audience. We are left with a reminder that, although now told and heard, this remains a fractured history. Death is imagined here as a beginning, as an impetus for new listeners, new historical filters. A void calls forth for new listeners.

The End of Listening?

The constitutive nature of historical grief, loss, and claiming of a slave past in *The Chaneysville Incident* remains a struggle to the end of the novel. As readers follow John's construction of a historical narrative that explains the Chaneysville Incident—which, incidentally, encompasses not just the death of the runaway slaves but also a scene of lynching and his struggles in his relationship with Judith, who is white and (according to John's repeated assertions) probably a descendant of slave owners—we come to understand that Bradley is dramatizing historical understanding and memory as wrapped up in grieving for the past and confronting one's self in the present. As John ponders earlier, "I wondered if I—not the historian, but I, whoever I was—really wanted to know."[99]

What complicates either of my interpretive choices for John—life with Judith or death at Old Jack's cabin—is that these alternatives flatten the complexity of the historical listening that he and, by extension, the listening reader have accomplished over the course of the text. Recall that in an earlier discussion with Judith about history and imagination, John denies that imagination plays any role in history. He clarifies the role of imagination by explaining that if a historian is "good, there's a point where all the facts just come together and the ideas come out. It's like a fire, smoldering, and then it catches, and the flame catches other things, and then it's like a forest fire."[100] At the time, John admits to Judith that there is no fire for or in him. He cannot link the facts to create a historical narrative about his father, about the runaway slave C. K., or about himself in all of it. That is, he cannot fully engage with the historical and personal archive. As in the initial moments of the novel, John in these final moments is cold, and we know by his own account that he fears freezing to death.

What happens to John and this new historical narrative at the end of the novel is ambiguous. John moves from being literally, critically, and personally cold in his work as a historian to standing before (or within) a huge fire that he himself has built, using as kindling the very historical materials he amassed over time. It is fire, Old Jack declares, that "gives a man say. Gives him final say. . . . Now, that ain't much say, an' it ain't the best kinda say, but it's bettern havin' no say at all. Because a man with no say is an animal. So a man has to be able to make a fire. . . . When he can do that, he can have some say."[101] Fire here literally consumes history—its materials and its (aural) processes and renders John a man who "has say."

Where Old Jack's notion of "final say" falls short, however, is in his insistence that "when the fire's gone, there ain't nothin' left, for nobody."[102] Instead, John hears historical understanding as what matters at the end of the novel. He is not so much concerned with the *what* of that understanding as he is with the *how*. How might Judith make sense of the smoke she sees rising over the Hill? Does she know that all of John's notes are feeding the flames? How can John make sense of what he now understands and believes—that a white man probably took the time to bury the slaves next to those they loved—revising his constant insistence on the pure hatred that exists between blacks and whites? Lastly, who, ultimately, is this or any history for? The novel's conclusion positions readers as ongoing listeners, desiring to know while simultaneously acknowledging that a complete knowing is impossible. The novel, then, is about the business of activating the voice of the past in the present, much like the recordings in *Remembering Slavery* and the drummer in *Sankofa*.

The Chaneysville Incident is also, however, very much concerned with the possibility that, as Saidiya Hartman notes upon her visit to Ghana's Cape Coast Castle, the fort featured in *Sankofa*, there are remains without stories, returns featuring the passage through trauma and without closure. For the purposes of this chapter's discussion, how do we write a history from the residue, from the traces of historical trauma heard audibly? These audible and sometimes inaudible remains become the impetus and source for the story. Ultimately, answers heard within rupture produce new questions, new reasons to listen. Largely, however, the impetus for this testimony is the recognition of the historical record's refusal to offer a neat resolution despite the imaginative listening done. The impetus for this testimony also entails a fear that there will be no listeners who will be able to perceive the possibilities of these traces in their resonant quiet.[103]

"New Ways to Make Us Listen"
. . . .
Aural Learning in the English Classroom

For the characters in James Baldwin's 1965 short story "Sonny's Blues," listening is learning, and one of their classrooms is a Greenwich Village club. The story's unnamed narrator visits the club to listen as his younger brother, Sonny, plays piano during a blues set, his first following a hiatus from music. As he listens, the narrator-brother notes his own limited knowledge of music. Additionally, he shares this realization: "All I know about music is that not many people ever really hear it. And even then, on the rare occasion when something opens within, and the music enters, what we mainly hear, or hear corroborated, are personal, private, vanishing evocations."[1] Sonny's brother perceives a tendency in the musical listener, even in moments in which the music serves as an ear-opener, to experience only fleeting revelations, emotions, and confirmation of and in the self.

As the performance progresses, the narrator continues to share his own realizations and evocations in relation to what he perceives in sound.[2] He identifies multiple points of listening active in this setting: not only is he listening in the audience—an audience that itself brings multiple points of listening to the scene—but the musicians, too, are listening as they perform. The narrator explains, "But the man who creates the music is hearing something else, is dealing with the roar rising from the void and imposing order in it as it hits the air."[3] As they play, then, the musicians onstage concurrently are listening—engaging with sound, crafting sound, and sounding music. According to the narrator, these musicians are also performing a lesson in listening. As Creole, the band's leader, plays his solo, the narrator shares his interpretation of Creole's music:

He began to tell us what the blues were all about. They were not about anything very new. He and his boys up there were keeping it new, at the risk of ruin, destruction, madness, and death, in order to find new ways to make us listen. For, while the tale of how we suffer, and how we are delighted, and how we may triumph is never new, it always must be heard. There isn't any other tale to tell, it's the only light we've got in all this darkness. And this tale, according to that face, that body, those strong hands on those strings, has another aspect in every country, and a new depth in every generation. Listen, Creole seemed to be saying, listen.[4]

Despite familiarity, despite a sense of knowledge already acquired, despite the "old" of the blues, the narrator perceives the need to listen. More precisely, what makes the blues new in this moment of hearing—for musician and music fan or audience member alike—is an active, renewing, risk-taking, and reflective listening as well as what the unique listener brings to the task. In "Sonny's Blues," listening is an ethical imperative. As the narrator explains, "while the tale of how we suffer, and how we are delighted, and how we may triumph is never new, it always must be heard."[5] This hearing, too, must remain mindful of the social context in which these listeners live. What resonance can this cultural listening have, "Sonny's Blues" seems to ask, in a world in which, just outside the doors of the club, "trouble stretched above us, longer than the sky?"[6]

Similar to Baldwin's fictional listening lesson, Julian Henriques details the intricate relationship between aural engagement and learning in his discussion of reggae sound system engineering practices in Jamaica. Through an apprenticeship model, novice sound engineers learn how to listen—in this case, how to monitor and evaluate the sound of a system—by working alongside seasoned sound engineers. In this context, listening emerges as a set of practices that aim to tune not only the sound but also the engineer as listener. If in the context of reggae sound engineering apprenticeships engineers are able to learn how to listen in ways that inform their performance, how then can students in an English or cultural studies classroom learn how to listen and leverage listening as an approach to their own learning as self-aware readers, writers, and critical thinkers?

Baldwin's and Henriques's lessons in listening set the stage for this chapter's focus on listening and learning in, specifically, the literature classroom. As Cathy Davidson describes, her language resonant with Baldwin's story, "Learning is the constant disruption of an old pattern, a breakthrough that substitutes something new for something old. And then the process starts again."[7] Listening is learning, a way of knowing that entails a set of practices that can be used to discern, reflect, question, and engage. If learning happens through intentional disruption, how might a listening pedagogy perform as an act of aural disturbance in the service of new learning? How might we design learning opportunities for students to develop listening habits of mind? How might we bring listening in to balance with the work of developing one's voice? How might we commit to becoming a better audience for each other?

As an educator, I have committed my teaching practices to designing a listening pedagogy, one that cultivates in my students a heightened awareness of the ways in which listening enhances their reading and writing practices.[8] I am committed to working with students to develop an advanced sonic literacy. As Michelle Comstock and Mary Hocks have explained, while sonic literacy is "the ability to identify, define, situate, construct, manipulate, and communicate our personal and cultural soundscapes," listening is the sensory process through which we develop sonic literacy: "Listening is an art, a conscious process of observing and defining sound. And like the art of writing, it is affected by one's place in and knowledge of a particular sonic environment as much as one's previous experiences with sonic forms. Recognizing both resonances and dissonances as cultural and individual is key to what we consider critical sonic literacy."[9] In my classes, I am interested in cultivating deliberate and enduring experiences through listening-inflected teaching and learning. Listening can be a difficult practice to introduce to a literature classroom because, if asked to identify the part of the body that is most associated with reading, most students focus on their eyes. Yet as I argue throughout this study, literature often calls on us to read in a multimodal way, particularly as listeners. An aural pedagogy is heavily involved in designing opportunities for students to undo their often *uni*modal sensory habits of mind in the service of developing multimodal habits of a listening mind.

A Listening Mind: The Course

In A Listening Mind, students study fiction, nonfiction, and poetry—some by the authors included in *Race Sounds*—alongside film, music, natural and human-crafted environments, and other multimedia forms in order to become increasingly attuned to the sounds, silences, vibrations, and other sonic elements enfolded in the printed word. While this is a multimedia course, I aim for my students to experience how listening enhances their engagement with the written word and to develop ways in which their aurally inflected reading practices can unmute words in print.

As the phrase and my course title suggest, I am invested in cultivating sonic interestedness and in challenging students to engage with literature in ways that are collaborative and cognitively (and otherwise) dissonant from their usual

English classroom habits of mind.[10] For my students, at least initially, writing is ruled by the heavily visual mantra "Show. Don't tell." They have received this feedback often on their writing and digested it fully, not only in humanities courses but also in mathematics and science courses, where our feedback language tends to emphasize the visual in that we ask students to make their understanding visible all the time. A Listening Mind, then, creates preconditions for an additional mode of learning. It aims to enhance students' aural attentiveness in general, particularly in relation to the printed word. As I design assessments and moderate the course, I keep in mind my own essential question as an educator: how might my scholarly interest in listening as a significant mode of cultural, social, and political engagement and action translate into sound learning opportunities for my students? The assignments students complete in the course, a few of which I share next, are my partial and constantly evolving response.

Close Listening

We begin the class with "Cradle Song" from Jason Moran's album *Artist in Residence*. Beginning with music takes students to a medium to which they expect to listen. In this way, we reflect on what they do when they listen to music and begin to lean on those listening habits in order to build their capacities for listening to other—and unexpectedly sonic—media. In "Cradle Song," Moran plays a Carl Maria von Weber–composed lullaby on piano unaccompanied; the urgent scratching of a closely miked pencil on paper writes slightly ahead of the calming melody. The song, a tribute to Moran's mother, who would stand over his shoulder taking notes as he practiced the piano as a child, makes writing audible and reminds us that the printed word resonates with sound. Thus, it allows us to begin exploring the possibilities of listening as an approach to reading and writing.

In the first month of the course, students practice low-stakes listening and writing. One of the writing prompts asks this question: What does your writing sound like? Students collect writing sounds by describing them in their listening journals—the tapping of laptop keys, silent fingertip swipes across a smartphone screen, the imagined sound of ink rolling across paper. One student remembered that in middle school she would crumple lined paper into a ball, flatten the paper out by hand, and then write on it in pen or pencil because she liked the sound her handwriting made across the newly textured surface. Students also wrote metaphors and similes about their writing to capture their posture as they entered the class. Metaphors and similes such as "the words a waterfall flowing from the pen" or "just like static" communicate both an attention to and a mindset toward writing that are instructive for me as a teacher.

Throughout the course but particularly early on, students go on short listening walks. Listening walks are based on soundwalks, a research tool that invites listeners to participate actively in a soundscape and improvise in and with the sounds they encounter there. Listening walks help students understand listening as a practice situated in a particular spatial and temporal context.[11] Students record in their own words what they hear and their reflections on their listening in their listening journals, discovering along the way and through my prompts that listening does not just happen through the ears. The sound of a truck rumbling by is indeed heard through the ears—and through vibrations felt throughout the body. Some of the students note that some sounds they hear also generate emotive or affective responses.

I also ask students to visit a space in which they feel most like themselves and tune in to its acoustics. They do the same in a space where they are less comfortable. We practice guided meditation. Students tune their attention to ecolistening—listening with intention to the natural or artificial environments in which we find ourselves. The idea is to notice the sounds that our ears no longer notice when we become so accustomed to the acoustics of a space. Rutger Zuydervelt's "Take a Closer Listen," an excerpt from the opening pages of Jonathan Safran Foer's *Extremely Loud and Incredibly Close*, an excerpt from John Francis's *The Ragged Edge of Silence*, and the *New York Times Magazine* prose and audio essay "Whisper of the Wild" by Kim Tingley are inspirations for these close-listening provocations. By listening to various sounds in various ways during the early weeks of the course, students become more attuned to sound by exercising and strengthening their habits of listening.

Sonic Material Culture

One of the assignments of the course involves work in what I call sonic material culture. This assignment asks students to explore the ways in which material culture affects, is experienced, or is understood specifically through the audible world.[12] Sonic material culture considers how objects help create cultural meaning through the sounds they make and the ways in which people make sense of those sounds. During this unit, we examine the work of African American artist Nick Cave, specifically, his Soundsuits—wearable works of art handcrafted from scavenged materials, found objects, recycled pieces, discarded materials, and other detritus from nature and culture. In 1992, in response to the

Rodney King beating and the subsequent Los Angeles riots, Cave began to create his first Soundsuit, *Twigs*, out of sticks he collected from a public park.[13] The piece evolved from stationary sculpture into a dynamic piece of wearable art. In a telephone conversation, Cave reflected:

> With the twigs, what I was doing with that incident which led to the LA riots—I was thinking about all the readings that I'd done and how that brought description to Rodney King's character. . . . Reading things such as "he was larger than life," "scary," "took ten men to bring him down," "worked out with prison weights" . . . things like that. . . . As a black male, I was really disturbed by these comments and these responses and I started to think about the fact that myself—I'm only protected within the privacy of my space and outside of that I can be profiled in a second.

Soundsuits are akin to traditional African ritual masks and garb. When in stationary display, the suits are impressive works of sculptural art; when worn during performance, they emit sound, offering dynamic audible and visual performances for the audience. In our conversation, Cave said that when he put on the suit for the first time and looked in the mirror, he thought: "'I've now built a second skin, this layer of protection to protect my spirit.' . . . When I started to move in the suit, it made sound, which led into the idea of the sonic protest: in order to be heard you've got to speak loud. But even before that, before you can be heard, sometimes you have to stop and listen."[14] Students discuss the ways in which Cave's suits pull audiences in to listen in order to attend to the surreal, audible protest he launches through the surprising sonic elements of these suits. Then they explore an array of sonic objects that include a Tibetan singing bowl, steel drum, shofar, typewriter, stethoscope, and boom box. They choose one of the items—one that either makes a sound (like a steel drum) or allows for access to sound (like a stethoscope)—and begin their research with a specific focus on how their selected item holds sonic cultural significance.

To research the stethoscope, for example, one student interviewed a cardiologist and a medical historian. She learned that sounds doctors hear through the stethoscope "comprise a language, spelling out diagnoses and prognoses" that provide "gateways to our understanding of the heart." Another student chose the steel drum, an instrument developed in the twentieth century in Trinidad and Tobago, and ended up discussing the innovation involved in reusing oil containers to produce a new cultural sound. One student's love of all things vintage led her to her father's manual typewriter and an essay combining family history and larger insights about education, workplaces, and mechanical writing. In each case, students realized that these sounds cannot be extricated from the material, social, and historical conditions that produce them.

Historical Sound Systems

In 1963 Bayard Rustin, one of the primary organizers of the March on Washington, arranged for an expensive sound system capable of being heard throughout the Mall to be set up on the evening before the march. That night, the system was destroyed; the Army Corps of Engineers rebuilt it in time for the march. Given the slate of performers scheduled to appear on the program as a prelude to Dr. King's speech, it is no wonder that Rustin wanted such a strong sound system. The March on Washington was a peaceful protest that brought approximately 250,000 people to Washington, D.C. While it is perhaps best remembered for King's "I Have a Dream" speech booming across the Mall, the march has a robust, complex sonic story of the civil rights movement even beyond King's delivery that day. It is a moment that affords students in this class an opportunity to explore the role music played in the march specifically and during the civil rights movement more generally.

How might we gain a fuller understanding of the march by listening to the musicians and songs selected to perform at this event? Students take time in this class to listen back to the march. Some of the questions we ask include: What song did you select? Who is the song's performer? Who are the writer and the composer? When was the song written? Have other musicians performed or recorded this song? What is your experience listening to the song? What do you find yourself thinking about as you listen? How do you feel? What do you notice? What do you hear in the song? What story can you tell about the March on Washington by using this source? Students select and research one song performed at the march and listen to it while contemplating the social, political, and cultural context in which it was performed that day.[15] They write to explain how the song exemplifies the politics and purpose of the march specifically and share what they have come to understand about the moment through this aural inquiry. Alongside learning how to listen in the present in their immediate environment, students in this course also practice how to think historically through sound and listening.

Following their sound work on the March on Washington, students complete a sonic history mini-project inspired by my work on *The Chaneysville Incident*. For this project, they think about this question: How might sound function as a way to narrate a specific historical moment?[16] I have assigned this project to follow the study of either *The Chaneysville Incident* or *Beloved*, but I would suggest it as a culminating assessment following the study of any historical fiction. Students choose a specific historical moment, compose a sound, and then create a museum card that, among others, answers the following key questions: What does this sound bring to our attention that we might not otherwise consider? What questions does this sound raise? What does this sound leave mute? If a student "writes," for instance, slavery through the crack of the whip, then she or he might focus on the violence and torture of that institution. If you "tell" slavery, though, from the code-laden singing that enslaved persons used to send messages to flee, then you have a different frame, a different point of listening from which to engage with the historical moment. One student used the opening sounds from *The Wizard of Oz* to sonically narrate the Dust Bowl. Another examined news reports and hip-hop music to listen back to the 1992 Los Angeles riots. One young woman interviewed her mother about her immigration experience from Guatemala; in her project, the sound of a train whistle signaled arrival to the United States and a new life.

Students worked on this assignment as part of their culminating assessment for the course. I assigned this work at the end of the course because it gave them an opportunity to delve into the work of a sound studies scholar: students drew on the listening skills they had developed over the term, returned to questions we had asked regarding listening to and interpreting written and recorded texts, framed their own questions for inquiry, and used sound technologies such as Audacity and GarageBand to amplify their historical sounds.

Listening in Print

One way that I encourage my students to cultivate habits of a listening mind is to have them produce a sonic reading of a printed text. This assignment, "Listening in Print," asks them to concentrate on reading a short printed text of any literary genre with aural attentiveness. Students revisit a moment they were assigned or chose from a text. As they reread the moment, they are to note the ways in which it sounds. To focus their listening, I provide these questions: What are the sonic tones you would associate with this moment? If a character is speaking, what does he or she sound like? How do we come to know differences between characters through sounds? What differences do you perceive and how can you hear them? What are the environmental and other sounds you imagine drifting through this moment? Students make note of what they "hear" and what they think about what they hear. Then they use these sounds to compose an audio recording of no more than one minute that sonically communicates their understanding of the moment from the text. As they work on the sound composition, they reflect on these questions: How can you help us listen to what you have heard through your reading as a listener? How might you create a composition that shares with another your experience of listening to the text? How might you share your listening?

For Baldwin's "Sonny's Blues," students have captured sounds of a school at the end of the day to think in detail about the narrator's soundscape as he walks from his classroom, through the halls, and out the doors of the New York City school where he teaches. They are also drawn to re-creating both how Sonny sounds and how the people with whom he lived earlier in the story perceive noise and nonsense when listening to his music. Recall that the music he made "didn't make any sense" to the people he lived with; they felt that living with Sonny "wasn't like living with a person at all, it was like living with sound."[17] While his music "was life or death to him," he stops playing the piano when he learns that his sound torments the family he lived with.[18] Students have also attempted to compose the vacuum of sound that, in the story, generates a silence that "must have been louder than the sound of all the music ever played since time began."[19] Interestingly, these are not moments students tend to perceive when they read the story for the first time. The first semester I taught this course, students delved right into the literature without developing listening habits through the exercises we now use at the start of the course. After the first reading, their annotations and discussion points focused largely on scenes where Sonny is playing music. Now that I create ways for students to learn step by step how to listen more effectively, by the time we read "Sonny's Blues" they are attuned to the work of engaging with a more complex sense of what constitutes sounds to listen for in print.

After students complete their compositions, we watch and listen to the trailer for Mendi and Keith Obadike's *Blues Speaker [for James Baldwin]*, a twelve-hour sound installation that uses the glass façade of the New School's University Center as a speaker to deliver the sound.[20] Engaging with this sound installation gives students an opportunity to think through compositions created by readers beyond those in the class and to consider what it means to amplify one's listening in public.

Reading Toni Morrison's *Jazz*, students have responded to the following passage at the end of the novel, where the narrator describes her subjects—potential characters in her narrative—not as objects to watch, not as fully developed photographs, but instead as "real":

When I see them now they are not sepia, still, losing their edges to the light of a future afternoon. Caught midway between was and must be. For me they are real. Sharply in focus and clicking. I wonder, do they know they are the sound of snapping fingers under the sycamores lining the streets? When the loud trains pull into their stops and the engines pause, attentive listeners can hear it. Even when they are not there, when whole city blocks downtown and acres of lawned neighborhoods in Sag Harbor cannot see them, the clicking is there.[21]

The sound compositions students have created in response to this moment capture the sounds of a film camera alongside sounds of heels clicking on a concrete sidewalk. Fingers snapping to a jazzy tune morph into the sounds of a clicking and screeching elevated train or the click of a click-tap keeping time in a jazz song. In class, we discuss the possibilities of capturing the sounds of a dark-room to think about the idea of pictures in the process of development. Students reflect on their decisions and on the experience of sharing an interpretation of a text through sound composition. Ultimately, this assessment aims to help them begin to think about reading and writing as multisensory activities. By extension, they begin to think about their sound compositions not as recordings to consume passively but as a situated experience that potentially affects their entire sensory range, crafted for a particular situated moment in the text.

Tuning in to Static

At the start of this course, many students describe their writing or their engagement with writing through the sonic figure of static. We try to engage with, then, rather than ignore or wish away that static. Alongside Moran's "Cradle Song," I play Lauryn Hill's single "The Miseducation of Lauryn Hill." The week of its release, her first solo album, *The Miseducation of Lauryn Hill*, debuted at number 1 on the *Billboard* chart.[22] Selling more than 12 million copies worldwide, *Miseducation* achieved both popular and critical acclaim, earning Hill five Grammy Awards, three American Music Awards, one Billboard Music Award, one Soul Train Award, and one MTV Video Music Award. The album synthesizes a striking range of musical genres, including rhythm and blues, soul, reggae, rap, hip-hop, and gospel. In "To Zion," a tribute to her first child, we hear martial drums and chants.

The thematic range—and Hill's ability to listen with dexterous fluidity across musical and other cultural texts—is equally impressive. The lyrics, most of which she wrote, feature personal and political concerns, allusions from popular culture, Egyptian mythology, the Bible (listen to the anthem-like "Everything Is Everything," where Hill declares, "Now hear this mixture / Where hip hop meets scripture"), and literature and history (the title of the album is an allusion to Carter Woodson's 1933 *The Mis-Education of the Negro*).[23] Her bluesy ballad "When It Hurts So Bad" recalls a blues tradition that sings of love, pain, and hate in the same space: "When it hurts so bad, when it hurts so bad / Why's it feel so good?" In this impressive range of sounds, Lauryn Hill creates music reminiscent of Stevie Wonder and the Queen of Soul herself, Aretha Franklin. In fact, in her song "The Final Hour," Hill "demands respect."

The title song, which is the official closing song of the album, in my mind's ear speaks most directly to the complex issues facing critics, artists, and other individuals in our postmodern world. The song opens with static coming from the needle of a record player on the vinyl's surface. From static, the song enters a beautiful, heartfelt, and intensely sung set of lyrics: "And deep in my heart the answer it was in me / And I made up my mind to define my own destiny."[24] Hill sings about the speed with which this world moves, rendering the unique complexity of the moment in this slow ballad. When we listen to "Miseducation" in class, the song pulls us into its lingering static for, even after the song proper ends, the static continues.[25] The term "static" bears some measure of attention here. It is a signifier for the noise that prevents—for example, in radio communication—auditory channels from being clear. It functions, then, as a metaphor for blockages. Yet in Hill's recording our swiftly changing world, an increasingly complex world, generates the need for—not the silencing of—this static, a sonic recall of the seemingly distant (vinyl) past. Rather than interference, static functions as a means to call on our ears to listen anew.

Here in the midst of speed, Hill slows down, slows her listeners down, and leads her audience's audition to attend to the static. This static—resonant with Nathaniel Mackey's discrepancy and skipping record, Toni Morrison's linguistically missed target, and Ralph Ellison's microphone and phonograph—plays along with the stylized piano and intense vocals, calling attention to the squeeze that the song's persona feels. Yet this static, lingering at the end of the song, also causes us to stand or stop in the moment—causes us to be static—in the midst of all this swift complexity. We are called on, then, to find a necessarily momentary equilibrium in which to listen and make sense until the next sound loop. The flourishing piano solo and intense vocals on Hill's recording are an attempt to record and listen to the traces of a sound that contains memories of a distant past—one archived in phonographs and vinyl records. Perhaps this sound contains its own history waiting to be listened to. I hear in it a potential site for individual negotiation in the midst of audible complexity. Equally importantly, I hear in this song the implied notion that listening can reeducate the miseducated. Learning is listening. Listening is an education.

Listening for Student Learning

At the end of the course, students compile listening portfolios reflecting on their learning. They have mentioned that their time in the course helped them pay more attention to the sounds around them: "My ears have been retrofitted by my experience in this class." Some became more in tune with their own sounds: "The world is too noisy. I need to focus in, to tune in to myself." Yet others found themselves "slowly opening . . . up to others" and becoming "more engaged with others' opinions even if they were different from" their own. Even though some entered the class resistant to, uncertain about, or "unnerved" by the thought of a listening English course, they felt by the end, in the words of one student: "Now I leave this class with a purpose and clearer understanding of the importance of listening to my own echo." In short, the groups of students who have taken this class reported having grown more attuned to multiple frequencies of reading, writing, and learning.

While I hoped students would grow as listeners, I did not anticipate that their perceptions of themselves as readers and writers would also shift. Students who previously described themselves as "just not an English student" or who began writing and reading assignments with self-defeating "I'm just not good at this" comments delved more deeply into the writing process and produced strikingly confident, nuanced pieces by term's end. In their reflections, my students remind me of the most essential questions: How, to borrow Carol Dweck's language, do we help students develop a growth, rather than a fixed, mindset where learning is concerned? How can we help them develop a *listening* mindset?[26] I advocate for listening—practiced as a dynamic, tinkering, beta-type approach to the study of literature and writing—as a compelling sonic mode of teaching and learning. Helping students learn to listen, to be attentive to others, and to be discerning of all the talk that comes their way can lead to enduring understandings about themselves and the ways in which they want to engage with and change their world.

"All Living Is Listening"

. . . .

Toward an Aurally Engaged Citizenry

On Tuesday, January 10, 2017, Barack Obama delivered his final address as president of the United States.[1] That evening in Chicago, he spoke of the racial divisiveness that continues to threaten American democracy, asserting that "we're not where we need to be. All of us have more work to do." At the core of the difficult work ahead lies this imperative: "Hearts must change." President Obama elaborates, his ideas resonating with Danielle Allen's notion of talking to strangers and Anna Deavere Smith's challenge to make "the broad jump towards the other," notions discussed earlier in *Race Sounds*. "For blacks and other minorities," Obama states, this change involves "tying our own struggles for justice to the challenges that a lot of people in this country face—the refugee, the immigrant, the rural poor, the transgender American, and also the middle-aged white man who from the outside may seem like he's got all the advantages, but who's seen his world upended by economic, cultural, and technological change." He continues, appealing to white Americans to acknowledge that "the effects of slavery and Jim Crow didn't suddenly vanish in the '60s; that when minority groups voice discontent, they're not just engaging in reverse racism or practicing political correctness; that when they wage peaceful protest, they're not demanding special treatment, but the equal treatment our Founders promised." President Obama identifies the need for citizens to listen particularly in the face of contention and distrust and practice communicating in ways that depend on listening, not on consensus, to occur.

While President Obama's remarks focus, ultimately, on the state of American democracy—a massive structure and ideal—he zooms in on the daily structures, platforms, and habits that tend to confirm rather than complicate our ways of being in that democracy. In the United States, the way personhood is represented in democratic structures and institutions is intertwined heavily with voice and the ability to speak. We are a nation of talk. When we cast our votes, we describe doing so as a way to have our voice heard. We emerged as a nation by *declaring* our independence. Yet we have developed a speaking voice at the expense of listening with a public purpose. We are unaware of the conversations we miss when we speak. And we tire of the conversations that do not immediately confirm our worldview, particularly those discussions concerning race and other social differences. Our fatigue stems not from a deep level of engagement with such talk but instead from our low-level listening fluency. We would do well to, in the words of Aaron Burr in Lin-Manuel Miranda's *Hamilton*, "Talk less. Smile more."[2] In order to become a more realized democracy, we need to talk less and *listen* more. We need to learn how to listen more effectively in public and private discourse.

As we witness between Pheoby and Janie, it is one thing to listen to friends. It is quite another to generate communication grounded in listening between Janie and the rest of the porchsitters or citizens. President Obama recognizes as much when he concedes in his remarks, "None of this is easy. For too many of us, it's become safer to retreat into our own bubbles, whether in our neighborhoods or college campuses or places of worship or our social media feeds, surrounded by people who look like us and share the same political outlook and never challenge our assumptions." It is especially difficult to listen when, as Andrew Dobson notes, "speaking has garnered the lion's share of attention, both in terms of the skills to be developed and the ways in which we should understand what improving it might entail."[3] Being engaged as a citizen, then, means grappling with sound through the difficult work of listening. Despite the difficulty involved, President Obama frames our full participation in listening to the other as a necessary "responsibility of citizenship" on which the health of the democracy depends.

I end with these epigraphic lines from Claudia Rankine's docupoetry, *Citizen: An American Lyric*:

All living is listening for a throat to open—
The length of its silence shaping lives.[4]

I hear in these lines a resonance with Obama's speech and his call for a democratic listening. These lines are attuned to what it means to be living in conversation as a citizen engaged in the work of democracy. They point to a desire for aural recognition—to be listened to and be afforded the chance to listen. Capturing the silence of listening in wait for a speaker's utterance, these lines listen toward the not yet spoken. Amplifying the need for and the urgency of this listening, they identify listening as a means to enable cultural, social, and political conversations. Our lives depend upon our deep understanding of this notion: all living is listening.

NOTES

Introduction

1. Marie Cardinal quoted in Toni Morrison, *Playing in the Dark: Whiteness and the Literary Imagination*, v.

2. Ibid., vi.

3. Ibid.

4. Ibid., vii.

5. For a discussion of fully attentive listening in the context of listening to recorded Islamic sermons, see Charles Hirschkind's *The Ethical Soundscape: Cassette Sermons and Islamic Counterpublics*.

6. Stuart Firestein, *Ignorance: How It Drives Science*, 4.

7. Nathaniel Mackey, *Paracritical Hinge: Essays, Talks, Notes, Interviews*, 313. As Julian Henriques also observes, "Listening requires attention, and is therefore likened to reading, including the reading of social, rather than literary, 'texts'"; see *Sonic Bodies: Reggae Sound Systems, Performance Techniques, and Ways of Knowing*, 97. While Henriques considers this aural "reading" applicable to social texts, I hear listening as an aurally resonant approach to reading African American texts, one that can, in part, allow for the reassessment of what we listen to as well as the consideration of what we are not listening to because of ideological and critical longings to hear particular and certain aspects of cultural expressivity.

8. Robert B. Stepto, *A Home Elsewhere: Reading African American Classics in the Age of Obama*, 151.

9. Ibid.

10. Ibid., 145.

11. Mackey, *Paracritical Hinge*, 313.

12. Bruce R. Smith, *The Key of Green: Passion and Perception in Renaissance Culture*, 32.

13. Ibid.

14. Ibid., 23.

15. James M. Robinson, ed., "Thunder, Perfect Mind."

16. Ibid.

17. Toni Morrison, *Jazz*, 229.

18. Steven Connor quoted in Ana María Ochoa Gautier, *Aurality: Listening and Knowledge in Nineteenth-Century Colombia*, 66.

19. Nathaniel Mackey, *Djbot Baghostus's Run*, 150.

20. Ibid.

21. Ibid.

22. Nathaniel Mackey, *Discrepant Engagement: Dissonance, Cross-Culturality, and Experimental Writing*, 19.

23. Mackey, *Djbot Baghostus's Run*, 155.

24. Ibid.

25. Tsitsi Jaji's current work in progress on classical music, performance, and African American literature, *Classic Black*, and Rita Dove's *Sonata Mulattica* engage with the relationship between black expressivity and classical music.

26. For Houston A. Baker, Jr., African American culture is a blues matrix, "a point of ceaseless input and output, a web of intersecting, crisscrossing impulses always in productive transit"; see *Blues, Ideology, and Afro-American Literature: A Vernacular Theory*, 3. For Henry Louis Gates, Jr., blackness is represented in the African American literary tradition as a discursive construct, the locus of which is the vernacular, "the black person's ultimate sign of difference, a blackness of the tongue"; see *The Signifying Monkey: A Theory of African-American Literary Criticism*, 41. According to Gates, it is the critic's role to produce meaning from this vernacular system by consulting "the ['speakerly text' or 'talking book'] regularly, to wrestle with its play of differences, not to invent a meaning, but rather to process a meaning from among the differences . . . only to return to explore the process once more" (xix). Each of these critics calls for an archaeological reading practice of sorts, because the African American literary tradition, like other literary traditions, Gates asserts, "at least implicitly, contains within it an argument for how it can be read" (xx).

27. Hortense J. Spillers, "Mama's Baby, Papa's Maybe: An American Grammar Book," 67.

28. See Alexander G. Weheliye's *Habeas Viscus: Racializing Assemblages, Biopolitics, and Black Feminist Theories of the Human* for a recent example.

29. George Lipsitz, *Dangerous Crossroads: Popular Music, Postmodernism, and the Poetics of Place*, 3.

30. Ibid.

31. Gemma Corradi Fiumara, *The Other Side of Language: A Philosophy of Listening*, 1.

32. Ibid., 11, 26.

33. Henriques, *Sonic Bodies*, 243.

34. Mitsuye Yamada in Mitsuye Yamada, Merle Woo, and Nellie Wong, *Three Asian American Writers Speak Out on Feminism*, 301.

35. Fred Moten, *In the Break: The Aesthetics of the Black Radical Tradition*, 67.

36. Ibid., 84. For an exception to this focus on reading as solely ocular, see Philip P. Schweighauser, *The Noises of American Literature, 1890–1985: Toward a History of Literary Acoustics*.

37. Fiumara, *Other Side of Language*, 57.

38. Jennifer Lynn Stoever, *The Sonic Color Line: Race and the Cultural Politics of Listening*, 4.

39. Jaji, *Africa in Stereo*, 17.

40. Carter Mathes, *Imagine the Sound: Experimental African American Literature after Civil Rights*, 10.

41. Ibid.

42. Nick Sousanis's graphic text, *Unflattening*, innovatively explores how to animate and get beneath the surface of the visual. In *Sonic Warfare: Sound, Affect, and the Ecology of Fear*, Steve Goodman proposes the notion of "unsound" to refer to, among other things, "that which is not yet audible" (191).

43. Peter Szendy, *Listen: A History of Our Ears*, 34.

44. Don Ihde, *Listening and Voice: Phenomenologies of Sound*, 15.

45. Ibid., 49.

46. Ibid., 92.

47. This moment in Los Angeles in 1992 is referred to in various ways—as a riot, an uprising, or a rebellion—depending on the speaker's point of view. In *Race Matters*, Cornel West asserts, "What happened in Los Angeles in April of 1992 was neither a race riot nor a class rebellion. Rather, this monumental upheaval was a multiracial, trans-class, and largely male display of justified social rage" (1). He goes on to say that "what we witnessed in Los Angeles was the consequence of a lethal linkage of economic decline, cultural decay, and political lethargy in American life. Race was the visible catalyst, not the underlying cause" (4). In this sentence, I use "civil disturbances" to capture the range of words that could apply and have been used to identify this moment. After this, I refer to this moment throughout the text alternatively as an uprising to acknowledge the reaction as embroiled in systems of oppression and as a riot to capture the elements of both racial rage and destruction at play.

48. Anna Deavere Smith quoted in Robin Bernstein, "Rodney King, Shifting Modes of Vision, and Anna Deavere Smith's *Twilight: Los Angeles, 1992*," 128. *Twilight* is one installation in an ongoing theater project Smith calls "On the Road: A Search for American Character."

49. Anna Deavere Smith, *Twilight: Los Angeles, 1992*, 67–68.

50. Elizabeth Alexander, "'Can You Be BLACK and Look at This?' Reading the Rodney King Video(s)," 83.

51. Ibid.

52. Anna Deavere Smith, "Anna Deavere Smith: Listening between the Lines."

53. Pope Brock, "Anna Deavere Smith."

54. Smith, "Anna Deavere Smith: Listening between the Lines."

55. Anne Anlin Cheng, *The Melancholy of Race: Psychoanalysis, Assimilation, and Hidden Grief*, 6.

56. Dale Mezzacappa, "Anna Deavere Smith Brings School-to-Prison Pipeline Play to Philadelphia."

57. Anna Deavere Smith quoted in Alia Wong, "How the Justice System Pushes Kids Out of Classrooms and into Prisons."

58. Ignoring gaps is not the purpose of an ethical listening. As Nick Sousanis writes (and draws) in his graphic critical text, "A gulf between us will always remain (and that separation is necessary). . . . Reaching across the gap to experience another's way of knowing takes a leap of the imagination." See *Unflattening*, 89.

59. Smith, *Twilight: Los Angeles, 1992*, xxiv.

60. Susan Bickford, *The Dissonance of Democracy: Listening, Conflict, and Citizenship*, 2.

61. Danielle S. Allen, *Talking to Strangers: Anxieties of Citizenship since "Brown v. Board of Education,"* 45–46.

62. "We are on the same wavelength." This metaphoric phrase to describe an understanding between two people, it turns out, has scientific validity. Neuroscientist Uri Hasson and the team at his Princeton University Listening Lab have found that in successful communication brains couple—that is, the speaker's fMRI image begins to mirror that of the listener. Using fMRI imaging to uncover what happens when people communicate with each other, Hasson's team compared the brain of a speaker telling a story as if to a friend with the brain of the listener receiving the story. The findings show that not only do brain images mirror each other but, as Hasson explained to me in a phone interview, the listener's brain "begins to anticipate that of the speaker" when a heightened understanding is reached. This brain coupling, he notes, "vanishes when participants fail to communicate. It disappears when they stop listening." Watch Uri Hasson's TED Talk, https://www.ted.com/talks/uri_hasson_this_is_your_brain_on_communication.

63. Mackey, *Paracritical Hinge*, 320.

1. "Our Literary Audience"

1. Alice Walker, *In Search of Our Mothers' Gardens*, 402.

2. Ibid., 405.

3. Daphne Mary Lamothe, *Inventing the New Negro: Narrative, Culture, and Ethnography*, 92.

4. Robert B. Stepto, "On Sterling A. Brown's Life and Career."

5. To add another contemporary of Hurston and Brown to the mix, I also refer to Langston Hughes as a listening poet. As Arnold Rampersad demonstrates, "In his willingness to stand back and record, with minimal intervention as a craftsman, aspects of the drama of black religion or black music, Hughes had clearly shown already that he saw his own art as inferior to that of either black musicians or religionists. . . . At the heart of his sense of inferiority . . . was the knowledge that he stood to a great extent outside the culture he worshiped"; see *The Life of Langston Hughes*, vol. 1, 64. Brown and Hurston both insist in their own ways and practices that they belong to the folk.

6. Peter Szendy, *Listen: A History of Our Ears*, 35.

7. Ibid., 36.

8. Zora Neale Hurston, "You May Go but This Will Bring You Back," my transcription. Hurston's description of her process of collecting cultural material accurately in the field brings to my mind Anna Deavere Smith's process of learning her characters. She credits her grandfather with teaching her "the kernel of all that I understand about acting." That kernel was contained in a sentence her grandfather liked to repeat: "If you say a word often enough it becomes you." Smith explains that "I take the words I can get and try to occupy them. Using the idea that my grandfather gave me . . . I borrow people for a moment, by borrowing their words. I borrow them for a moment to understand something about them, and to understand something about us. By 'us,' I mean humans. The way you think about walking in somebody's shoes, I'm walking in somebody's words." See Emily Wilson, "Turning Stories into Communities: Interview with Playwright Anna Deavere Smith." http://www.alternet.org/story/151152

/turning_stories_into_communities%3A_interview_with_playwright_anna_deavere
_smith?page=0%2C1

9. Sarah Pink, *Doing Sensory Ethnography*, 1. While Pink acknowledges the importance and possibilities of sound for ethnographic work, she nonetheless maintains that sound cannot express meaning as powerfully as visual media. Her construction of meaning also overlooks the somatic aspects of sound and the fact that sound can require attentiveness in different ways.

10. Daphne A. Brooks, "'Sister, Can You Line It Out?' Zora Neale Hurston and the Sound of Angular Black Womanhood," 617.

11. Ibid., 623.

12. Melvin Dixon's found poem, "Zora Neale Hurston: 'I'll See You When Your Trouble Gets Like Mine,'" incorporates lines from Hurston's recording. Dedicated to Robert Hemenway, Alice Walker, and Sherley Ann Williams, the poem demonstrates the process of literary inheritance and Dixon's listening to this cultural figure. The last two stanzas of the poem follow: "When Lomax asked me how, I told him / I just get in with the people. / If they sing I take part / until I learn all the verses. / Then, when it is in my memory, / I take it with me wherever I go. / Now you, children, line by line, / Can take it from there" (lines 19–26). The poem ends with an invitation to listen. See Dixon, *Change of Territory*.

13. See Henry Louis Gates's influential analysis of Hurston in *The Signifying Monkey: A Theory of African-American Literary Criticism*, 196. It is notable that although Gates acknowledges Hurston's work as an anthropologist and attributes her acquisition of an "oral base" to that work, he does not examine the central function of listening in her use and learning of that oral base in her novel.

14. Brooks, "Sister, Can You Line It Out?" 623.

15. Zora Neale Hurston, *Their Eyes Were Watching God*, 1, 2.

16. Ibid., 3.

17. Ibid.

18. Ibid., 10.

19. Saidiya Hartman, "The Time of Slavery," 72.

20. Hurston, *Their Eyes Were Watching God*, 2.

21. For an analysis of hunger in the fiction of Hurston, Richard Wright, and Toni Morrison, see Andrew Warnes, *Hunger Overcome? Food and Resistance in Twentieth-Century African American Literature*.

22. Danielle S. Allen, *Talking to Strangers: Anxieties of Citizenship since "Brown v. Board of Education,"* xxi.

23. Hurston, *Their Eyes Were Watching God*, 56.

24. Ibid., 17.

25. Kate Lacey, *Listening Publics: The Politics and Experience of Listening in the Media Age*, 179.

26. Hurston, *Their Eyes Were Watching God*, 53–54.

27. Ibid., 7.

28. Ibid., 75.

29. Ibid., 77.

30. Ibid., 88.

31. See, for instance, Barbara Johnson, "Metaphor, Metonymy and Voice in *Their Eyes Were Watching God*," and Karla F. C. Holloway, *The Character of the Word: The Texts of Zora Neale Hurston.*

32. Mary Helen Washington in Hurston, *Their Eyes Were Watching God*, xiv.

33. Mae G. Henderson developed her seminal essay into a book-length treatment of this influential trope: *Speaking in Tongues and Dancing Diaspora: Black Women Writing and Performing.*

34. Jennifer Lynn Stoever also identifies the listener as a trope in black literature. See *The Sonic Color Line: Race and the Cultural Politics of Listening*, 17.

35. If we consider her role as listener in the context of a philosophy of listening, Pheoby embodies listening as what Gemma Corradi Fiumara calls "a genuinely inter-active propensity, in the sense that [she] determines what [Janie] will say as much as [Janie] determines it, with the innumerable tensions that are created in a bipersonal field"; see *The Other Side of Language: A Philosophy of Listening*, 145.

36. Hélène Cixous quoted in Alice Rayner, "The Audience: Subjectivity, Community and the Ethics of Listening," 15.

37. Hurston, *Their Eyes Were Watching God*, 6.

38. Monisha Pasupathi and Ben Rich, "Inattentive Listening Undermines Self-Verification in Personal Storytelling," 1079.

39. Ibid., 1080.

40. Hurston, *Their Eyes Were Watching God*, 286.

41. Maurice Merleau-Ponty quoted in Susan Bickford, *The Dissonance of Democracy: Listening, Conflict, and Citizenship*, 23.

42. Lacey, *Listening Publics*, 179.

43. Ibid.

44. Hurston, *Their Eyes Were Watching God*, 182–183.

45. Reading of Pheoby's growth as well as Janie's figurative description of her conversation with Pheoby as "mah tongue is in mah friend's mouth" in the twenty-first century reverberates with current studies of effective conversations, listening, and what neuroscientist Uri Hasson refers to as brain coupling. Hasson's ongoing work on listening and the brain and Hurston's narration of Janie's conversation with Pheoby raise questions for me about how these two areas of inquiry—cognitive neuroscience and literary and cultural studies—might hold conversations with each other.

46. Robert Coles, *The Call of Stories: Teaching and the Moral Imagination*, 19.

47. See Bruce R. Smith, *The Key of Green: Passion and Perception in Renaissance Culture*, 173.

48. Sterling A. Brown, "Our Literary Audience," 114.

49. Ibid.

50. Ibid., 122.

51. See Nicole L. B. Furlonge, "An Instrument Blues-Tinged: Listening, Language and the Everyday in Sterling Brown's 'Ma Rainey.'"

52. Regina Bendix, *In Search of Authenticity: The Formation of Folklore Studies*, 9.

53. Ibid., 10.

54. Ibid., 21.

55. See Sonya Posmentier, "Blueprints for Negro Reading: Sterling Brown's Study Guides."

56. Gayl Jones likens the transition from Dunbar to Brown to the development in the Spanish ballad, one that progresses "in the movement from subjective to sentimental elements, through objective images and narration, to a scenic style in which dialogued elements predominate in dramatic situations"; see *Liberating Voices: Oral Tradition in African American Literature*, 32–33.

57. Robert Stepto, "'When de Saints Go Ma'chin' Home': Sterling Brown's Blueprint for a New Negro Poetry," 940.

58. Ibid., 948.

59. Ibid., 949.

60. Jean-François Lyotard quoted in Julian Wolfreys, *Critical Keywords in Literary and Cultural Theory*, 98.

61. Lyotard quoted in Peter Mendelsund, *What We See When We Read*, 39.

62. Lyotard quoted in Wolfreys, *Critical Keywords*, 101.

63. Emily J. Lordi, *Black Resonance: Iconic Women Singers and African American Literature*, 100.

64. Hazel V. Carby, "It Jus Be's Dat Way Sometime: The Sexual Politics of Women's Blues," 233. For more on Ma Rainey's life, her impact on classic blues, and her vocal stylings, see Sandra R. Lieb, *Mother of the Blues: A Study of Ma Rainey*. Lieb also quotes Sterling Brown's poem "Ma Rainey" in full, noting that it "captured the marvelous power of her performance" (13).

65. Poet Marilyn Chin reads Bessie Smith's "Backwater Blues" here: https://www.loc.gov/poetry/poetry-of-america/american-identity/marilynchin-bessiesmith.html.

66. Although unnamed in Brown's flood poems, Bessie Smith wrote and performed several of the songs at the heart of his poems in response to the 1927 Mississippi river flood: "Homeless Blues," which her pianist Porter Grainger composed in direct response to the flood, and "Backwater Blues," whose sales and distribution markedly increased following the great flood.

67. Angela Y. Davis, *Blues Legacies and Black Feminism: Gertrude "Ma" Rainey, Bessie Smith, and Billie Holiday*, 109.

68. For Davis, songs like "Backwater Blues" "transcend the particular circumstances that inspire them and become metaphors about oppression while the aesthetic distance achieved through this music forges a consciousness that imagines community among the people who share glimpses of the possibility of eventually moving beyond this oppression"; ibid., 111. According to Rainey's biographer, Sandra Lieb, Smith was known more for socially conscious song lyrics than was Rainey. Also, in his analysis of Dinah Washington's 1958 recording of "Backwater Blues," Guthrie P. Ramsey, Jr., suggests how an artist's covering of a song reflects the changing significance and image of the blues vocalist. Washington's version of the song differs from Bessie Smith's recording and Ma Rainey's performance as remembered in Brown's poem. Washington recorded the song at the Newport Jazz Festival. Her performance, Ramsey asserts, "provides an excellent instance of the centering of black female subjectivity within the logic of this piece's formal procedures"; see *Race Music: Black Cultures from Bebop to*

Hip-Hop, 59. Washington performs the song as a hard bop piece and pays homage to Smith at the start of the recording. Her personal politics are clearly present in the last lines: "Somebody, somebody please tell me, where's a poor, poor girl like me to go, / Can't you see I'm tired and I don't feel like moving no more, / But if I ever get my nerves settled down, I'll be a mean so and so." In Washington's cover, the song remembers the flood but also adds a personal dimension. There is a sense that she is talking about the historical moment but also about the struggles she is going through as a black woman performer. Her cover reminds me of the shift in meaning and social significance that occurred when Aretha Franklin covered Otis Redding's "Respect." See chapter 3 for further discussion.

69. Paul Oliver quoted in Stephen E. Henderson, "The Heavy Blues of Sterling Brown: A Study in Craft and Tradition," 36.

70. Davis, *Blues Legacies and Black Feminism*, 110.

71. In "Living with Music," Ralph Ellison writes, "Bessie Smith might have been a 'blues queen' to society at large, but within the tighter Negro community where the blues were part of a total way of life . . . she was a priestess, a celebrant who affirmed the values of the group"; see *Living with Music: Ralph Ellison's Jazz Writings*, ed. Robert G. O'Meally, 131. Also, Mary sings "Backwater Blues" in *Invisible Man*. We witness this elevated status of priestess in Robert Hayden's "Homage to the Empress of the Blues." Bessie Smith is also mentioned in Ann Petry's *The Street* and represented in Sherley Anne Williams's *Some One Sweet Angel Chile*. British writer Jackie Kay muses, "The fascinating thing about the voice of Bessie Smith, for all its blueness, is its total lack of sentimentality. She can sing unnerving, sad songs without a note of self-pity. It is the very flatness of her voice, singing about tragedies, that so moves us. It is not in any way the voice of the victim"; see *Bessie Smith: Outlines*, 72–73. Bessie Smith and her "Backwater Blues" lyrics and recording provided a muse for generations of writers.

72. National Public Radio, "Intersections: August Wilson, Writing to the Blues."

73. Ibid.

74. Studs Terkel, "An Interview with James Baldwin," 3.

75. Mary Bogumil, *Understanding August Wilson*, 19.

76. While Ursa worries that her voice has changed, Cat assures her, "Not for the worse. Like Ma [Rainey], for instance, after all the alcohol and men, the strain made it better, because you could tell what she'd been through. You could hear what she'd been through"; Jones, *Corregidora*.

77. Ma Rainey, the Mother of the Blues, also takes center stage at the conclusion of Houston A. Baker's *Modernism and the Harlem Renaissance*. This relationship between Ma Rainey and critical ideas is visualized and sounded in *Modernism*, which features a black-and-white photograph of Ma Rainey on its cover. The photograph repeats at the conclusion of the monograph. In addition to Rainey's photographic image, Baker reprints in full Sterling Brown's poem "Ma Rainey." Baker regards the poem as expressing "the essence of black discursive modernism" and serving as "the indisputably modern moment in Afro-American discourse" (92–93). As critics have noted, however, his emphasis on Brown's poetic accomplishment frames Rainey as significant *because* she is the subject of Brown's poetry and, indirectly, the subject of Baker's critical discourse. Baker asks his readers to recall Brown's voice as they "listen" to the poem on the page.

78. See "Sterling Allen Brown Reading his Poems with Comment in the Recording Laboratory, July 9, 1973," https://www.loc.gov/item/94838831.

79. Steven C. Tracy, "A Reconsideration: Hearing Ma Rainey," 85.

80. See Gayl Jones, *Liberating Voices*, and Sherley Anne Williams, "The Blues Roots of Contemporary Afro-American Poetry," in Michael S. Harper and Robert B. Stepto, eds., *Chant of Saints: A Gathering of Afro-American Literature, Art, and Scholarship*, 123–135, for detailed discussions of elements and strategies characteristic of blues poetics.

81. Sterling A. Brown, *The Collected Poems of Sterling A. Brown*, ed. Michael S. Harper, 68. In-text references are to lines from this edition.

82. Henderson, "The Heavy Blues of Sterling Brown," 37.

83. Christopher Small, *Musicking: The Meanings of Performing and Listening*, 29.

84. See, for instance, Lauryn Hill's *MTV Unplugged No. 2.0*.

85. I draw here on my understanding of Peter Szendy's discussion of musical arrangements in *Listen*. Szendy demonstrates that transcriptions are encoded with the experience of the arranger's listening. While he is talking about musical arrangements and their transcription onto the page specifically, I find his idea useful when examining texts like Brown's poem, which I read as a literary score.

86. Rayner, "The Audience," 23.

87. For a blues-tinged reading of his poem, listen to Sterling A. Brown, "Ma Rainey."

88. Fred Moten, *In the Break: The Aesthetics of the Black Radical Tradition*, 62. This centrality of necessary mourning recalls Moten's notion of "black mo'nin'." He asserts that the performance of "mo(ur)nin(g)" is central to black radical tradition and performance. Suggesting that the sound of mourning is central to representations of black tortured bodies, he sees this sonic presence as a site of resistance and possibility.

89. Bessie Smith's recording of "Backwater Blues" also enacts this moan.

90. Lacey, *Listening Publics*, 179.

91. See Angela Naimou, *Salvage Work: U.S. and Caribbean Literatures amid the Debris of Legal Personhood*.

2. "To Hear the Silence of Sound"

1. Ralph Ellison, *Invisible Man*, 3.

2. Ibid.

3. Ibid., 6.

4. While the sonic plays an important role in delimiting Invisible Man's personhood, as this chapter will illuminate, Salomé Voegelin reminds us that such a "sonic sensibility is not anti-visual" but instead activates "the multidimensionality, temporality, and complexity of the visual, making it ready to receive multimodal work"; see *Listening to Noise and Silence: Towards a Philosophy of Sound Art*, 127.

5. Ellison, *Invisible Man*, 340–341.

6. Robert G. O'Meally, ed., *Living with Music: Ralph Ellison's Jazz Writings*, 4. Ellison's essay "Living with Music" was first published in *High Fidelity* magazine. Beginning in 1958, *High Fidelity* was geared toward recorded music lovers, and its articles influenced consumer taste in music and musical equipment. It is not surprising, then, that Ellison makes a point of mentioning in his essay the type of radio he owned (a Philco) and other equipment. Not only was he knowledgeable, but he was also writing for an

audience that wanted to know what equipment to purchase. He was affecting not only the singing taste of the neighbor he discusses in his essay but also the buying tastes of his and the magazine's readers.

7. Ibid., 5.

8. For a detailed account of noise ordinances in New York City, see Lilian Radovac's "The 'War on Noise': Sound and Space in La Guardia's New York."

9. O'Meally, ed., *Living with Music*, 5.

10. Ibid., 6.

11. Ibid., 10.

12. Ibid.

13. See David L. Morton, Jr., *Off the Record: The Technology and Culture of Sound Recording in America*, for a history of the development of high fidelity.

14. Ibid., 11.

15. Ellison, *Invisible Man*, 7.

16. In a different context and toward different ends, Jentery Sayers examines the importance of tinkering in English classrooms. He notes that tinkering allows us in the realm of letters to think about what *Invisible Man* learns: adaptability in planning, constant negotiation of materials and contexts, resistance to ready-made plans, collaboration between different kinds of knowledge, and a perspective from outside of the traditional practitioners. "Embracing tinkering's inexpert, tactical, and situational experimentation lends itself well to introducing students of literature and language to otherwise unfamiliar modes of learning." See "Tinker-Centric Pedagogy in Literature and Language Classrooms," 279.

17. O'Meally, ed., *Living with Music*, 12. Also see Richard Brody, "Ralph Ellison's Record Collection."

18. O'Meally, ed., *Living with Music*, 11.

19. Ibid.

20. Jonathan Sterne, *The Audible Past: Cultural Origins of Sound Reproduction*, 225.

21. O'Meally, ed., *Living with Music*, 11. Later, when he moves to a more suitable apartment, Ellison notes with melancholy that all his equipment is stored in a closet and only one wire is visible.

22. Mark Goble, *Beautiful Circuits: Modernism and the Mediated Life*, 164.

23. O'Meally, ed., *Living with Music*, 12.

24. Ibid.

25. Ellison, *Invisible Man*, 8.

26. Alexander G. Weheliye, *Phonographies: Grooves in Sonic Afro-Modernity*, 46–56. Throughout his essays, Ellison reflects on his negotiations between sound and writing. See, for instance, "The Golden Age, Time Past," in O'Meally, ed., *Living with Music*, 60.

27. Weheliye, *Phonographies*, 50.

28. Ellison, *Invisible Man*, 340–341.

29. Ibid.

30. Ibid.

31. Ibid.

32. Ibid., 334.

33. Ibid., 340.

34. Invisible Man would have enjoyed the developments in virtual audio technology: "virtual audio offers a 360-degree aural space. Second, this three-dimensional space simulates the actual movement of sound in an environment, mapping sound's passage from a virtual source through a particular acoustic environment to the ear, which . . . is . . . represented in its fully fleshy uniqueness." See Frances Dyson, *Sounding New Media: Immersion and Embodiment in the Arts and Culture*, 139.

35. There are resonances here with James Baldwin. For a discussion of Baldwin as a listener, see Josh Kun, *Audiotopia: Music, Race, and America*.

36. Henriques, *Sonic Bodies*, 29.

37. Ellison, *Invisible Man*, 6. Meta DuEwa Jones extends this notion, saying that "the trumpeter's virtuosic scat also made a poetry out of being inaudible"; see *The Muse Is Music: Jazz Poetry from the Harlem Renaissance to Spoken Word*, 187.

38. Listen to Armstrong here: http://www.youtube.com/watch?v=gHLTl2cMCQk.

39. See O'Meally, ed., *Living with Music*. Eric J. Sundquist also discusses the history of this song in *Cultural Contexts for Ralph Ellison's "Invisible Man,"* 115–116.

40. This recalls for me Char Davies's comment: "Always what was important to me was the notion of being immersed in enveloping space, and the sensation that you're fully enveloped, . . . it's not about interactivity but the fact that you are spatially encompassed and spatially surrounded—it's all around—and that's what sound is." Quoted in Dyson, *Sounding New Media*, 107.

41. Ellison, *Invisible Man*, 8–9.

42. Ibid.

43. The sermon also includes an allusion to the biblical Jonah story. While Invisible Man's descent might be mistaken for a plumbing of and for ultimate and essential sounds of blackness, the sermon he hears specifically contains, as Kimberly W. Benston demonstrates, complex difference and tension that ultimately suggest blackness as "not . . . a node of absolute essence but, rather, the (re)discovery of the subversive ambiguity of any expressive act"; see *Performing Blackness: Enactments of African-American Modernism*, 10. For a full analysis of the sermon, see pp. 7–10. Performance poet Tracie Morris's "Black but Beautiful" is a riff on Ellison's "Black Is, Black Ain't." See Meta Jones's reading of Morris's poem and her performance aesthetic in *The Muse Is Music*, 186–189.

44. Ellison, *Invisible Man*, 8–9.

45. In her punctuated discussion of *Invisible Man*, Jennifer DeVere Brody, too, brings attention to the ellipses. She notes the way the ellipses attune us more precisely to this novel's auditory play. "For, if we read the typography of *Invisible Man*," Brody instructs, "the ellipsis appears as the first (in)co-*hear*-ent mark in the text—an initializing site/cite of trouble . . . perforating that page and our passive 'silent' reading." See *Punctuation: Art, Politics, and Play*, 74–75, my emphasis.

46. Ellison, *Invisible Man*, 10.

47. Ibid.

48. Later in the novel, Mary, the woman who takes Invisible Man in in Harlem, alludes to Bessie Smith and Mahalia Jackson: "It's you young folks what's going to make the changes. . . . Y'all's the ones. You got to lead and you got to fight and move us all on up a little higher. And I tell you something else, it's the ones from the South that's got to do it, them what knows the fire and ain't forgot how it burns. Up here too

many forgits. They finds a place for theyselves and forgits the ones on the bottom. Oh, heap of them talks about doing things, but they done really forgot. No, it's you young ones what has to remember and take the lead" (255). See also Guthrie P. Ramsey, Jr., on Mahalia Jackson's signature song, "Move on Up," in *Race Music: Black Cultures from Bebop to Hip-Hop*, 52–56.

49. Ellison, *Invisible Man*, 12.

50. Ibid., 580–581.

51. Ibid., 581.

52. John Shepherd, *Music as Social Text*, 90. Also, to recall Don Ihde's assertion, "an inquiry into the auditory is also an inquiry into the invisible. Listening makes the invisible present"; *Listening and Voice: Phenomenologies of Sound*, xxi.

53. This figure differs from Jennifer Lynn Stoever's listening ear, a hegemonic listening that functions to police the sonic color line. See *The Sonic Color Line: Race and the Cultural Politics of Listening*, 7–8.

54. Susan Schmidt Horning, *Chasing Sound: Technology, Culture, and the Art of Studio Recording from Edison to the LP*, 111.

55. Ibid.

56. Sterne, *Audible Past*, 22.

57. Mark Katz, *Capturing Sound: How Technology Has Changed Music*, 40–41.

58. Ellison, *Invisible Man*, 341.

59. Ibid.

60. Ibid.

61. Ibid., 345.

62. Ibid.

63. Ibid.

64. Ibid., 347.

65. Ibid., 6.

66. Ibid., 581.

67. R. Murray Schafer quoted in Andra McCartney, "Soundwalking: Creating Moving Environmental Sound Narratives," 179. In "Living with Music," Ellison uses similar language in describing his experience with his neighbor. Unlike the other sounds in his neighborhood as acoustic space, this woman's singing voice "got beneath the skin and worked into the very structure of one's consciousness" (O'Meally, ed., *Living with Music*, 5). Emphasizing the intensity of the acoustic space, Ellison describes the singer's vocal vibrations as tactile: they touch his physical and psychological being. The singer's voice inhabits Ellison so much so that it deeply affects his view of himself as a writer on any given day: "I was forced to listen, and in listening I soon became involved to the point of identification. If she sang badly I'd hear my own futility in the windy sound; if well, I'd stare at my typewriter and despair that I would ever make my prose so sing" (9–10). Here and in the novel Ellison's listening is, to borrow David Burrows's phrase, a "full-bodied hearing" (quoted in McCartney, "Soundwalking," 179).

68. Shelley Trower, *Senses of Vibration: A History of the Pleasure and Pain of Sound*, 133.

69. Steve Goodman discusses a "politics of frequency"; see *Sonic Warfare: Sound, Affect, and the Ecology of Fear*, xvii.

70. Ellison, *Invisible Man*, 579.

71. Ibid., 581.

72. Ibid.

73. Ibid., 439.

74. Ibid., 443.

75. Morton, *Off the Record*, 134.

76. Emily Thompson quoted in Jim Drobnick, *Aural Cultures*, xiv. The separation that Invisible Man describes between himself—the source of the sound—and his voice—the sound itself—during the Brotherhood rally is another instance of acousmatic listening in the text.

77. "Ralph Ellison: An American Journey."

78. Ralph Ellison quoted in Jill Lepore, *The Story of America: Essays on Origins*, 18 n. 8.

79. Veit Erlmann, *Reason and Resonance: A History of Modern Aurality*, 15.

3. When Malindy Listens

1. Farah Jasmine Griffin, "When Malindy Sings: A Meditation on Black Women's Vocality," 104.

2. Ibid. In such moments, what is heard in the black singing voice is the expression of cultural value and political potential. In *Blackness and Value: Seeing Double*, Lindon Barrett hears this voice as "a site of the active production of meaning" and "the preeminent sign of the production of cultural value in African American communities" (76, 58). This voice, he asserts, allows "African Americans to enter or subvert symbolic, legal, material, and imaginative economies to which we are most usually denied access" (57).

3. Griffin, "When Malindy Sings," 113.

4. Ibid., 110–111.

5. Gayl Jones quoted in Madhu Dubey, *Signs and Cities: Black Literary Postmodernism*, 87.

6. In Jones's novel *Mosquito*, the title character possesses a perfect auditory memory. Mosquito is the archive keeper for the spiritual organization the Daughters of Nzingha, a collective that gathers stories from the African diaspora and from friends from other locations across the globe as part of its Minder of the World project. She longs for a future in which "it be possible to tell a true jazz story, where the peoples that listens can just enter the story and start telling it and adding things wherever they wants. The story would provide the jazz foundation, the subject, but they be improvising around that subject or them subjects and be composing they own jazz story" (93).

7. In *Monstrous Intimacies: Making Post-Slavery Subjects*, Christina Sharpe corrects the persistent reading of Gram as enslaved. She notes that Gram was born in 1888, the actual year of Brazilian emancipation and seventeen years after the passage of the 1871 Free Womb Law. That is, even though Gram speaks as if she was enslaved, she was never legally Corregidora's slave. For reference, readings of Gram as enslaved include Jennifer Cognard-Black, "'I Said Nothing': The Rhetoric of Silence and Gayl Jones's *Corregidora*," and Elizabeth Swanson Goldberg, "Living the Legacy: Pain, Desire, and Narrative Time in Gayl Jones's *Corregidora*."

8. See Peter Manso, "Chronicle of a Tragedy Foretold." For Morrison's influence as an editor on black letters, see Hilton Als, "Ghosts in the House: How Toni Morrison Fostered a Generation of Black Writers."

9. See Harper's interview with Gayl Jones in Michael S. Harper and Robert B. Stepto, eds., *Chant of Saints: A Gathering of Afro-American Literature, Art, and Scholarship*, 352–375, 357–359.

10. Ibid.

11. Ibid.

12. Ibid.

13. Stephanie Li, *Something Akin to Freedom: The Choice of Bondage in Narratives by African American Women*, 6.

14. Gayl Jones, *Corregidora*, 40. Hurston's *Their Eyes Were Watching God* provides one answer to this question. When Janie belittles Joe Starks on the porch of their store, she is publicly ostracized and critiqued, and Joe takes it quite seriously. Seemingly, too, the force of Janie's public critique of Joe leads to his demise.

15. Ibid., 6.

16. Ibid., 46.

17. Michael S. Harper, *History Is Your Own Heartbeat: Poems*. *Corregidora* is littered with intimate brutality or what Christina Sharpe terms monstrous intimacies. She describes it as "a text in which the primal scenes of slavery emerge as those familial and legal entanglements that were central to the transformative enterprise of making some persons into kin and some into property"; *Monstrous Intimacies*, 28.

18. Carolyn Cooper, *Noises in the Blood: Orality, Gender, and the "Vulgar" Body of Jamaican Popular Culture*, 58. Later, after dreaming that she has given birth to Corregidora, Ursa proclaims, "*I am Ursa Corregidora. I have tears for eyes. I was made to touch my past at an early age. I found it on my mother's tiddies. In her milk. Let no one pollute my music. I will dig out their temples. I will pluck out their eyes.*" See Jones, *Corregidora*, 77. She ingests the past through her mother's milk.

19. Sharpe, *Monstrous Intimacies*, 39.

20. Jones, *Corregidora*, 44.

21. Jean-Luc Nancy speaks of "pure resonance," what he explains as "a becoming-different, one differentiated by this resonance of onself: to hear oneself, as a body, a cavity, sounding to oneself as another." See *Listening*, 89.

22. Jones, *Corregidora*, 40.

23. Toni Morrison quoted in Emily J. Lordi, *Black Resonance: Iconic Women Singers and African American Literature*, 138. Lordi also examines *Corregidora* alongside "Strange Fruit" and the haunting nature of both, comparing not Ursa but Jones to Billie Holiday.

24. Sherley Anne Williams, "Returning to the Blues: Esther Phillips and Contemporary Blues Culture," 817.

25. Listen to Nina Simone's performance of the song: https://www.youtube.com /watch?v=_5xmCFSU7xg.

26. Jones, *Corregidora*, 44.

27. See Nina Sun Eidsheim, *Sensing Sound: Singing and Listening as Vibrational Practice*.

28. Goldberg, "Living the Legacy," 447.

29. Jones, *Corregidora*, 96.

30. Ibid., 148.

31. Ibid., 54.

32. Ibid., 44.

33. Ibid., 45.

34. Ibid., 72. This moment in the novel resonates for me with Hortense J. Spillers's important question: "We might well ask if [the] phenomenon of marking and branding actually 'transfers' from one generation to another, finding its various symbolic substitutions in an efficacy of meanings that repeat the initiating moments?" See *Black, White, and in Color: Essays on American Literature and Culture*, 207.

35. Similar to Ursa, Jones grew up in a house where she heard older relatives telling stories, under different circumstances, of course: "I think it's important that we—my brother and I—were never sent out of the room when grown-up people were talking. So we heard their stories. So I've always heard stories of people generations older than me. I think that's important." See Harper and Stepto, eds., *Chant of Saints*, 352.

36. Jones, *Corregidora*, 22.

37. James Alan McPherson's figure of writing and recording on the brain in "The Story of a Scar," in *Elbow Room*, comes to mind: "You know everything. . . . A black mama birthed you, let you suck her titty, cleaned your dirty drawers, and you still look at us through paper and movie plots. . . . 'Now this is the way it happened.' . . . I want you to write it on whatever part of your brain that ain't already covered with page print" (141).

38. Jones, *Corregidora*, 9. In her interview with Harper, Jones recounts an exchange she had with her mother during which she shared her decision not to have children. Her mother asked, "What about the generations?" See Harper and Stepto, eds., *Chant of Saints*, 374. Jones realized then that such a decision, though personal, was also tied up with all the connections across generations—those who came before and those in the present. She develops a metaphor for this personal decision in the novel.

39. Ibid., 101.

40. Ibid., 110.

41. Ibid.

42. Ibid., 123.

43. Ibid., 124.

44. Ibid.

45. Ibid., 129.

46. Ibid., 131.

47. Kevin Quashie, *The Sovereignty of Quiet: Beyond Resistance in Black Culture*, 22.

48. Jones, *Corregidora*, 102.

49. Recall the moment when a five-year-old Ursa asks, "*You telling the truth, Great Gram?*" Great Gram slapped her, asserting, "*When I'm telling you something, don't you ever ask if I'm lying.*" In her next sentence, she returns to her compulsory leaving of evidence through storytelling: "*Because they didn't want to leave no evidence of what they done—so it couldn't be held against them.*" See Jones, *Corregidora*, 14.

50. As Gemma Corradi Fiumara notes in *The Other Side of Language: A Philosophy of Listening*, "the willingness to keep alive [an] orientation towards openness is the

genuine basis for every question. The very notion of question is sustained by an open-ness—presumably as openness towards listening to the answer" (36).

51. Jones, *Corregidora*, 100, 101, 103.

52. Lauri Siisiäinen, *Foucault and the Politics of Hearing*, 92.

53. Jones, *Corregidora*, 132.

54. Ibid., 60. The selective, spare use of italics here is worthy of note as they are instructional, leading the reader toward words that should receive emphasis in their reading.

55. Ibid., 59.

56. Ralph Ellison, "Richard Wright's Blues," in *Shadow and Act*, 80.

57. Jones, *Corregidora*, 103.

58. See Don Ihde, *Listening and Voice: Phenomenologies of Sound*, 137.

59. See Siisiäinen, *Foucault and the Politics of Hearing*.

60. Jones, *Corregidora*, 67.

61. Ibid.

62. Ibid., 76.

63. Ibid., 54.

64. Ibid., 67.

65. Homi K. Bhabha, *The Location of Culture*, 10.

66. Ibid.

67. Jones, *Corregidora*, 184.

68. Ibid., 185.

69. Ibid., 183.

70. Ibid., 52.

71. Ibid., 183.

72. Ibid., 184.

73. Ibid.

74. Ibid., 45.

75. This moment is full of audacious hope—*audax* from the Latin means "bold, daring," and *auris* is "ear." *Auris* in some ancient texts can mean "judgment." The definition of judgment is in reference to rhetorical use (what we understand or do when we use our ears). Thus, the hope I hear in this moment in the text is full of listening force, and it also resonates with Brandon LaBelle's assertion that "to give one's ear is to invest in the making of a future public"; see *Lexicon of the Mouth: Poetics and Politics of Voice and the Oral Imaginary*, x.

76. Christopher Small, *Musicking: The Meanings of Performing and Listening*, 50.

77. Ibid.

78. James Baldwin quoted in Josh Kun, *Audiotopia: Music, Race, and America*, 88. On a personal note, I love it that Baldwin recognizes so greatly the importance of a single person by equating one person with the world.

79. Lyndon B. Johnson, "Remarks at a Ceremony at the Lincoln Memorial."

80. Aretha Franklin with David Ritz, *Aretha: From These Roots*, 112. The Library of Congress added "Respect" to the National Recording Registry in 2002.

81. Brian Ward, *Just My Soul Responding: Rhythm and Blues, Black Consciousness, and Race Relations*, 345.

82. "Perhaps more than any other recording, it was . . . chart-topping version of . . . 'Respect' in 1967 which swelled the trickle of overtly engaged, political soul songs into a flood"; ibid., 361–362.

83. Ibid., 301. Peter Guralnick credits Franklin's vocal stylings to the emergence of new meaning: "Aretha is so Aretha—in her emotional tone, her touch and intonation, in her unprompted leaps of notes and faith, the way she fractures syllables and elicits new meaning." Quoted in ibid., 348–349.

84. See Sherley Anne Williams, *Some One Sweet Angel Chile*, 53. Such a call for Aretha to sing resonates with the call to Ma Rainey in Brown's poem.

85. Bettye LaVette, *A Woman Like Me*, 25–27.

86. Ibid.

87. I draw here again on Peter Szendy's discussion of musical arrangements. While Szendy is talking about musical arrangements and their transcription onto the page specifically, I find his idea useful when reflecting on LaVette's and Franklin's interpretive work, each bringing a song to the microphone, stage, sheet music, and recording studio as a result of her active listening.

88. McCartney credits Bach's Bourrée in E minor as the song's inspiration, a piece he and George Harrison learned to play when they were young. Says McCartney, "Part of its structure is a particular harmonic thing between the melody and the bass line which intrigued me. Bach was always one of our favourite composers; we felt we had a lot in common with him. . . . I developed the melody on guitar based on the Bach piece and took it somewhere else, took it to another level, then I just fitted the words to it." See Barry Miles, *Paul McCartney: Many Years from Now*, 485.

89. Listen, for instance, to Ray Charles's "America": https://www.youtube.com /watch?v=TRUjr8EVgBg. The music of "Blackbird" features a number of time signature changes. The phrase "Blackbird singing in the dead of night" is in 3/4, while much of the remainder of the song switches between 4/4 and 2/4.

90. LaVette, *A Woman Like Me*, 233. It was during the Hollywood Bowl performance that Eric Gardner, a major music manager, heard LaVette sing and asked her to sign with him.

91. LaVette's story, of course, differs in detail from McCartney's story about the song. According to McCartney, the American civil rights movement of the 1950s and 1960s inspired the lyrics of "Blackbird": "I had in mind a black woman, rather than a bird. Those were the days of the civil rights movement, which all of us cared passionately about, so this was really a song from me to a black woman, experiencing these problems in the States: 'Let me encourage you to keep trying, to keep your faith, there is hope.' As is often the case with my things, a veiling took place so, rather than say 'Black woman living in Little Rock' and be very specific, she became a bird, became symbolic, so you could apply it to your particular problem." Quoted in Kenneth Womack, *The Beatles Encyclopedia: Everything Fab Four*, 153.

92. Although she is inspired by the Beatles' music and recognizes that many people she sings for now think of the music of the Beatles as the music of their youth, LaVette told the crowd at Café Carlyle that evening that she views the Beatles and the British invasion as a nemesis. In this comment, she also speaks for black musicians whose

songs disappeared from the airwaves as the Beatles and their imitators flooded the American pop music scene.

93. See also Emily Lordi's examination of "popular female singers not as passive muses with raw, natural, or ineffable talent, but as experimental artists who innovate black expressive possibilities right alongside their literary peers." *Black Resonance*, 151.

4. "If I Allow Myself to Listen"

1. David Bradley, *The Chaneysville Incident*, 214.

2. Ibid.

3. Particularly regarding slavery in the United States, Michel-Rolph Trouillot writes that it "has both officially ended, yet continues in many complex forms"; *Silencing the Past: Power and the Production of History*, 146–147.

4. Bradley, *The Chaneysville Incident*, 214.

5. Ibid., ix.

6. For example, historians Shane White and Graham White assert that "for nearly three centuries of African American history, much of what was distinctive about black culture was to be found in the realm of sound, a characteristic that was particularly clear in the hours in which slaves were not toiling for their owner. Above all else, slave culture was made to be heard." See *The Sounds of Slavery: Discovering African American History through Songs, Sermons, and Speech*, ix.

7. Sam Wineburg, *Historical Thinking and Other Unnatural Acts: Charting the Future of Teaching the Past*, ix.

8. Ibid.

9. Ibid.

10. Bradley, *The Chaneysville Incident*, 283.

11. Ibid., 264.

12. Hortense J. Spillers, *Black, White, and in Color: Essays on American Literature and Culture*, 179.

13. Salamishah Tillet, *Sites of Slavery: Citizenship and Racial Democracy in the Post–Civil Rights Imagination*, 3, 5.

14. Frederick Douglass, *Narrative of the Life of Frederick Douglass, An American Slave*, in *The Narrative and Selected Writings*, ed. Michael Meyer, 28–29.

15. Ibid., 29.

16. Ibid.

17. Ibid., 29. In *Culture on the Margins: The Black Spiritual and the Rise of American Cultural Interpretation*, Jon Cruz uses the term "ethnosympathy" to describe Douglass' longing for his audience to hear these sounds as vocalized, human songs of sorrow. For Cruz, the ability to ethnosympathize was a pivotal kind of emotive recognition that slaves were human beings. Additionally, the recognition that slaves were human beings enabled people to hear these songs *as* songs.

18. Douglass, *Narrative*, 28–29.

19. In *Ugly Feelings*, Sianne Ngai examines her notion of racial animatedness in relation to Douglass' text. Citing William Lloyd Garrison's preface to *Narrative* and his assertion of the text's power to intensely move the reader, she concludes, "the affective ideologeme of animatedness foregrounds the degree to which emotional qualities

seem especially prone to sliding into *corporeal* qualities where the African-American subject is concerned, reinforcing the notion of race as a truth located, quite naturally, in the always obvious, highly visible body" (95). My examination of Douglass' text, however, extends Ngai's discussion of racial animatedness in that, instead of his words functioning as the site of animatedness, the sounds represented therein activate feeling rather than corporeal change in him. While these animated emotions belong to Douglass, he suggests that the songs hold the power to move the listener to emotional and political action.

20. Harriet A. Jacobs, *Incidents in the Life of a Slave Girl*, 29, 45.

21. Ibid., 34. Jacobs's recounting here reminds me of the song Ursa sings about "mister" in *Corregidora*. See my discussion of the song in chapter 3.

22. See Deborah M. Garfield, "Earwitness: Female Abolitionism, Sexuality, and *Incidents in the Life of a Slave Girl*."

23. Daphne A. Brooks, "'Puzzling the Intervals': Blind Tom and the Poetics of the Sonic Slave Narrative," 3.

24. Such texts, including Dolores Kendrick's *The Women of Plums: Poems in the Voices of Slave Women*, Ishmael Reed's *Flight to Canada*, Robert Hayden's "Middle Passage," and Sherley Anne Williams's *Dessa Rose*, attempt to render slavery audible or less writerly—and thus authentically and intimately connected to—contemporary ears. In Tom Feelings's *The Middle Passage: White Ships/Black Cargo*, a black-and-white rendering of an enslaved woman in a slave ship covering her ears from the trauma happening to and around her resonates with me as well as an *image* that posits listening as a potential site of historical resistance or refusal. Writers also are invested in representing slavery in operatic form. Toni Morrison wrote the libretto for her opera, *Margaret Garner*, and Wynton Marsalis created *Blood on the Fields*.

25. See Ira Berlin, Marc Favreau, and Steven F. Miller, eds., *Remembering Slavery: African Americans Talk about Their Personal Experiences of Slavery and Emancipation*. The 2003 HBO special *Unchained Memories: Readings from the Slave Narratives* also uses some of the same archived materials found in *Remembering Slavery* and features dramatic readings by African American actors and celebrities. One key difference between these two collections, however, is that *Remembering Slavery* was produced as a radio special available as a book-and-CD set, while *Unchained Memories* includes visual images of former slaves and visualized dramatic readings.

26. See Robin D. G. Kelley, "Foreword," in *Remembering Slavery*, ed. Berlin, Favreau, and Miller, xxii. Kelley's scholarship repeats this notion of the importance of hearing the folk—with the critic as conduit. See, for example, his *Yo' Mama's DisFunktional! Fighting the Culture Wars in Urban America*.

27. I use the solidus or slash here in "re/wound" to highlight the wordplay between rewound, as in a tape rewinding, and (re)wound, as in a history whose perpetual presence also replays its wound or wounding. My use of the slash recalls Jennifer DeVere Brody's discussion of it in *Punctuation: Art, Politics, and Play*, 106.

28. See Michael W. Harris, *The Rise of Gospel Blues: The Music of Thomas Andrew Dorsey in the Urban Church*.

29. Beyoncé performed "Take My Hand, Precious Lord" at the 2015 Grammys. Behind her onstage, performers posed in a "hands up, don't shoot" gesture to reference

the murder of Michael Brown, an unarmed black man shot by police in Ferguson, Missouri.

30. See National Public Radio's 2000 interview with Michael Harris, "Take My Hand, Precious Lord."

31. Ibid.

32. Mark M. Smith, ed., *Hearing History: A Reader*, xiii.

33. Steven Feld, "Acoustemology," in *Keywords in Sound*, ed. David Novak and Matt Sakakeeny, 12.

34. Robert B. Stepto refers to Old Jack as one of the master storytellers who are "custodians of the prompting tales" in the African American literary tradition, characters who pass from knowing to possessing the tale. He puts Bradley's Old Jack in league with Charles Chesnutt's Uncle Julius and Ernest Gaines's Miss Jane Pittman. See *A Home Elsewhere: Reading African American Classics in the Age of Obama*, 154.

35. Bradley, *The Chaneysville Incident*, 23.

36. See the discussion of "the silence of sound" in *Invisible Man* in chapter 2.

37. As I read this scene and listen to Mrs. Turner, her wail acts on me as a sonic allusion, rewinding my mind's ear to Toni Morrison's first novel, *The Bluest Eye*, and Geraldine's reaction to Pecola when she sees the disheveled girl standing in her living room. I am reminded, too, of the internalized racism of an earlier Mrs. Turner in Zora Neale Hurston's *Their Eyes Were Watching God*. This moment, as well as the fire motif that runs throughout portions of *The Chaneysville Incident*, also recalls for me Matthew 14:41–43: "The Son of man shall send forth his angels, and they shall gather out of his kingdom all things that offend, and them which do iniquity; And shall cast them into a furnace of fire: there shall be wailing and gnashing of teeth. Then shall the righteous shine forth as the sun in the kingdom of their Father. Who hath ears to hear, let him hear."

38. Bradley, *The Chaneysville Incident*, 23.

39. Of course, this wail also reminds me of Aunt Hester's shrieks in Douglass' *Narrative*. But the circumstances of and meanings layered in her screams are quite and importantly different, and it is ethically imperative to recognize that difference and listen through it. For discussions of Aunt Hester's punishment and Douglass' rendering of it, particularly as spectacle, see Saidiya Hartman, *Scenes of Subjection: Terror, Slavery, and Self-Making in Nineteenth-Century America*, 4, and Fred Moten, *In the Break: The Aesthetics of the Black Radical Tradition*, 1–24.

40. Bradley, *The Chaneysville Incident*, 38.

41. Ibid., 40.

42. Ibid., 62.

43. Ibid., 63. For a discussion of "Sonny's Blues," see chapter 5.

44. Ibid. This moment recalls for me these lines from Lucille Clifton's *good woman: poems and a memoir 1969–1980*: "in populated air / our ancestors continue. / i have seen them. / i have heard / their shimmering voices / singing" (221).

45. Bradley, *The Chaneysville Incident*, 1.

46. Ibid.

47. Jean-Luc Nancy, *Listening*, 6.

48. Consider, for instance, Toni Morrison's treatment of the past in "Sites of Memory" as held in spaces from which slavery in particular can be experienced—re/wound and replayed—again and again.

49. Steven Connor, "Edison's Teeth: Touching Hearing," 159.

50. Bradley, *The Chaneysville Incident*, 382.

51. Ibid. As readers, we are left to wonder how Old Jack comes to live alone on this side of the Hill in the first place. George L. Henderson notes that "what is missing in the novel . . . is the history of how Old Jack came to be left alone and let be in the landscape, or territory, he calls home. There is an implicit romanticization, reification even, of the rural, of the homestead." See "South of the North, North of the South: Spatial Practices in David Bradley's *The Chaneysville Incident*," 134. Ernest Gaines's *The Autobiography of Miss Jane Pittman* is similar in this omission. Both Bradley and Gaines, however, resist the idea of a unitary teller who issues from the folk. For instance, they make it clear that there is no such thing as an individual's own story. Stories, that is, are the property of the community.

52. Old Jack's approach contrasts sharply with the figure of Great Gram in *Corregidora*, who slaps Ursa when she poses a question about the narrative Great Gram insists that she learn, remember, and pass down to the next generation. For Great Gram, such questions and veering narratives are acts of defiance.

53. Bradley, *The Chaneysville Incident*, 383.

54. Ibid.

55. Henderson, "South of the North," 135.

56. Bradley, *The Chaneysville Incident*, 383.

57. Ibid.

58. Ibid., 159.

59. Ibid., 158–160.

60. Struggling with the uncertainty that listening introduces to historical practice, with the notion of what stands as evidence in history, and with linking listening to imagination, John attempts vigorously to exclude imaginative listening altogether from his work as a historian reconstructing the Chaneysville Incident.

61. As Mary Warnock suggests in *Imagination and Time*, "it is an essential feature of imagination that it enables us to think about things that are absent, including things which no longer exist or do not yet exist. It is thus only through imagination that a man has a concept of himself as having a history which is not yet finished" (22).

62. Bradley, *The Chaneysville Incident*, 112.

63. These fragments resonate with John's memory of the Hill upon his return: "I knew nothing about the Hill any longer, I had made it my business not to know. But now suddenly, inexplicably, I was curious, and so I thought for a moment, pulling half-remembered facts from the back of my mind—scraps of information—and made extrapolations." Ibid., 17.

64. See Madhu Dubey, *Signs and Cities: Black Literary Postmodernism*, 179.

65. Bradley, *The Chaneysville Incident*, 151.

66. Ibid., 152.

67. In this stance, Mrs. Washington grieves and espouses notions about modern change as detrimental to black communal cohesion similar to those of writers such as Gloria Naylor and Toni Morrison. For a fuller discussion of these texts and issues, see Dubey, *Signs and Cities.*

68. Bradley, *The Chaneysville Incident*, 146–147.

69. As Michel-Rolph Trouillot asserts in *Silencing the Past*, "unearthing of silences, and the historian's subsequent emphasis on the retrospective significance of hitherto neglected events, requires not only extra labor at the archives—whether or not one uses primary sources—but also a project linked to an interpretation" (58–59).

70. See historians Ronald Takaki and Studs Terkel for examples of the importance of history written from multiple perspectives and voices. See also Chimamanda Ngozi Adichie's TED Talk, "The Danger of a Single Story."

71. See the National Research Council's *How People Learn: Brain, Mind, Experience, and School* for a discussion of the crucial role that cognitive dissonance plays in the process of learning.

72. Bradley, *The Chaneysville Incident*, 268. As we witness in this novel, not every character who comes in contact with history worries about filling the gaps. Contrasting with John is the Judge, who comments, "I've never studied [history], but I delved into it. Enough to know that it was not a subject that appealed to me. There were too many differences of opinion, too many gaps, too many hidden motivations, too many coincidences. . . . I found it frustrating" (186). The Judge's shallow descent into history recasts John's early fears as part of a healthy curiosity to know.

73. I can't help but think, too, of the "hot" and "cold" responses that children give when providing clues, telling guessers whether they are getting closer to the target or the answer.

74. Don Ihde, *Listening and Voice: Phenomenologies of Sound*, 134.

75. Bradley, *The Chaneysville Incident*, 394.

76. Matthew Wilson, "The African American Historian: David Bradley's *The Chaneysville Incident*," 99.

77. See Diana Taylor, *The Archive and the Repertoire: Performing Cultural Memory in the Americas*, 19, 21.

78. Bradley, *The Chaneysville Incident*, 144.

79. Ibid., 142.

80. Judith is not his sole listener, however, for the reader, as I have discussed, also functions as part of his listening audience.

81. None of the black women in the novel understands either, and John does not give anyone else the opportunity to show otherwise. For instance, he does not talk openly with his mother and shows anger toward her.

82. Bradley, *The Chaneysville Incident*, 384.

83. Ibid., 411.

84. Ibid., 394.

85. Perhaps we witness her "thirsty listening" here. Like Hurston, Bradley uses these mundane modes—food, drink, other small social rituals—as moments on which engagement and understanding turn.

86. See Stepto, *A Home Elsewhere.*

87. Bradley, *The Chaneysville Incident*, 394.

88. Ibid.

89. Szendy, *Listen*, 5–6.

90. Bradley, *The Chaneysville Incident*, 401.

91. Ibid., 430.

92. For an examination of Bradley's novel in terms of the connections between historical inquiry and death, see Ashraf H. A. Rushdy, *Remembering Generations: Race and Family in Contemporary African American Fiction*, 68–98.

93. Bradley, *The Chaneysville Incident*, 431.

94. Critics have read this moment in different ways based on a misreading of what happens to the folio. John F. Callahan discusses such misreadings and then offers a corrective reading of his own in *In the African-American Grain: The Pursuit of Voice in Twentieth-Century Black Fiction*. Also, John's burning of the materials implies a burning of Bradley's novel as well, suggesting the multiple possibilities of the act of writing a fictional history or a fiction informed by history.

95. Bradley, *The Chaneysville Incident*, 432.

96. Ibid., 431.

97. Ibid., 432.

98. Ibid.

99. Ibid., 223.

100. Ibid., 268.

101. Ibid., 42.

102. Ibid.

103. See Saidiya Hartman, *Lose Your Mother: A Journey along the Atlantic Slave Route*. For a full study of quiet in African American literature, see Kevin Quashie's *The Sovereignty of Quiet: Beyond Resistance in Black Culture*.

5. "New Ways to Make Us Listen"

1. James Baldwin, "Sonny's Blues," in *Going to Meet the Man*, 137.

2. Actually, he does this throughout the entire short story, which is a sonic text long before we enter the Greenwich Village club.

3. Baldwin, "Sonny's Blues," 137.

4. Ibid., 139.

5. Ibid.

6. Ibid., 140.

7. Cathy N. Davidson, *Now You See It: How Technology and Brain Science Will Transform Schools and Business for the 21st Century*, 5.

8. For other scholar-educators who are invested in developing sonically engaged students and citizens, see Steph Ceraso at http://stephceraso.com/ and Jentery Sayers at http://www.jenterysayers.com/.

9. See Michelle Comstock and Mary E. Hocks, "Voice in the Cultural Soundscape: Sonic Literacy in Composition Studies."

10. Rather than a Howard Gardner "disinterestedness." See Gardner's essay, for example, "Reclaiming Disinterestedness for the Digital Era."

11. See Andra McCartney, "Soundwalking: Creating Moving Environmental Sound Narratives."

12. See Jonathan Sterne, *The Audible Past: Cultural Origins of Sound Reproduction*.

13. Black artists have invoked the Rodney King beating in their work in different ways. Two examples: Spike Lee opens *Malcolm X* with the videotape of the beating, complete with its original audio, and Portia Cobb's video *No Justice, No Peace! Young, Black, ImMEDIAte!* layers images from the televised beating with repeated tapping noises, juxtaposed with a repetitive voice: "56 times in 87 seconds," the number of blows dealt and the duration of the violence.

14. I was fortunate to speak with Nick Cave via telephone from his home in New York City prior to the exhibit and performance, *Heard NY*, in April 2013. For *Heard NY*, Cave transformed Grand Central Terminal's Vanderbilt Hall with a herd of thirty colorful life-size horses that broke into choreographed movement—or "crossings"—twice a day. They were accompanied by live music. Creative Time and MTA Arts for Transit presented the project as part of a series of events celebrating the centennial of Grand Central Station.

15. See "Dream Songs: The Music of the March on Washington" for one resource.

16. See Mark M. Smith, *How Race Is Made: Slavery, Segregation, and the Senses*.

17. Baldwin, "Sonny's Blues," 126.

18. Ibid.

19. Ibid.

20. Including "slow moving harmonies, language from Baldwin's writings, ambient recordings from the streets of Harlem, and an inventory of sound contained in" the short story, the piece invites visitors to walk through its amplified soundscape, all enacting Baldwin's emphasis on the connective power of listening. See http://www.obadike.com/.

21. Toni Morrison, *Jazz*, 227.

22. *The Miseducation of Lauryn Hill* contrasts with Hill's second solo effort, *MTV Unplugged No. 2.0*. Most of the songs on this second album feature only her voice, accompanied by acoustic guitar. The album received mixed reviews. While some critics praised Hill's passion and honesty, others, interestingly enough, called the songs unlistenable. Nevertheless, the album reached platinum status.

23. For the story and controversy surrounding the authorship of the songs on Hill's album, see Laura Checkoway, "Inside 'The Miseducation of Lauryn Hill.'" http://www.rollingstone.com/music/news/inside-the-miseducation-of-lauryn-hill-20080826.

24. My transcription.

25. In the video to "The Miseducation of Lauryn Hill," the world is imagined as a record playing on a phonograph and Hill is the needle of the record player.

26. See Carol S. Dweck, *Mindset: The New Psychology of Success*.

"All Living Is Listening"

1. Barack Obama, "Final Address as President of the United States."

2. Lin-Manuel Miranda, *Hamilton*.

3. Andrew Dobson, *Listening for Democracy: Recognition, Representation, Reconciliation*, 2. In the classroom or office, one example of such speaking-centric atten-

tion would be to suggest that students or colleagues talk more to demonstrate their engagement.

4. Claudia Rankine, *Citizen: An American Lyric*, 112. These lines, part of "Long Form Birth Certificate," meditate on the commencement of Obama's presidency. Taking the oath of office, he speaks, inscribing the silence, "the length of the silence becoming a living."

BIBLIOGRAPHY

Abbate, Carolyn. "Sound Object Lessons." *Journal of the American Musicological Society* 69, no. 3 (2016): 793–829.

Abel, Elizabeth, Barbara Christian, and Helene Moglen, eds. *Female Subjects in Black and White: Race, Psychoanalysis, Feminism.* Berkeley: University of California Press, 1991.

Abreu, Martha. "Slave Mothers and Freed Children: Emancipation and Female Space in Debates on the 'Free Womb' Law, Rio de Janeiro, 1871." *Journal of Latin American Studies* 28, no. 3 (October 1996): 567–580.

Adichie, Chimamanda Ngozi. "The Danger of a Single Story." TED Talk, 2009. http://www.ted.com/talks/chimamanda_adichie_the_danger_of_a_single_story.html.

Alexander, Elizabeth. "'Can You Be BLACK and Look at This?' Reading the Rodney King Video(s)." *Public Culture* 7 (1994): 77–94.

Allen, Danielle S. *Talking to Strangers: Anxieties of Citizenship since "Brown v. Board of Education."* Chicago: University of Chicago Press, 2006.

Als, Hilton. "Ghosts in the House: How Toni Morrison Fostered a Generation of Black Writers." October 27, 2003. http://www.newyorker.com/magazine/2003/10/27/ghosts-in-the-house.

Anzaldúa, Gloria. *Borderlands/"La Frontera": The New Mestiza.* San Francisco: Aunt Lute Books, 2012.

Armstrong, Paul B. *Conflicting Readings: Variety and Validity in Interpretation.* Chapel Hill: University of North Carolina Press, 1990.

Baker, Houston A., Jr. *Blues, Ideology, and Afro-American Literature: A Vernacular Theory.* Chicago: University of Chicago Press, 1988.

———. *Modernism and the Harlem Renaissance.* Chicago: University of Chicago Press, 1987.

Baldwin, James. *Going to Meet the Man.* 1965; reprint New York: Vintage, 1995.

———. *The Price of the Ticket: Collected Nonfiction, 1948–1985.* New York: St. Martin's Press, 1985.

Barrett, Lindon. *Blackness and Value: Seeing Double.* New York: Cambridge University Press, 1998.

Barthes, Roland. "Listening." In *The Responsibility of Forms: Critical Essays on Music, Art, and Representation*, trans. Richard Howard, 245–260. Berkeley: University of California Press, 1985.

Bavelas, Janet B., Linda J. Coates, and Trudy Johnson. "Listeners as Co-Narrators." *Journal of Personality and Social Psychology* 79, no. 6 (2000): 941–952.

The Beatles. "Blackbird." *The White Album*. Capitol, 1968.

Beavers, Herman. "Documenting Turbulence: The Dialectics of Chaos in *Invisible Man*." In *Ralph Ellison and the Raft of Hope: A Political Companion to "Invisible Man,"* ed. Lucas E. Morel, 193–217. Lexington: University Press of Kentucky, 2004.

Bendix, Regina. *In Search of Authenticity: The Formation of Folklore Studies*. Madison: University of Wisconsin Press, 1997.

Bennett, Jane. *Vibrant Matter: A Political Ecology of Things*. Durham, N.C.: Duke University Press, 2010.

Benston, Kimberly W. *Performing Blackness: Enactments of African-American Modernism*. New York: Routledge, 2000.

Berlin, Ira, Marc Favreau, and Steven F. Miller, eds. *Remembering Slavery: African Americans Talk about Their Personal Experiences of Slavery and Emancipation*. New York: New Press, 2000.

Bernstein, Robin. "Rodney King, Shifting Modes of Vision, and Anna Deavere Smith's *Twilight: Los Angeles, 1992*." *Journal of Dramatic Theory and Criticism* 14, no. 2 (2000): 121–134.

Bhabha, Homi K. *The Location of Culture*. London: Routledge, 1994.

Bickford, Susan. *The Dissonance of Democracy: Listening, Conflict, and Citizenship*. Ithaca, N.Y.: Cornell University Press, 1996.

Blesser, Barry, and Linda-Ruth Salter. *Spaces Speak. Are You Listening? Experiencing Aural Architecture*. Cambridge, Mass.: MIT Press, 2009.

Bogumil, Mary. *Understanding August Wilson*. Columbia: University of South Carolina Press, 2011.

Bone, Martyn. "The (Extended) South of Black Folk: Intraregional and Transnational Migrant Labor in *Jonah's Gourd Vine* and *Their Eyes Were Watching God*." *American Literature: A Journal of Literary History, Criticism, and Bibliography* 79, no. 4 (December 2007): 753–779.

Bradley, David. *The Chaneysville Incident: A Novel*. New York: Harper and Row, 1981.

Brathwaite, Kamau. *ConVERSations with Nathaniel Mackey*. Staten Island, N.Y.: We Press, 1999.

Brock, Pope. "Anna Deavere Smith." *People*, August 30, 1993. http://people.com/archive/anna-deavere-smith-vol-40-no-9/.

Brody, Jennifer DeVere. *Punctuation: Art, Politics, and Play*. Durham, N.C.: Duke University Press, 2008.

Brody, Richard. "Ralph Ellison's Record Collection." *New Yorker*, March 12, 2014. http://www.newyorker.com/culture/richard-brody/ralph-ellisons-record-collection.

Brooks, Daphne A. *Bodies in Dissent: Spectacular Performances of Race and Freedom, 1850–1910*. Durham, N.C.: Duke University Press, 2006.

———. "'Puzzling the Intervals': Blind Tom and the Poetics of the Sonic Slave Narrative." In *The Oxford Handbook of the African American Slave Narrative*, ed. John Ernest, 391–413. Oxford: Oxford University Press, 2014.

———. "'Sister, Can You Line It Out?' Zora Neale Hurston and the Sound of Angular Black Womanhood." *Amerikanstudien/American Studies* 55, no. 4 (2010): 617–626.

Brown, David P. *Noise Orders: Jazz, Improvisation, and Architecture*. Minneapolis: University of Minnesota Press, 2006.

Brown, Sterling A. "Ma Rainey." *The Poetry of Sterling A. Brown*, CD compiled by Yusef Jones. Smithsonian Folkways, 1995.

———. "Negro Folk Expression: Spirituals, Seculars, Ballads, and Work Songs." In *A Son's Return: Selected Essays of Sterling A. Brown*, ed. Mark A. Sanders, 243–264. Boston: Northeastern University Press, 1996.

———. "Our Literary Audience." In *Speech and Power: The African-American Essay and Its Cultural Content from Polemics to Pulpit*, ed. Gerald Early, vol. 2, 69–78. Hopewell, N.J.: Echo Press, 1993.

———, Arthur P. Davis, and Ulysses Lee, eds. *The Negro Caravan: Writings by American Negroes*. New York: Arno Press, 1969.

Bull, Michael. "Thinking about Sound, Proximity and Distance in Western Experience: The Case of Odysseus's Walkman." In *Hearing Cultures: Essays on Sound, Listening and Modernity*, ed. Veit Erlmann, 173–190. Oxford: Berg, 2004.

———, and Les Back, eds. *The Auditory Culture Reader*. New York: Berg, 2003.

Callahan, John F. *In the African-American Grain: The Pursuit of Voice in Twentieth-Century Black Fiction*. Urbana: University of Illinois Press, 1988.

Carby, Hazel V. "It Jus Be's Dat Way Sometime: The Sexual Politics of Women's Blues." In *Gender and Discourse: The Power of Talk*, ed. Alexandra Dundas Todd and Sue Fisher, 227–242. Norwood, N.J.: Ablex Publishing Corporation, 1988.

———. "The Politics of Fiction, Anthropology, and the Folk: Zora Neale Hurston." In *History and Memory in African-American Culture*, ed. Geneviève Fabre and Robert G. O'Meally, 28–44. New York: Oxford University Press, 1994.

Carter, Paul. "Ambiguous Traces, Mishearing, and Auditory Space." In *Hearing Cultures: Essays on Sound, Listening and Modernity*, ed. Veit Erlmann, 43–63. Oxford: Berg, 2004.

Cave, Nick. Personal interview. April 18, 2013.

Chanan, Michael. *Repeated Takes: A Short History of Recording and Its Effects on Music*. New York: Verso, 1995.

Checkoway, Laura. "Inside 'The Miseducation of Lauryn Hill.'" *Rolling Stone*, August 26, 2008. http://www.rollingstone.com/music/news/inside-the-miseducation-of-lauryn -hill-20080826.

Cheng, Anne Anlin. *The Melancholy of Race: Psychoanalysis, Assimilation, and Hidden Grief*. New York: Oxford University Press, 2000.

———. *Second Skin: Josephine Baker and the Modern Surface*. New York: Oxford University Press, 2001.

Chesnutt, Charles. *The Conjure Woman and Other Conjure Tales*. Ed. Richard H. Brodhead. 1899; reprint, Durham, N.C.: Duke University Press, 1995.

Chion, Michel. *Audio-Vision: Sound on Screen*. Ed. and trans. Claudia Gorbman. New York: Columbia University Press, 1990.

———. *Film, a Sound Art*. Trans. Claudia Gorbman. New York: Columbia University Press, 2009.

Chow, Rey, and James A. Steintrager, eds. *The Sense of Sound*. Special issue of *Differences: A Journal of Feminist Cultural Studies* 22, nos. 2–3 (Summer–Fall 2011).

Cixous, Hélène. *The Hélène Cixous Reader*. Ed. Susan Sellers. New York: Routledge, 1994.

Classen, Constance. *The Deepest Sense: A Cultural History of Touch*. Urbana: University of Illinois Press, 2012.

Clifford, James. "Diasporas." *Cultural Anthropology* 9, no. 3 (1994): 302–338.

Clifton, Lucille. *good woman: poems and a memoir 1969–1980*. New York: BOA Editions, 1987.

Cognard-Black, Jennifer. "'I Said Nothing': The Rhetoric of Silence and Gayl Jones's *Corregidora*." *NWSA Journal* 13, no. 1 (Spring 2001): 40–60.

Coles, Robert. *The Call of Stories: Teaching and the Moral Imagination*. New York: Houghton Mifflin, 1990.

Comstock, Michelle, and Mary E. Hocks. "Voice in the Cultural Soundscape: Sonic Literacy in Composition Studies." June 5, 2009. http://www.bgsu.edu/cconline/comstock_hocks/technological literacy.htm.

Connor, Steven. "Edison's Teeth: Touching Hearing." In *Hearing Cultures: Essays on Sound, Listening and Modernity*, ed. Veit Erlmann, 153–172. Oxford: Berg, 2004.

Cooper, Carolyn. *Noises in the Blood: Orality, Gender, and the "Vulgar" Body of Jamaican Popular Culture*. Durham, N.C.: Duke University Press, 1995.

Cox, Christoph, and Daniel Warner, eds. *Audio Culture: Readings in Modern Music*. New York: Continuum, 2004.

Cox, Trevor. *The Sound Book: The Science of the Sonic Wonders of the World*. New York: W. W. Norton, 2014.

Cruz, Jon. *Culture on the Margins: The Black Spiritual and the Rise of American Cultural Interpretation*. Princeton, N.J.: Princeton University Press, 1999.

——, and Justin Lewis, eds. *Viewing, Reading, Listening: Audiences and Cultural Reception*. Boulder, Colo.: Westview Press, 1994.

Danticat, Edwidge. *Create Dangerously: The Immigrant Artist at Work*. Princeton, N.J.: Princeton University Press, 2010.

Davidson, Cathy N. *Now You See It: How Technology and Brain Science Will Transform Schools and Business for the 21st Century*. New York: Penguin, 2012.

Davis, Angela Y. *Blues Legacies and Black Feminism: Gertrude "Ma" Rainey, Bessie Smith, and Billie Holiday*. New York: Pantheon, 1998.

DeNora, Tia. *Beethoven and the Construction of Genius: Musical Politics in Vienna, 1792–1803*. Berkeley: University of California Press, 1995.

Derrida, Jacques. *Archive Fever: A Freudian Impression*. Trans. Eric Prenowitz. Chicago: University of Chicago Press, 1996.

Dixon, Melvin. *Change of Territory*. Lexington, Ky.: Callaloo Poetry, 1983.

Dobson, Andrew. *Listening for Democracy: Recognition, Representation, Reconciliation*. London: Oxford University Press, 2014.

Donlon, Jocelyn Hazelwood. *Swinging in Place: Porch Life in Southern Culture*. Chapel Hill: University of North Carolina Press, 2001.

Douglass, Frederick. *The Narrative and Selected Writings*. Ed. Michael Meyer. 1845; reprint New York: Modern Library, 1984.

Dove, Rita. *Sonata Mulattica: Poems*. New York: W. W. Norton, 2010.

"Dream Songs: The Music of the March on Washington." *New Yorker*, August 28, 2013. http://www.newyorker.com/culture/culture-deskdream-songs-the-music-of-the -march-on-washington.

Drobnick, Jim, ed. *Aural Cultures*. Toronto: YYZ Books, 2004.

Dubey, Madhu. "Narration and Migration: *Jazz* and Vernacular Theories of Black Women's Fiction." *American Literary History* 10, no. 2 (Summer 1998): 291–316.

———. *Signs and Cities: Black Literary Postmodernism*. Chicago: University of Chicago Press, 2003.

DuBois, W.E.B. *Souls of Black Folk*. New York: Library of America, 1986.

duCille, Ann. *The Coupling Convention: Sex, Text, and Tradition in Black Women's Fiction*. New York: Oxford University Press, 1993.

———. "Phallus(ies) of Interpretation: Toward Engendering the Black Critical 'I.'" *Callaloo* 16, no. 3 (Summer 1993): 559–573.

———. "'Who Reads Here?' Back Talking with Houston Baker." *Novel* 26, no. 1 (Fall 1992): 97–105.

Dunn, Leslie C., and Nancy A. Jones, eds. *Embodied Voices: Representing Female Vocality in Western Culture*. Cambridge: Cambridge University Press, 1994.

Dweck, Carol S. *Mindset: The New Psychology of Success*. New York: Ballantine Books, 2007.

Dyer, Richard. *White: Essays on Race and Culture*. New York: Routledge, 1997.

Dyson, Frances. *Sounding New Media: Immersion and Embodiment in the Arts and Culture*. Berkeley: University of California Press, 2009.

Eidsheim, Nina Sun. *Sensing Sound: Singing and Listening as Vibrational Practice*. Durham, N.C.: Duke University Press, 2015.

Ellison, Ralph. *Invisible Man*. 1952; reprint New York: Vintage International, 1990.

———. *Shadow and Act*. New York: Random House, 1995.

Ellsworth, Elizabeth. *Places of Learning: Media, Architecture, Pedagogy*. New York: Routledge, 2004.

Eng, David L., and David Kazanjian, eds. *Loss: The Politics of Mourning*. Berkeley: University of California Press, 2003.

Ensslen, Klaus. "Fictionalizing History: David Bradley's *The Chaneysville Incident*." *Callaloo* 11, no. 2 (Spring 1988): 280–296.

Erlmann, Veit. *Reason and Resonance: A History of Modern Aurality*. Philadelphia: Zone Books, 2010.

———, ed. *Hearing Cultures: Essays on Sound, Listening and Modernity*. Oxford: Berg, 2004.

Feelings, Tom. *The Middle Passage: White Ships/Black Cargo*. New York: Penguin, 2018.

Feld, Steven. "Acoustemology." In *Keywords in Sound*, ed. David Novak and Matt Sakakeeny, 12–21. Durham, N.C.: Duke University Press, 2015.

———. "From Ethnomusicology to Echo-Muse-Ecology: Reading R. Murray Schafer in the Papua New Guinea Rainforest." *Soundscape Newsletter* 8 (June 1994): 9–13.

Felman, Shoshana, and Dori Laub. *Testimony: Crises of Witnessing in Literature, Psychoanalysis, and History*. New York: Routledge, 1992.

Firestein, Stuart. *Ignorance: How It Drives Science*. Oxford: Oxford University Press, 2012.

Fiumara, Gemma Corradi. *The Other Side of Language: A Philosophy of Listening.* Trans. Charles Lambert. London: Routledge 1990.

Foer, Jonathan Safran. *Extremely Loud and Incredibly Close.* New York: Mariner Books, 2006.

Fonteneau, Yvonne. "Ralph Ellison's *Invisible Man*: A Critical Reevaluation." *World Literature Today* 64 (Summer 1990): 408–412.

Forsthoefel, Andrew. *Walking to Listen: 4,000 Miles across America, One Story at a Time.* New York: Bloomsbury, 2017.

Francis, John. *The Ragged Edge of Silence: Finding Peace in a Noisy World.* New York: National Geographic, 2011.

Franco, Dean. "Working through the Archive: Trauma and History in Alejandro Morales's *The Rag Doll Plagues*." *PMLA* 120, no. 2 (March 2005): 375–387.

Frankenfield, H. C. "The Floods of 1927 in the Mississippi Basin." Monthly Weather Review Supplement. Washington, D.C.: U.S. Department of Agriculture Weather Bureau, 1927.

Franklin, Aretha, with David Ritz. *Aretha: From These Roots.* New York: Villard, 1999.

Furlonge, Nicole L. B. "An Instrument Blues-Tinged: Listening, Language and the Everyday in Sterling Brown's 'Ma Rainey.'" *Callaloo* 21, no. 4 (Fall 1998): 969–984.

Gabbin, Joanne V. *Sterling A. Brown: Building the Black Aesthetic Tradition.* Westport, Conn.: Greenwood Press, 1985.

Gaines, Ernest J. *The Autobiography of Miss Jane Pittman: The Famous, Inspiring Story of One Woman's Courageous Battle for Freedom.* New York: Bantam, 1982.

Gardner, Howard. "Reclaiming Disinterestedness for the Digital Era." In *From Voice to Influence: Understanding Citizenship in a Digital Age*, ed. Danielle Allen and Jennifer Light, 232–253. Chicago: University of Chicago Press, 2015.

Garfield, Deborah M. "Earwitness: Female Abolitionism, Sexuality, and *Incidents in the Life of a Slave Girl*." In *Harriet Jacobs and "Incidents in the Life of a Slave Girl": New Critical Essays*, ed. Deborah M. Garfield and Rafia Zafar, 100–130. London: Cambridge University Press, 1996.

Gates, Henry Louis, Jr. *The Signifying Monkey: A Theory of African-American Literary Criticism.* New York: Oxford University Press, 1988.

Gilmore, Paul. *Aesthetic Materialism: Electricity and American Romanticism.* Stanford, Calif.: Stanford University Press, 2009.

Gilroy, Paul. "Between the Blues and the Blues Dance: Some Soundscapes of the Black Atlantic." In *The Auditory Culture Reader*, ed. Michael Bull and Les Back, 381–395. New York: Berg, 2003.

———. *The Black Atlantic: Modernity and Double Consciousness.* Cambridge, Mass.: Harvard University Press, 1993.

Glenn, Cheryl, and Krista Ratcliffe, eds. *Silence and Listening as Rhetorical Arts.* Carbondale: Southern Illinois University Press, 2011.

Goble, Mark. *Beautiful Circuits: Modernism and the Mediated Life.* New York: Columbia University Press, 2010.

Godøy, Rolf Inge, and Marc Leman, eds. *Musical Gestures: Sound, Movement, and Meaning.* New York: Routledge, 2010.

Goldberg, Elizabeth Swanson. "Living the Legacy: Pain, Desire, and Narrative Time in Gayl Jones's *Corregidora*." *Callaloo* 26, no. 2 (2003): 446–472.

Goodale, Greg. *Sonic Persuasion: Reading Sound in the Recorded Age*. Urbana: University of Illinois Press, 2011.

Goodman, Steve. *Sonic Warfare: Sound, Affect, and the Ecology of Fear*. Cambridge, Mass.: MIT Press, 2009.

Gopnik, Adam. "Music to Your Ears: The Quest for 3-D Recording and Other Mysteries of Sound." *New Yorker*, January 28, 2013. http://www.newyorker.com/magazine /2013/01/28/music-to-your-ears.

Graham, Maryemma, and Amritjit Singh, eds. *Conversations with Ralph Ellison*. Jackson: University Press of Mississippi, 1995.

Griffin, Farah Jasmine. "When Malindy Sings: A Meditation on Black Women's Vocality." In *Uptown Conversation: The New Jazz Studies*, ed. Robert G. O'Meally, Brent Hayes Edwards, and Farah Jasmine Griffin, 102–125. New York: Columbia University Press, 2004.

Guralnick, Peter. *Sweet Soul Music: Rhythm and Blues and the Southern Dream of Freedom*. New York: Harper and Row, 1986.

Handel, Stephen. *Listening: An Introduction to the Perception of Auditory Events*. Cambridge, Mass.: MIT Press, 1989.

Harper, Michael S. *History Is Your Own Heartbeat: Poems*. Urbana: University of Illinois Press, 1971.

———, ed. *The Collected Poems of Sterling A. Brown*. New York: Harper and Row, 1989.

———, and Robert B. Stepto, eds. *Chant of Saints: A Gathering of Afro-American Literature, Art, and Scholarship*. Urbana: University of Illinois Press, 1979.

Harris, Michael W. *The Rise of Gospel Blues: The Music of Thomas Andrew Dorsey in the Urban Church*. New York: Oxford University Press, 1992.

Harrison, Daphne Duval. *Black Pearls: Blues Queens of the 1920s*. New Brunswick, N.J.: Rutgers University Press, 1988.

Hartman, Saidiya. *Lose Your Mother: A Journey along the Atlantic Slave Route*. New York: Farrar, Straus and Giroux, 2007.

———. *Scenes of Subjection: Terror, Slavery, and Self-Making in Nineteenth-Century America*. New York: Oxford University Press, 1997.

———. "The Time of Slavery." *South Atlantic Quarterly* 101, no. 4 (Fall 2002): 757–777.

Hasson, Uri. Personal interview. June 24, 2016.

———. TED Talk, February 2016. https://www.ted.com/talks/uri_hasson_this_is_your _brain_on_communication.

Hayden, Robert. *Collected Poems*. Ed. Frederick Glaysher. New York: Liveright, 1997.

Henderson, George L. "South of the North, North of the South: Spatial Practices in David Bradley's *The Chaneysville Incident*." In *Keep Your Head to the Sky: Interpreting African American Home Ground*, ed. Grey Gundaker, 113–143. Charlottesville: University Press of Virginia, 1989.

Henderson, Mae G. *Speaking in Tongues and Dancing Diaspora: Black Women Writing and Performing*. New York: Oxford University Press, 2014.

Henderson, Stephen E. "The Heavy Blues of Sterling Brown: A Study in Craft and Tradition." *Black American Literature Forum* 14, no. 1 (1980): 32–44.

Hendy, David. *Noise: A Human History of Sound and Listening*. New York: HarperCollins, 2013.

Henriques, Julian. *Sonic Bodies: Reggae Sound Systems, Performance Techniques, and Ways of Knowing*. New York: Bloomsbury, 2009.

Hill, Lauryn. *The Miseducation of Lauryn Hill*. Sony, 1998.

Hirsch, Marianne. *Family Frames: Photography, Narrative, and Postmemory*. Cambridge, Mass.: Harvard University Press, 1997.

Hirschkind, Charles. *The Ethical Soundscape: Cassette Sermons and Islamic Counterpublics*. New York: Columbia University Press, 2006.

Holloway, Karla F. C. *The Character of the Word: The Texts of Zora Neale Hurston*. Westport, Conn.: Greenwood Press, 1987.

———. *Legal Fictions: Constituting Race, Composing Literature*. Durham, N.C.: Duke University Press, 2014.

hooks, bell. *Talking Back: Thinking Feminist, Thinking Black*. Boston: South End Press, 1989.

Horning, Susan Schmidt. *Chasing Sound: Technology, Culture, and the Art of Studio Recording from Edison to the LP*. Baltimore: Johns Hopkins University Press, 2013.

Hughes, Langston. *The Collected Poems of Langston Hughes*. Ed. Arnold Rampersad. New York: Vintage, 1995.

———. *Not without Laughter*. 1930; reprint New York: First Collier Books, 1969.

Hurston, Zora Neale. *Dust Tracks on a Road*. In *Zora Neale Hurston: Folklore, Memoirs, and Other Writings*, ed. Cheryl A. Wall, 556–808. New York: Library of America, 1995.

———. *Their Eyes Were Watching God*. 1937; reprint New York: Harper and Row, 1990.

———. "You May Go but This Will Bring You Back." In *The Norton Anthology of African American Literature Audio Companion*, ed. Henry Louis Gates, Jr., and Valerie A. Smith. New York: W. W. Norton, 1996.

———. *Zora Neale Hurston: A Life in Letters*. Ed. Carla Kaplan. New York: Anchor Books, 2003.

Hutchinson, George. *The Harlem Renaissance in Black and White*. Cambridge, Mass.: Harvard University Press, 1995.

Ihde, Don. *Listening and Voice: Phenomenologies of Sound*. Athens, Ohio: Ohio University Press, 1976.

Jacobs, Harriet A. *Incidents in the Life of a Slave Girl*. Ed. L. Marie Child. 1861; reprint Cambridge, Mass.: Harvard University Press, 1987.

Jaji, Tsitsi Ella. *Africa in Stereo: Modernism, Music, and Pan-African Solidarity*. New York: Oxford University Press, 2014.

Johnson, Barbara. "Metaphor, Metonymy and Voice in *Their Eyes Were Watching God*." In *Black Literature and Literary Theory*, ed. Henry Louis Gates, Jr. New York: Methuen, 1984.

Johnson, Lyndon B. "Remarks at a Ceremony at the Lincoln Memorial." February 12, 1967. http://www.presidency.ucsb.edu/ws/?pid=28549.

Jones, Gayl. *Corregidora*. Boston: Beacon Press, 1975.

———. *Liberating Voices: Oral Tradition in African American Literature*. Cambridge, Mass.: Harvard University Press, 1991.

———. *Mosquito*. Boston: Beacon Press, 1999.

Jones, Meta DuEwa. *The Muse Is Music: Jazz Poetry from the Harlem Renaissance to Spoken Word*. Urbana: University of Illinois Press, 2013.

Jourdain, Robert. *Music, the Brain, and Ecstasy: How Music Captures Our Imagination*. New York: HarperCollins, 1997.

Kahn, Douglas. *Noise, Water, Meat: A History of Sound in the Arts*. Cambridge, Mass.: MIT Press, 1999.

———, and Gregory Whitehead, eds. *Wireless Imagination: Sound, Radio, and the Avant-Garde*. Cambridge, Mass.: MIT Press, 1992.

Katz, Mark. *Capturing Sound: How Technology Has Changed Music*. Berkeley: University of California Press, 2004.

Kay, Jackie. *Bessie Smith: Outlines*. Bath, U.K.: Absolute Press, 1997.

Keizer, Arlene R. *Black Subjects: Identity Formation in the Contemporary Narrative of Slavery*. Ithaca, N.Y.: Cornell University Press, 2004.

Kelley, Robin D. G. "Foreword." In *Remembering Slavery: African Americans Talk about Their Personal Experiences of Slavery and Emancipation*, ed. Ira Berlin, Marc Favreau, and Steven F. Miller, vii–x. New York: New Press, 2000.

———. *Yo' Mama's DisFunktional! Fighting the Culture Wars in Urban America*. Boston: Beacon Press, 1998.

Kendrick, Dolores. *The Women of Plums: Poems in the Voices of Slave Women*. New York: William Morrow, 1989.

Kun, Josh. *Audiotopia: Music, Race, and America*. Berkeley: University of California Press, 2005.

LaBelle, Brandon. *Acoustic Territories: Sound Culture and Everyday Life*. New York: Bloomsbury, 2010.

———. *Lexicon of the Mouth: Poetics and Politics of Voice and the Oral Imaginary*. New York: Bloomsbury, 2014.

Lacey, Kate. *Listening Publics: The Politics and Experience of Listening in the Media Age*. Cambridge: Polity Press, 2013.

Lamothe, Daphne Mary. *Inventing the New Negro: Narrative, Culture, and Ethnography*. Philadelphia: University of Pennsylvania Press, 2008.

LaVette, Bettye. "Blackbird." Hollywood Bowl, 2011. https://www.youtube.com/watch?v=J0bOgP5lYBg.

———. Personal interview. February 26, 2013.

———. *A Woman Like Me*. New York: Blue Rider Press, 2012.

Lepore, Jill. *The Story of America: Essays on Origins*. Princeton, N.J.: Princeton University Press, 2012.

Leppert, Richard. *The Sight of Sound: Music, Representation, and the History of the Body*. Berkeley: University of California Press, 1993.

———. "The Social Discipline of Listening." In *Aural Cultures*, ed. Jim Drobnick, 19–35. Toronto: YYZ Books, 2004.

———, and Susan McClary. *Music and Society: The Politics of Composition, Performance, and Reception*. Cambridge: Cambridge University Press, 1989.

Li, Stephanie. *Something Akin to Freedom: The Choice of Bondage in Narratives by African American Women*. New York: SUNY Press, 2011.

Lieb, Sandra R. *Mother of the Blues: A Study of Ma Rainey*. Boston: University of Massachusetts Press, 1981.

Lipsitz, George. *Dangerous Crossroads: Popular Music, Postmodernism, and the Poetics of Place*. London: Verso, 1994.

Lordi, Emily J. *Black Resonance: Iconic Women Singers and African American Literature*. New Brunswick, N.J.: Rutgers University Press, 2005.

Luciano, Dana. "Passing Shadows: Melancholic Nationality and Black Critical Publicity in Pauline E. Hopkins's *Of One Blood*." In *Loss: The Politics of Mourning*, ed. David L. Eng and David Kazanjian, 148–187. Berkeley: University of California Press, 2003.

Lyotard, Jean-François. *The Postmodern Explained: Correspondence 1982–1985*. Ed. Julian Pefanis and Morgan Thomas, trans. Don Barry, Bernadette Maher, Julian Pefanis, Virginia Spate, and Morgan Thomas. Minneapolis: University of Minnesota Press, 1992.

Mackey, Nathaniel. *Discrepant Engagement: Dissonance, Cross-Culturality, and Experimental Writing*. Cambridge: Cambridge University Press, 1993.

———. *Djbot Baghostus's Run*. Los Angeles: Sun and Moon Press, 1993.

———. *Paracritical Hinge: Essays, Talks, Notes, Interviews*. Madison: University of Wisconsin Press, 2005.

Manso, Peter. "Chronicle of a Tragedy Foretold." July 19, 1998. http://www.nytimes.com/1998/07/19/magazine/chronicle-of-a-tragedy-foretold.html?mcubz=0.

Mathes, Carter. *Imagine the Sound: Experimental African American Literature after Civil Rights*. Minneapolis: University of Minnesota Press, 2015.

McCartney, Andra. "Soundwalking: Creating Moving Environmental Sound Narratives." In *The Oxford Handbook of Mobile Music Studies*, ed. Sumanth Gopinath and Jason Stanyek, vol. 2, 212–237. Oxford: Oxford University Press, 2014.

McDowell, Deborah E., and Arnold Rampersad, eds. *Slavery and the Literary Imagination*. Baltimore: Johns Hopkins University Press, 1989.

McPherson, James Alan. *Elbow Room*. 1977; reprint New York: Fawcett, 1986.

Mead, Margaret, and James Baldwin. *A Rap on Race*. New York: Dell, 1971.

Mendelsund, Peter. *What We See When We Read*. New York: Vintage, 2014.

Merleau-Ponty, Maurice. *Phenomenology of Perception*. New York: Humanities Press, 1962.

Mezzacappa, Dale. "Anna Deavere Smith Brings School-to-Prison Pipeline Play to Philadelphia." February 9, 2016. http://thenotebook.org/latest0/2016/02/09/anna-deavere-smith-brings-her-school-to-prison-pipeline-play-to-philadelphia.

Miles, Barry. *Paul McCartney: Many Years from Now*. New York: Holt, 1998.

Miranda, Lin-Manuel. *Hamilton*. Atlantic Records, 2015.

Moraga, Cherríe, and Gloria Anzaldúa, eds. *This Bridge Called My Back: Writings by Radical Women of Color*. New York: Kitchen Table Press, 1984.

Morrison, Toni. *Beloved*. New York: Alfred A. Knopf, 1987.

———. *The Dancing Mind*. New York: Alfred A. Knopf, 1996.

———. *Jazz*. New York: Plume, 1993.

———. *Playing in the Dark: Whiteness and the Literary Imagination*. New York: Vintage, 1992.

Morton, David L., Jr. *Off the Record: The Technology and Culture of Sound Recording in America*. New Brunswick, N.J.: Rutgers University Press, 2000.

——. *Sound Recording: The Life Story of a Technology*. Westport, Conn.: Greenwood Press, 2004.

Moten, Fred. "Black Op." *PMLA* 123, no. 5 (October 2008): 1743–1747.

——. *In the Break: The Aesthetics of the Black Radical Tradition*. Minneapolis: University of Minnesota Press, 2003.

Moya, Paula M. L., and Michael R. Hames-García, eds. *Reclaiming Identity: Realist Theory and the Predicament of Postmodernism*. Berkeley: University of California Press, 2000.

Nadel, Alan. *Invisible Criticism: Ralph Ellison and the American Canon*. Iowa City: University of Iowa Press, 1988.

Nagai, Michelle. "Listen Compose Listen: A Study of Perception, Process and the Spaces between in Two Works Made from Listening." *Organised Sound* 16, no. 3 (2011): 211–219.

Naimou, Angela. *Salvage Work: U.S. and Caribbean Literatures amid the Debris of Legal Personhood*. New York: Fordham University Press, 2015.

Nancy, Jean-Luc. *Listening*. New York: Fordham University Press, 2007.

National Public Radio. "Intersections: August Wilson, Writing to the Blues." March 1, 2004. http://www.npr.org/templates/story/story.php?storyId=1700922.

——. "Take My Hand, Precious Lord." Interview with Michael Harris, January 17, 2000. http://www.npr.org/2000/01/17/1069272/take-my-hand-precious-lord.

National Research Council. *How People Learn: Brain, Mind, Experience, and School*. 1999; reprint New York: National Academies Press, 2000.

Ngai, Sianne. *Ugly Feelings*. Cambridge, Mass.: Harvard University Press, 2005.

Obadike, Mendi. "Low Fidelity: Stereotyped Blackness in the Field of Sound." PhD dissertation, Duke University, 2005.

Obama, Barack. "Final Address as President of the United States." January 10, 2017. http://www.latimes.com/politics/la-pol-obama-farewell-speech-transcript-20170110-story.html.

Ochoa Gautier, Ana María. *Aurality: Listening and Knowledge in Nineteenth-Century Colombia*. Durham, N.C.: Duke University Press, 2014.

O'Meally, Robert G., ed. *Living with Music: Ralph Ellison's Jazz Writings*. New York: Modern Library, 2002.

——, Brent Hayes Edwards, and Farah Jasmine Griffin, eds. *Uptown Conversation: The New Jazz Studies*. New York: Columbia University Press, 2004.

Orr, Elaine Neil. *Subject to Negotiation: Reading Feminist Criticism and American Women's Fictions*. Charlottesville: University Press of Virginia, 1997.

Pasupathi, Monisha, and Ben Rich. "Inattentive Listening Undermines Self-Verification in Personal Storytelling." *Journal of Personality* 73, no. 4 (August 2005): 1051–1085.

Peterson, Nancy J. *Against Amnesia: Contemporary Women Writers and the Crises of Historical Memory*. Philadelphia: University of Pennsylvania Press, 2001.

Pink, Sarah. *Doing Sensory Ethnography*. London: Sage, 2009.

Posmentier, Sonya. "Blueprints for Negro Reading: Sterling Brown's Study Guides." In *A Companion to the Harlem Renaissance*, ed. Cherene Sherrard-Johnson, 119–136. New York: Wiley Blackwell, 2015.

Quashie, Kevin. *The Sovereignty of Quiet: Beyond Resistance in Black Culture*. New Brunswick, N.J.: Rutgers University Press, 2012.

Rabinowitz, Peter J. *Before Reading: Narrative Conventions and the Politics of Interpretation*. Ithaca, N.Y.: Cornell University Press, 1987.

Radano, Ronald Michael. *Lying up a Nation: Race and Black Music*. Chicago: University of Chicago Press, 2003.

———, and Philip V. Bohlman, eds. *Music and the Racial Imagination*. Chicago: University of Chicago Press, 2000.

Radovac, Lilian. "The 'War on Noise': Sound and Space in La Guardia's New York." In *Sound Clash: Listening to American Studies*, ed. Kara Keeling and Josh Kun, 289–316. Baltimore: Johns Hopkins University Press, 2012.

"Ralph Ellison: An American Journey." Directed by Avon Kirkland and Elise Robertson. Arlington, Va.: Public Broadcasting Service, 2002.

Rampersad, Arnold. *The Life of Langston Hughes*. 2 vols. New York: Oxford University Press, 2002.

Ramsey, Guthrie P., Jr. *Race Music: Black Cultures from Bebop to Hip-Hop*. Berkeley: University of California Press, 2003.

Rankine, Claudia. *Citizen: An American Lyric*. Minneapolis: Graywolf Press, 2014.

Rapaport, Herman. "Archive Trauma." *Diacritics* 28, no. 4 (1998): 68–81.

Rasula, Jed. "Understanding the Sound of Not Understanding." In *Close Listening: Poetry and the Performed Word*, ed. Charles Bernstein, 233–261. Oxford: Oxford University Press, 1998.

Ratcliffe, Krista. *Rhetorical Listening: Identification, Gender, Whiteness*. Carbondale: Southern Illinois University Press, 2006.

Rayner, Alice. "The Audience: Subjectivity, Community and the Ethics of Listening." *Journal of Dramatic Theory and Criticism* 7, no. 2 (Spring 1993): 3–24.

Reed, Ishmael. *Flight to Canada: A Novel*. New York: Simon and Schuster, 1976.

Robinson, James M., ed., "Thunder, Perfect Mind." Nag Hammadi, Gnostic Society Library, March 23, 2005. http://www.gnosis.org/naghamm/thunder.html.

Ross, Marlon B. *Manning the Race: Reforming Black Men in the Jim Crow Era*. New York: New York University Press, 2004.

Ross, Posnock, ed. *The Cambridge Companion to Ralph Ellison*. New York: Cambridge University Press, 2005.

Rowell, Charles H., ed. *Special Issue on Sterling A. Brown*. Callaloo 21, no. 4 (1998).

Rushdy, Ashraf H. A. *Remembering Generations: Race and Family in Contemporary African American Fiction*. Chapel Hill: University of North Carolina Press, 2001.

Rustin, Nichole T., and Sherrie Tucker, eds. *Big Ears: Listening for Gender in Jazz Studies*. Durham, N.C.: Duke University Press, 2008.

Sanders, Mark A. *Afro-Modernist Aesthetics and the Poetry of Sterling A. Brown*. Athens: University of Georgia Press, 1999.

Sankofa. Directed by Haile Gerima. 1993; Washington, D.C.: Mypheduh Films, 2003.

Savage, Barbara Dianne. *Broadcasting Freedom: Radio, War, and the Politics of Race, 1938–1948*. Chapel Hill: University of North Carolina Press, 1999.

Sayers, Jentery. "Tinker-Centric Pedagogy in Literature and Language Classrooms." In

Collaborative Approaches to the Digital in English Studies, ed. Laura McGrath, 279–300. Logan: Utah State University Press, 2013.

Schweighauser, Philip P. *The Noises of American Literature, 1890–1985: Toward a History of Literary Acoustics*. Gainesville: University Press of Florida, 2006.

Sharpe, Christina. *Monstrous Intimacies: Making Post-Slavery Subjects*. Durham, N.C.: Duke University Press, 2010.

Shepherd, John. *Music as Social Text*. New York: Polity Press, 1991.

Siisiäinen, Lauri. *Foucault and the Politics of Hearing*. New York: Routledge, 2013.

Small, Christopher. *Musicking: The Meanings of Performing and Listening*. Middletown, Conn.: Wesleyan University Press, 1998.

Smith, Anna Deavere. "Anna Deavere Smith: Listening between the Lines." New School at Commonweal, June 23, 2011. http://tns.commonweal.org/podcasts/anna-deavere-smith/#.Weq7mhOPLBl.

——. *Talk to Me: Listening between the Lines*. New York: Random House, 2000.

——. *Twilight: Los Angeles, 1992*. New York: Anchor, 1994.

Smith, Bessie. "Backwater Blues." Columbia 14195-D, 1927.

Smith, Bruce R. *The Key of Green: Passion and Perception in Renaissance Culture*. Chicago: University of Chicago Press, 2009.

Smith, Mark M. *How Race Is Made: Slavery, Segregation, and the Senses*. Chapel Hill: University of North Carolina Press, 2006.

——, ed. *Hearing History: A Reader*. Athens: University of Georgia Press, 2004.

Sousanis, Nick. *Unflattening*. Cambridge, Mass.: Harvard University Press, 2015.

Spillers, Hortense J. *Black, White, and in Color: Essays on American Literature and Culture*. Chicago: University of Chicago Press, 2003.

——. "Mama's Baby, Papa's Maybe: An American Grammar Book." *Diacritics* 17, no. 2 (Summer 1987): 65–81.

Standley, Fred L., and Louis H. Pratt, eds. *Conversations with James Baldwin*. Jackson: University Press of Mississippi, 1989.

Stepto, Robert B. *A Home Elsewhere: Reading African American Classics in the Age of Obama*. Cambridge, Mass.: Harvard University Press, 2010.

——. "On Sterling A. Brown's Life and Career." http://www.modernamericanpoetry.org/content/robert-stepto-sterling-browns-life-and-career.

——. "'When de Saints Go Ma'chin' Home': Sterling Brown's Blueprint for a New Negro Poetry." *Callaloo* 21, no. 4 (1998): 940–949.

Sterne, Jonathan. *The Audible Past: Cultural Origins of Sound Reproduction*. Durham, N.C.: Duke University Press, 2003.

Stoever, Jennifer Lynn. *The Sonic Color Line: Race and the Cultural Politics of Listening*. New York: New York University Press, 2016.

——. "Splicing the Sonic Color-Line: Tony Schwartz Remixes Postwar Nueva York." *Social Text 102* 28, no. 1 (Spring 2010): 59–85.

Sundquist, Eric J. *Cultural Contexts for Ralph Ellison's "Invisible Man."* New York: St. Martin's Press, 1991.

Szendy, Peter. *Listen: A History of Our Ears*. New York: Fordham University Press, 2008.

Takaki, Ronald. *A Different Mirror: A History of Multicultural America.* Boston: Back Bay Books, 2008.

Tate, Claudia. "Notes on the Invisible Women in Ralph Ellison's *Invisible Man.*" In *Speaking for You: The Vision of Ralph Ellison,* ed. Kimberly W. Bentson, 253–266. Washington, D.C.: Howard University Press, 1987.

Taylor, Diana. *The Archive and the Repertoire: Performing Cultural Memory in the Americas.* Durham, N.C.: Duke University Press, 2003.

Terkel, Studs. "An Interview with James Baldwin." In *Conversations with James Baldwin,* ed. Fred L. Standley and Louis H. Pratt, 3–23. Jackson: University Press of Mississippi, 1989.

———. *Working: People Talk about What They Do All Day and How They Feel about What They Do.* New York: New Press, 1997.

Thompson, Emily. *The Soundscape of Modernity: Architectural Acoustics and the Culture of Listening in America, 1900–1933.* Cambridge, Mass.: MIT Press, 2004.

Tidwell, John Edgar, and Mark A. Sanders, eds. *Sterling A. Brown's "A Negro Looks at the South."* Oxford: Oxford University Press, 2007.

———, and Steven C. Tracy, eds. *After Winter: The Art and Life of Sterling A. Brown.* Oxford: Oxford University Press, 2009.

Tillet, Salamishah. *Sites of Slavery: Citizenship and Racial Democracy in the Post–Civil Rights Imagination.* Durham, N.C.: Duke University Press, 2012.

Tingley, Kim. "Whisper of the Wild." March 15, 2012. http://www.nytimes.com/2012/03/18/magazine/is-silence-going-extinct.html?pagewanted=all&_r=0._

Tracy, Steven C. "A Reconsideration: Hearing Ma Rainey." *MELUS* 14, no. 1 (Spring 1987): 85–90.

Trouillot, Michel-Rolph. *Silencing the Past: Power and the Production of History.* Boston: Beacon Press, 1997.

Trower, Shelley. *Senses of Vibration: A History of the Pleasure and Pain of Sound.* New York: Bloomsbury, 2012.

Unchained Memories: Readings from the Slave Narratives. Written by Mark Jonathan Harris, directed by Ed Bell and Thomas Lennon, performances by Angela Bassett, Don Cheadle, Ossie Davis, Ruby Dee, et al. New York: HBO, 2003.

van Maas, Sander, ed. *Thresholds of Listening: Sound, Technics, Space.* New York: Fordham University Press, 2015.

Varela, Francisco J., Evan Thompson, and Eleanor Rosch. *The Embodied Mind: Cognitive Science and Human Experience.* Cambridge, Mass.: MIT Press, 1997.

Vazquez, Alexandra T. *Listening in Detail: Performances of Cuban Music.* Durham, N.C.: Duke University Press, 2013.

Voegelin, Salomé. *Listening to Noise and Silence: Towards a Philosophy of Sound Art.* New York: Bloomsbury, 2010.

Walker, Alice. *In Search of Our Mothers' Gardens.* New York: Harvest, 1983.

Wall, Cheryl A. *Worrying the Line: Black Woman Writers, Lineage, and Literary Tradition.* Chapel Hill: University of North Carolina Press, 2005.

Ward, Brian. *Just My Soul Responding: Rhythm and Blues, Black Consciousness, and Race Relations.* Berkeley: University of California Press, 1998.

Warnes, Andrew. *Hunger Overcome? Food and Resistance in Twentieth-Century African*

American Literature. Athens: University of Georgia Press, 2004.

Warnock, Mary. *Imagination and Time*. Oxford: Blackwell Publishers, 1994.

Weheliye, Alexander G. *Habeas Viscus: Racializing Assemblages, Biopolitics, and Black Feminist Theories of the Human*. Durham, N.C.: Duke University Press, 2014.

———. *Phonographies: Grooves in Sonic Afro-Modernity*. Durham, N.C.: Duke University Press, 2005.

West, Cornel. *Race Matters*. New York: Vintage, 1993.

White, Shane, and Graham White. *The Sounds of Slavery: Discovering African American History through Songs, Sermons, and Speech*. Boston: Beacon Press, 2005.

Wild Women Don't Have the Blues. Directed by Christine Dall. San Francisco: California Newsreel, 1989.

Williams, Sherley Anne. "The Blues Roots of Contemporary Afro-American Poetry." In *Chant of Saints: A Gathering of Afro-American Literature, Art, and Scholarship*, ed. Michael S. Harper and Robert B. Stepto, 123–135. Urbana: University of Illinois Press, 1979.

———. *Dessa Rose: A Novel*. New York: HarperCollins, 1986.

———. "Returning to the Blues: Esther Phillips and Contemporary Blues Culture." *Callaloo* 14 (1991): 816–828.

———. *Some One Sweet Angel Chile*. New York: William Morrow, 1982.

Wilson, August. *Ma Rainey's Black Bottom: A Play in Two Acts*. New York: Plume, 1985.

Wilson, Emily. "Turning Stories into Communities: Interview with Playwright Anna Deavere Smith." May 31, 2011. http://www.alternet.org/story/151152/turning_stories_into_communities%3A_interview_with_playwright_anna_deavere_smith?page=0%2C1.

Wilson, Matthew. "The African American Historian: David Bradley's *The Chaneysville Incident*." *African American Review* 29, no. 1 (Spring 1995): 97–107.

Wineburg, Sam. *Historical Thinking and Other Unnatural Acts: Charting the Future of Teaching the Past*. Philadelphia: Temple University Press, 2001.

Wolfreys, Julian. *Critical Keywords in Literary and Cultural Theory*. London: Palgrave Macmillan, 2004.

Womack, Kenneth. *The Beatles Encyclopedia: Everything Fab Four*. Santa Barbara, Calif.: Greenwood Press, 2014.

Wong, Alia. "How the Justice System Pushes Kids Out of Classrooms and into Prisons." *Atlantic*, December 28, 2016. https://www.theatlantic.com/education/archive/2016/12/anna-deavere-smith-shares-notes-from-the-field/511589/.

Woodson, Carter G. *The Mis-Education of the Negro*. 1933; reprint New York: Tribeca, 2013.

Yamada, Mitsuye, Merle Woo, and Nellie Wong. *Three Asian American Writers Speak Out on Feminism*. Seattle: Red Letter Press, 2003.

Zuydervelt, Rutger. "Take a Closer Listen." *Orion*, March/April 2012. https://orionmagazine.org/article/take-a-closerlisten/.

INDEX

acousmatic, 56
acoustemology, 88
Alexander, Elizabeth, 12
Allen, Danielle, 14–15, 24
American Grammar. *See* Spillers, Hortense J.
Armstrong, Louis, 1; "(What Did I Do to Be So) Black and Blue?," 48
audible reciprocity, 59
audience, 35–36. *See also* Rayner, Alice
audiographic archive, 60
aural ignorance, 2. *See also* Firestein, Stuart
aural relationship between author and reader, 6
aurality, 21; of the flesh, 65
authenticity, 29

"Backwater Blues," 30–31, 36, 38
Baker, Houston A., 122n26
Baldwin, James, 32; "Rap on Race," 13; "Sonny's Blues," 17, 90, 107–108, 115
Beatles, The, 78–79, 137n92
Bendix, Regina, 29
Bhabha, Homi K., 73
Bickford, Susan, 14
black feminism, 62
black female vocalist: as listener, 60, 64–80
black feminist criticism: and voice, 26
black listenership, 28, 29
black literature, 7–8, 10, 29; and black listenership, 34
black vernacular, 98, 99, 122n26
black women: and sterilization, 62

black women's vocality, 59–60
"Blackbird," 78–80
blackness: ideas of, 2, 9, 17; "blackness of blackness," 48–49
blues, the, 71; in *Corregidora*, 73–75; and Medusa, 72
blues poetry, 33
Bogumil, Mary, 32
Bradley, David: *The Chaneysville Incident*, 16, 81–106; historical understanding, 105; sonic figure of wind, 92–94, 103; and telephone, 91, 95, 96–97
Brody, Jennifer DeVere, 131n45
Brooks, Daphne, 22–23, 84
Brown, Sterling A.: "Ma Rainey," 16, 30, 33; "Our Literary Audience," 28–29; recording of poetry reading, 37–38

Café Carlyle (NYC), 77, 79
Carby, Hazel, 30–31
Cardinal, Marie, 1–2
Cave, Nick: and Soundsuits, 111–112
Cheng, Anne, 13
citizenship: and listening, 10, 14–15, 83, 120. *See also* listening
Cixous, Hélène, 26
Connor, Steven, 5; and telephone wire, 91, 95
Cooper, Carolyn, 63
cultural politics of frequency, 55–56
cultural salvage, 40

Davidson, Cathy, 108
Davis, Angela, 31, 32
democracy: and listening, 15, 83, 119–120

163

dissonance, 98, 109
Dixon, Melvin, 125n12
Dobson, Andrew, 120
Dorsey, Thomas A.: "Take My Hand,
  Precious Lord," 86–87
Douglass, Frederick: *Narrative of the Life
  of Frederick Douglass*, 83–84
Dweck, Carol, 118

ellipses, 49
Ellison, Ralph: and Albert Erskine, 57;
  embodied listening, 41–42; high fidelity (hi-fi), 43–45; inner ear, 44, 51; inner
  eye, 51; *Invisible Man*, 16; "Living with
  Music," 42–45; lower frequencies, 55–56;
  silence of sound, 54; tape recorder,
  56–58; as thinker-tinker, 44; vibrational
  listening, 41–45
embodied listening, 30, 35, 41–58, 60–63
Erlmann, Veit, 58
evidence, 66–70, 96–100

Feld, Steven, 88
Firestein, Stuart: ignorance in science, 2
Fiumara, Gemma Corradi: listening and
  logos, 7–8, 9
Franklin, Aretha: "Respect," 75–77
Free Womb Law (Brazil), 63

Gates, Henry Louis, 122n26
Gender: and embodied listening, 45,
  60–63
Gerima, Haile, 85. See also *Sankofa*
Goble, Mark, 45
Goldberg, Elizabeth, 65
Griffin, Farah Jasmine: listening, 59;
  "When Malindy Sings," 59–60. *See also*
  black women's vocality

Hamilton (Lin-Manuel Miranda), 120
Harper, Michael S., 61, 62
Harris, Michael, 86–87
Hartman, Saidiya, 23–24, 106
Hasson, Uri: Listening Lab, 15, 124n62
healing, 71
hearing, 2

Henderson, George, 93
Henderson, Mae: "speaking in tongues,"
  26
Henderson, Stephen, 33
Henriques, Julian: listening as learning,
  108, 118; sonic *logos*, 7; sonic dominance, 47
Hill, Lauryn: "Miseducation of Lauryn
  Hill," 116–118
historical listening, 82, 83, 95, 105
historical trauma, 63
hlysnan, 2. *See also* listening
Holloway, Karla: and *Their Eyes Were
  Watching God*, 25
Horning, Susan Schmidt, 51
Hurston, Zora Neale: ethnographic listening, 21–23; hungry listening, 23, 28;
  personification, 27; Pheoby as listener,
  23–25, 26; *Their Eyes Were Watching God*,
  16, 23–28

Ihde, Don: phenomenology of listening,
  10, 27, 98
inquiry, 2
interdisciplinary, 3, 8, 17
interior acoustics, 66–68
invisibility: and the sonic, 16, 41, 45, 54–55

Jacobs, Harriet: *Incident in the Life of a
  Slave Girl*, 83, 84
Jaji, Tsitsi, 9
Johnson, Barbara: and *Their Eyes Were
  Watching God*, 25
Jones, Gayl: *Corregidora*, 16, 59–75; free
  verse blues, 33; inner listening, 66–73;
  Mosquito, 133n6; storyhearers, 61; verb
  choice, 61; vocal strain, 62–63, 65; writer
  versus storyteller, 61

Kelley, Robin D. G., 85
knowledge, 2, 20; historical knowledge, 63,
  93–94; prior knowledge, 30

Lacey, Kate, 24, 28, 39
Lamothe, Daphne, 19
Lavette, Bettye, 77–80

Lipsitz, George, 7
listener: as trope, 26
listening: as agency, 10, 26–27, 60, 93;
  and citizenship, 10, 14–15, 83, 120; as
  co-narration, 27; cooperative, 101; cultural politics of, 25–28; habit of friendship, 27; and empathy, 13; *entendre*
  (Jean-Luc Nancy), 2, 90; and ethics,
  13–14, 56–58; *hlysnan*, 2; and identity, 5;
  and imagination, 105, 106; and interpretation, 93; learned activity, 11; as learning, 107–109; pedagogy, 10, 108–109;
  as reading, 22, 30; to self, 75; as social
  action, 70, 75; storylisteners, 3; as triangulated, 42, 45; types of, 10
listening ear, 9, 132n53
listening in print, 1, 3–6, 30, 114–116
Listening Mind, 17, 109–110
listening poet, 20
listening studies, 17
listening walks, 111
logos, 7–8
Lordi, Emily, 138n93
loss, 37–39, 61–63, 97; historical loss, 71;
  listening to, 64–66
lower frequencies, 55–56. *See also* Ellison,
  Ralph
Lyotard, Jean-François, 30

Mackey, Nathaniel, 15; discrepant listening, 5–6; *Djbot Bhaghostus' Run*, 5–6;
  inventory of traces, 5
Mathes, Carter, 9–10
Mead, Margaret, 13
memory, 5, 21–22, 65–68
Merleau-Ponty, Maurice, 27
McCartney, Paul, 78, 79, 137n88, 137n91
microphone, 51–55; as listening
  technology, 52
moaning, 38, 90
Moby-Dick: "whiteness of whiteness," 48
Moran, Jason: and "Cradle Song," 110
Morrison, Toni, 61, 64; *Beloved*, 114; *Jazz*,
  4–5, 115; "Playing in the Dark," 1–2. See
  also *Nag Hammadi*
Moten, Fred: ensemble of senses, 9

Nag Hammadi, 4–5
Nancy, Jean-Luc, 2, 10, 90. *See also*
  listening
noise, 42–43, 62–63, 115, 117; in the
  blood, 63

Obama, Barack, 17, 119–120
Oliver, Paul, 31

phonograph, 16, 42–48, 117
Pink, Sarah: sensory ethnography, 21–22
Posmentier, Sonya, 29

Quashie, Kevin: and quiet, 69
questions: as listening habit, 2, 69.
  See also inquiry

race, 1–3, 9–10, 45, 63, 89–90, 100
radio, 56, 97, 117
Rainey, Gertrude "Ma," 32; as effective lis-
  tener, 39
Rankine, Claudia: *Citizen*, 17, 120
Rayner, Alice, 35–36
resonance, 37–38, 55, 63
Rustin, Bayard, 113

Sankofa, 85–88
Schafer, R. Murray: hearing and touch, 55
sensory cultural engagement, 10
Siisiäinen, Lauri: paradox of listening,
  69–70
silence, 89, 90
Simone, Nina, 64
slavery, 60–61; and evidence, sexual
  abuse, 72–73; in *The Chaneysville Incident*, 81–88; in *Corregidora*, 60; nineteenth-century Brazil, 60, 63; sound
  history and, 83–88
Small, Christopher, 33–34; musicking, 75
Smith, Anna Deavere: "broad jump
  towards the other," 13; listening process,
  12; *Twilight: Los Angeles*, 11–15
Smith, Bessie, 31; as muse, 32
Smith, Bruce: early modern England and
  literacy, 4; unairing, 4
Smith, Mark, 88

THE NEW AMERICAN CANON